POLITICAL ECONOMY FOR SOCIALISM

Also by Makoto Itoh

THE BASIC THEORY OF CAPITALISM

THE VALUE CONTROVERSY (*co-author with I. Steedman and others*)

THE WORLD ECONOMIC CRISIS AND JAPANESE CAPITALISM

VALUE AND CRISIS

Political Economy for Socialism

Makoto Itoh
Professor of Economics
University of Tokyo

St. Martin's Press

© Makoto Itoh 1995

All rights reserved. No reproduction, copy or transmission of this publication may be made without written permission.

No paragraph of this publication may be reproduced, copied or transmitted save with written permission or in accordance with the provisions of the Copyright, Designs and Patents Act 1988, or under the terms of any licence permitting limited copying issued by the Copyright Licensing Agency, 90 Tottenham Court Road, London W1P 9HE.

Any person who does any unauthorised act in relation to this publication may be liable to criminal prosecution and civil claims for damages.

First published in Great Britain 1995 by
MACMILLAN PRESS LTD
Houndmills, Basingstoke, Hampshire RG21 2XS
and London
Companies and representatives
throughout the world

A catalogue record for this book is available
from the British Library.

ISBN 0–333–55337–3 hardcover
ISBN 0–333–55338–1 paperback

10	9	8	7	6	5	4	3	2	1
04	03	02	01	00	99	98	97	96	95

Printed and bound in Great Britain by
Antony Rowe Ltd
Chippenham, Wiltshire

First published in the United States of America 1995 by
Scholarly and Reference Division,
ST. MARTIN'S PRESS, INC.,
175 Fifth Avenue,
New York, N.Y. 10010

ISBN 0–312–12564–X

Library of Congress Cataloging-in-Publication Data
Itoh, Makoto, 1936–
Political economy for socialism / Makoto Itoh.
p. cm.
Includes bibliographical references and index.
ISBN 0–312–12564–X
1. Socialism. 2. Communism. I. Title.
HX36.I85 1995
335—dc20   94–46182
                                        CIP

Contents

Preface vii
Introduction: Socialism at Stake xiii

PART I IDEAS

1 Origins of Socialism 3
  Formation of various concepts of socialism 3
  Communist ideas as natural right 7
  Utopian socialism 10

2 Modern Socialism 18
  Owenism 18
  Fabianism 20
  Marxism 22

PART II THEORIES

3 Marx's Socialism 31
  Historical materialism 33
  Socialism in *The Communist Manifesto* 38
  The labour theory of value and socialism 44
  On the division of labour 57
  The functions of surplus labour 62
  How to secure dynamic flexibility 77
  Conclusion 81

4 Market Economy and Socialism 83
  Theoretical critiques of a socialist economy 83
  Theoretical defences of the rationality of a socialist economy 93
  Arguments for market socialism 105
  The Recent debates on the market and socialism 117
  Multiplicity of the models of a socialist economy 128

PART III REALITIES

5 The Nature of the Soviet Type of Society — 143
Anomalies in the Soviet order — 143
Marxist critiques: the real nature of the Soviet type of societies — 147
Arguments for reforms and the future of socialism — 153

6 Achievements and Crisis — 160
The Soviet type of planned economy — 160
The basic conditions for growth — 164
Stagnation and crisis — 166

7 The Reforms and Systemic Change — 176
Perestroika and the Russian tragedy — 176
Eastern European revolutions and systemic change — 189
Economic reforms in China — 201

Concluding Remarks — 213

Notes — 217

Bibliography — 228

Index — 234

Preface

This volume is an introduction to contemporary Marxist political economy for socialism, and discusses the various notions of socialism, several theories concerning the socialist economic order, as well as the actual reality of the socialist economies and their recent systemic changes. The book is profoundly concerned with conceptualising the perplexing processes of the recent dissolution of Soviet-type socialism, and with drawing conclusions about possible alternative economic orders for the future. These issues clearly require much co-operative re-examination by political economists across the world, and so this volume does not even pretend to be a comprehensive and standard guide. The author, however, is convinced that this sort of work should be undertaken from many different perspectives so as to promote international co-operation leading to the revival of the hope for a better future for human societies in the direction of socialism.

A few words on how the author came to write this book might also be appropriate. During my stay in Oxford in the summer of 1987, and while writing *The World Economic Crisis and Japanese Capitalism* (1990), I considered two possibilities for future work: one was to write a book on the Political Economy of Money and Finance, the other was this volume. Andrew Glyn decisively recommended that I should do the latter. I hesitated at the time since my work hitherto has been mainly on the basic theory of the capitalist economy, for instance, *Value and Crisis* (1980) and *The Basic Theory of Capitalism* (1988). I felt more comfortable with, and better qualified to undertake, work on money and finance.

Naturally, I had been intensely interested in the issues of socialism while studying Marxist political economy. For instance, I strongly encouraged the publication of Paul Sweezy's *Post-Revolutionary Society* (1980) in Japanese, translated it, and wrote an afterword (1980). In this afterword, addressed to Japanese readers, I argued that the development of Sweezy's thought since he wrote his book on *Socialism* (1949), should be seen as a serious attempt to understand the growth and deterioration of the Soviet type of society on the basis of Marxist political economy. However, I did not make clear my own position with respect to Sweezy's novel conception of the Soviet type of society as a post-revolutionary (non-socialist) class society. Part of the reasons for this was my own lack of preparation to deal with this issue. Consequently, I began a more concentrated study of these questions and started to write essays on them. I then became increasingly aware of the fact that contemporary issues regarding socialism were indeed closely related to Marx's fundamental theories of political economy, as well as to his historical materialism. One result of this realisation was the addendum 'Part IV: Socialism' to *The Basic Theory of Capitalism*.

However, since I am not qualified to do historical and empirical research into the actually existing socialist countries by using any of their original languages, I have been reluctant to treat my work on socialism as fully professional. Knowing my doubts, Andrew Glyn insisted that I should be bold enough to venture into a new field and work on the issues regarding socialism, rather than money and finance which is an old and established field of research. Although I was still attracted by the latter, I was eventually persuaded to do the former as Perestroika unfolded and the Eastern European revolutions occurred. Andrew Glyn's comments and encouragement were extremely helpful in producing this volume.

Further to this, Nobuo Okishio, while collaborating with me on a book on *Economic Theories and Contemporary Capitalism* (1987, in Japanese), suggested that if I undertook this project I should also re-examine the socialist economic calculation debate, including Hayek's critique of socialism. In the chapter on socialism in the above-mentioned book, Okishio asserted that socialism has to incorporate commodity production as an important channel for the participation of members of society in decision-making regarding production. I maintained that socialism should exclude commodity production in the long run, and in so far as a socialist society must employ market processes for a period of time it should strive to limit the scope and functions of the market. The extensive discussions I have had with Okishio on my book on *Contemporary Socialism* (1992, in Japanese) served as preparation for this volume and were very useful.

In re-examining the socialist economic calculation debate, I found Don Lavoie's *Rivalry and Central Planning* (1985) an interesting and stimulating contribution, though it clearly supports the Austrian critique of the rationality of a centrally planned socialist economy. It was also gratifying to read Lavoie's acknowledgement of myself as a person whose 'approach to Marxian scholarship had a significant impact on this book'.

A further unexpected development in the gestation of this project was a long letter from Bob Rowthorn in October 1991, commenting mainly on the final chapter of my *Basic Theory of Capitalism*. Rowthorn and Okishio tend to agree broadly in their theoretical views, as is also the case on the theory of skilled labour. In the letter, among several other comments, Rowthorn opposed my view that a socialist economy should aim at the abandonment of the law of value. According to Rowthorn, complex economies, which generate independent information for enterprises and the state, necessarily require markets, regardless of who owns or controls the means of production.

In a reply in November 1991, I wondered if Rowthorn was not too influenced by Hayek, and argued that I could accept the idea of market socialism provided that it was presented as one of many possible patterns of socialism suitable for advanced countries at the present time. However, I could not accept it as an abstract general principle. As a matter of historical record, is it not the case that the Soviet planned economy worked and achieved high economic growth for decades? My further question was: what kind of information is particularly difficult to deal with in a centrally planned economy with public prices?

In his reply in April 1992, Rowthorn confirmed that he was in favour of state intervention and public planning and against the so-called 'free market' economies. He raised three questions for us to consider: (1) what kind of market do we need? (2) what kind of activities should be regulated primarily by markets? (3) what forms of conscious collective control are needed to complement and shape market forces for desirable social ends? In a further reply in May 1992, I remarked that these three questions are very pertinent, and that one could add the following two: (1) how can we ensure economic efficiency, motivation and incentives for innovation in the public sector complementing the market? (2) why can we not extend the non-market public sphere beyond certain limits?

Our dialogue took a more extensive and direct form when Rowthorn visited Tokyo in July 1993, based on his reading of the initial parts of the manuscript of this volume. Rowthorn has continued to read the manuscript and to provide comments, a process not a little facilitated by e-mail. All his comments and arguments have served to broaden and deepen my study and rethinking of the political economy for socialism, which have crystallised in this volume.

Although I still could not fully agree with the view of Okishio and Rowthorn that Marx's perception of socialism as a system without markets is infeasible and irrational for complex economies, I became more aware of the need to reconsider the issue of employing and/or replacing the forms and functions of the market economy in socialism. The fruitful and enjoyable exchanges with Rowthorn helped me crystallise the suggestions and issues considered in this volume. For example, did Marx really believe in a centrally planned economy as a necessary part of socialism? What are the theoretical implications of Marx's theories of the capitalist market economy for socialism? More specifically, how should we assess the original and the recent socialist economic calculation debates, in the light of the recent developments in the Marxist theories of value? How can we explain the conditions for the viability of the Soviet type of centrally planned economy and the causes of its crisis? This volume contains my attempts to answer these problems.

My fundamental position on the issue of market economy and socialism was formed gradually and is presented in this volume. I can now summarise it as follows: (1) Marx's view of a society of association of free persons without a market can still be the ultimate goal aimed at by socialists for the distant future. Theoretically this view is deducible from the negation of the principles of the capitalist market economy. The theoretical foundation of socialism must always be a critical analysis of the capitalist market economy. (2) The Soviet type of centrally planned economy, which excluded the market, had a degree of viability under certain historical conditions. Although this society should not be identified with the view of Marx and the Marxists about socialism in general, not to mention ideal socialism, we should not reject it as completely irrational. It may, for instance, serve as a possible path to industrialisation for underdeveloped economies under certain conditions, provided that there is social consensus among people. (3) In order to achieve desirable social ends beyond the limitations of capitalism, and after the collapse of Soviet socialism, alternative models of socialism must not be narrowly limited to a single 'correct' solution, at least not for the foreseeable future. The possible combination of planning, economic co-operation and markets, as well as various forms of property ownership in firms, should be flexibly chosen by the people for the people.

The social democratic current has social ends very similar to those of the socialist current. Consequently, many socialists have co-operated with and participated in social democratic movements. The dogmatic rejection of social democracy in the name of 'orthodox' Marxism is no longer appropriate. However, so long as social democracy bases itself on the private ownership of firms and the means of production, its social system founded on equalising income through taxation will be politically unstable and vulnerable to capitalist attack, particularly in periods of economic depression. We are now witnessing this in not a few social democratic countries. Socialism, by contrast, must aim at the public ownership of firms and the important means of production, even if it assumes the form of market socialism. Socialism intends to overcome the weaknesses of social democracy, sometimes by passing through the social democratic stage itself. In a similar vein, the models of market socialism can be variable, and can be subjected to a process of intensifying socialisation.

In the process of forming this position, I had the opportunity to visit China in 1986 and 1991, East Germany, Poland, Czechoslovakia, and Hungary in 1990, and I was able to gather information on the past historical experiences and the current systemic changes in these countries. Many political economists in these countries indeed helped me to understand the realities of past and present, as well as their attempts at reconsidering theory.

In Japan, I enjoyed and took advantage of communicating with Masayuki Iwata, Masanori Kikuchi, Keimei Satoh, Momo Iida, Makoto Noguchi, Michiaki Obata and Makoto Nishibe among others, in the preparation of this volume. As in my previous books and papers, I have extensively drawn on the innovative contributions of Kozo Uno and his followers in Japan, which aim at restructuring Marxist economic theories. Normally, such theories are employed in the analysis of the capitalist economy, however, in this volume they were used to discuss the issues pertinent to socialism.

I was fortunate to have Costas Lapavitsas from the University of London as a visiting colleague at the University of Tokyo in 1993–4. He kindly helped me with the language problems in writing this volume, while also discussing extensively the substance of many parts of the manuscript.

I wish to state my sincere acknowledgements to all the persons and friends mentioned above who helped me to prepare this volume, though I am certainly responsible for whatever imperfections it may contain. I can only hope that this work is of some interest and use to a broader readership, and serves, against the current, to support the international effort to reconstruct political economy for socialism.

Tokyo, Summer 1994　　　　　　　　　　　　　　　　　MAKOTO ITOH

Introduction: Socialism at Stake

Socialism is now generally regarded as an old and failed social order. In 1991, hard on the heels of the Eastern European revolutions of 1989, the USSR, the motherland of 'socialist' countries, was dissolved. The very idea of socialism is now at stake. This is a heartbreaking historical experience, in view of the huge effort expended and the sacrifices made by innumerable people in the hope of achieving socialism. Is it really high time to bid farewell to the socialist belief in historical progress, to workers' socialist movements, to socialist political activity, as well as to socialist intellectual work in a variety of fields? Were socialist assertions and movements a votive offering to *nihil*, since they just dreamed of a rationally infeasible society? These questions are a major concern for a wide range of people as the failure of socialism and the victory of the capitalist market economy are hailed throughout the world. This volume steps forward and attempts to answer these problems, as well as to reconsider the present-day feasibility of political economy for socialism.

Until recently, and in retrospect, the 20th century seemed a century of socialist revolutions. The Russian Revolution took place in the largest country in the world during the First World War. This revolution spread to Eastern Europe, as well as to North Korea, during the last phase of the Second World War. Then the Chinese Revolution triumphed in 1949 in the world's most populous country. Successive revolutions in Indochina, Cuba, Portugal's former African colonies, the Horn of Africa, Southern Yemen, Iran, and Nicaragua sooner or later came to declare for socialism. All in all about 30 percent of the earth's area and about 35 percent of its population belonged to such 'socialist' societies. As long as the problems of exploitation, alienation and discrimination against workers, and the expropriation and oppression of the people of the third world, could not be successfully solved under capitalism (not even mentioning the cruel and irrational disasters of Great Depressions and World Wars), socialism appeared as a hopeful way out. In this respect, the Russian Revolution was widely believed to be an epoch-making event, a turning point in world history from the old capitalist to the emerging socialist era.

Meanwhile, until the 1960s few, if any serious critical studies of the Soviet type of 'socialist' politico–economic order were made by Marxists across the world. As the Soviet style of centrally planned economy was largely applied to Eastern European countries, China and other socialist countries, the centrally planned economy was thought of as the only possible model for a socialist economy. Consequently, it was also generally believed that the main direction of advance in world history was toward such a type of economy accompanied by an expanding role for the state. Keynesianism and welfare policies in advanced capitalist countries were in broad accord with this socialist view.

In the last decade of the 20th century, however, such belief in the progress of history has been deeply shaken. It has become clear that the ideal of a socialist revolution achieving the self-liberation of people from exploitative capitalist oppression, and making working people the real masters of a society was far from being fully realised in the Soviet type of societies. Beneath the privileged position of the mighty party and state bureaucracy, working people were generally depoliticised, excluded from decision-making mechanisms at various levels, and oppressed in a non-democratic social system. This reality was repeatedly criticised and condemned, even from within Soviet-type societies, particularly since the 1970s. Was it not true that the socialist aim of the withering away of the state was being betrayed by reality? Economic growth in 'socialist' countries became very stagnant despite their belief that it would naturally surpass the economic growth of capitalism. It became especially clear that a widening gap in consumption existed between the advanced capitalist and the 'socialist' countries.

Thus, socialism, in a historical crisis since the 1970s, was unexpectedly driven into a defensive position and underwent severe trials. As we shall see in Part III of this volume, the Chinese economic reforms since 1978, the Eastern European revolutions of 1989, as well as Perestroika and the dissolution of the USSR, were all results of this crisis. Despite all their different features they have one common policy element namely, to open the door to western countries and to revitalise the economy by reintroducing the market. As a whole, post-revolutionary societies which aimed at socialism failed to make the centrally planned economic system work and have turned, more or less, toward the vitality of market principles.

A revival of neo-liberal policies, which emphasise the vitality of the free market economy, has also occurred in the capitalist world since the end of the 1970s through the process of the world economic crisis. Keynesianism and welfare state policies were thus abandoned. The economic role of the state was intentionally reduced, many public enterprises were privatised, and trade unions were weakened in the 1980s. Developments in micro-electronic (ME) information technologies made possible smaller and more mobile units of investment, multiplied the types and models of consumer durables produced by a conveyor belt-type mass production system, promoted the international competitive activities of multinationals, and thus provided a strong economic basis for the neo-liberal trend in the capitalist world.

This trend in the capitalist world greatly influenced Eastern Europe, the Soviet Union, and China, as they were all strongly conscious of the increasing gap in consumption relative to that in advanced capitalist countries, or even in the Newly Industrialising Economies (NIEs). The Eastern European revolutions and the dissolution of the USSR followed this trend, and were broadly celebrated as a victory of capitalism over socialism. Ironically, the 20th century, which seemed to initiate a transition in world history toward socialism, is concluding with a wave of reaction against it. Socialism is indeed in crisis as our century is approaching its end. The socialist movement and ideological and theoretical socialist activities in capitalist countries have been badly shaken by the failure of the 'socialist' system in the USSR and Eastern Europe. The neo-liberal *laissez faire* reaction in the capitalist world fosters these difficulties of socialism and feeds on them.

However, capitalist development on the basis of a market economy is far from realising a harmonious and stable economic order. Even in Japan, model of the most advanced and prosperous capitalist country, capitalist development is so exploitative and oppressive as to make not a few workers die from overwork (karoshi), or suffer from a syndrome of chronic fatigue. At the same time, capitalist development has widened the unevenness in the distribution of assets through bubbles (speculative expansion of stock market and dealings in real estate), exacerbated the unevenness of regional development, broadened wage differentials, and extended the scale of ecological destruction. A critique of the capitalist market economy based on Marx's analysis still seems fundamentally proper and sound, and even more appropriate in the recently revitalised market economy.[1]

In this regard, the relevance of socialist thought and theory, which aims at overcoming the historical limitations of the workings of capitalism, has actually increased as far as the capitalist world is concerned. The rebirth and steady growth of western Marxist political economy reflect this relevance. Indeed, if we are witnessing the end of history and the final victory of the capitalist market economy, what can we expect for the 21st century? So long as our societies are driven by the interests of capitalist enterprises on the basis of market principles we cannot even hopĕ for fundamental solutions to the deepening economic crisis and dire poverty of third world countries, to the process of ecological destruction, and to the devastation of unemployed, or atomised, individuals forced to repeat alienated labour and to consume under the wage form. Is this not too pessimistic a perspective for the future given the potential creative power of human beings'?

We have thus to ask again whether socialism in its ideas and theories is really dead and gone. Dealing with this problem requires, above all, a re-examination of how feasible socialist political economy is, and, further, considerable co-operation with other social science disciplines. In an attempt to tackle this challenging issue, this volume will adopt the following four points of view: Marxism is one among many types of socialism; there is a variety of social formations compatible with democratic socialism; a centrally planned economy is one option among many social formations; contradictions in capitalism even today remain the basis for socialism.

Firstly, Marx's socialism appeared as one among many traditions of socialism, and intended to strengthen the ideas and theoretical foundations of the socialist current. The Soviet type of centralised socialism was, at most, a particular form of Marxism. Thus, there are three possible ways in which to oppose the popular view of identifying the failure of the Soviet social system with the failure of socialism. (1) The Soviet social system was not in accord with the basic propositions of Marxism and its socialist character has been rejected even by Marxist theorists, as we shall see in Chapter 5. (2) The Soviet case shows a failure of a particular pattern of Marxism, and should not be over-generalised as a failure of Marxism as such. (3) The failure of the Soviet system, and the resultant difficulties in Marxism, are not tantamount to the failure of the entire socialist tradition. It could even be argued that the broad tradition of socialism and Marxism can now be liberated from the dogmatic bondage of Soviet orthodoxy, as well as from the energy-consuming struggle against the Soviet orthodoxy, so as to become the source of our hopes for the future. It seems feasible to use Marx's own thought and theories in order to criticise the distortions in the Soviet type of centralised social system, and to provide direction toward a humanistic and democratic socialism.

Secondly, the failure of the Soviet type of socialism offers us a good opportunity to consider a wide range of possible options of social formations for democratic socialism. Just as Soviet orthodoxy demanded that we should believe in a single scientifically correct road, in the Soviet direction and leading straight to socialism, so the alternative views of socialism also tended to assume an ideal unique socioeconomic formation for socialism. Although Marx's thought and theories suggest that the abstract ideas of socialism derive from the principles of the capitalist economy, these theories basically present us with a variety of possibilities as far as the concrete strategic programme of socialist economic construction is concerned, depending on the actual political and economic conditions of each society.

In the case of capitalism, we are readily aware of different historical stages and types of socioeconomic development at the concrete level of research, which should be distinguished from the abstract level of study of the basic theoretical model of the capitalist market economy. Thus, the basic principles of political economy, the stages theory of capitalist development, and actual empirical analyses, were systematically distinguished into three levels of research by K. Uno (1897–1977), an original Japanese Marxist economist.[2] A variety of socioeconomic systems and forms of organisation can appear in the concrete process of socialist development. These forms would depend, for instance, on the degree and the manner of combining plan and market in different spheres of economic activity, on the degree of decentralisation, on the concrete forms of workers' self-management, and the concrete forms of public ownership of land and means of production. It is clearly untenable to identify the Soviet type of centrally planned economy as the single 'proper' model of a uniquely defined scientific socialism matching the basic principles of socialism. On the contrary, we should utilise Marx's economic theories as social science in order to liberate socialism from such rigid dogmatism.

Thirdly, the question has to be confronted whether we can still include the centrally planned economy among the several strategically possible forms of a viable socialist economy. This relates to the assessment of the historical experience of the Soviet type of economy. The oppressive domination of the party and state bureaucrats cannot be condoned. But how can we explain the continuous economic growth which took place for over half a century in the Soviet Union? Does this fact not suggest the rational viability of comprehensive economic planning under certain conditions? There may well exist democratic social systems, or self-governing organisations among people, which could implement comprehensive economic planning.

In a controversy over socialist economic calculation, a number of economists, including L. von Mises (1881–1973) and F.A. Hayek (1899–

1992), denied the rational viability of a socially planned economy. As we shall see in Chapter 4, they refused to admit that there were theoretical grounds for rational economic calculation in an economy where means of production were publicly owned and distributed outside the market. F.M. Taylor and O. Lange, among others, opposed this, and attempted to derive a solution for the problem defending the rational feasibility of a centrally planned economy. However, the theoretical problem concerning the rational viability of a planned economy without a market for means of production has remained unsolved, and has been the keynote in the recent process of social reforms in Eastern Europe, the Soviet Union and China.

We have to take note of the objective achievements in the rate of economic growth, industrialisation, security of employment, the social system of education, medical services, and general level of welfare in the Soviet Union, and we have to clarify the historical conditions which made them possible. This issue is also important in understanding why, in our own time, the Soviet system fell into crisis and collapsed. One factor seems to be crucial namely, co-operation with and support for the social system by the majority of working people. The recent social events in Eastern Europe and the Soviet Union showed us the fragility of the centralised socialist economic system when it loses people's support.

Fourthly, how should we assess the so-called victory of capitalism? In particular, the Japanese economy is generally seen as a highly successful model in the capitalist world. Is there a really ideal and harmonious economic order in Japan? The answer must be a definite 'no'. In Japan many unacceptable socioeconomic phenomena can be witnessed owing to the priority given to the untrammelled pursuit of profit by private enterprises in a market economy. Especially under the neoliberal policies of the 1980s, Japan faced increased unevenness in asset wealth and personal income, the instability of a bubble-ridden economy, continuous politico–economic scandals, the deepening fatigue of working people, the rapid decline of the birth-rate to 1.46 per woman, and spreading ecological destruction. Japan's foreign policies and international contributions tend to be guided by the narrow interests of leading business and political circles, and always tend to follow the US lead in order to secure access to the large American market for Japanese commodities. The economic welfare of working people in Japan, as in the rest of the world, is usually disregarded. The present Japanese social order cannot serve as an ideal model for the 21st century.[3]

Nevertheless, socialism in Japan is also in severe historical crisis. In

1989, Sohyo (The General Council of Trade Unions in Japan), the left national centre of trade unions, influenced by the restructuring of the capitalist economy since the middle of the 1970s, dissolved itself and formed a new national centre for Japanese unions, Rengo (The Confederation of All Private-Sector Trade Unions). Relying on a co-operative attitude by workers, Japanese firms have increased their competitive power in the world market, and revitalised the domestic market by introducing ME information technologies. The heightened prestige of the Japanese model of capitalism abroad tended to weaken the influence of socialism within Japan. The failure of 'socialism' in Eastern Europe and the Soviet Union has aggravated the difficulties of socialism in Japan.

Thus, as Japan has reached a leading position in the capitalist world it has become unprecedently difficult, but also acquired global significance, to confirm once again the feasibility of socialism even in this country. Political economy for socialism must always be founded upon the critique of the capitalist economy, especially of capitalism's most advanced model. At the same time, such political economy must attempt to find constituent elements of socialism in the progress of technology and social organisation of an advanced capitalist economy.

Bearing these four points of view in mind, this volume attempts a reconsideration of political economy for socialism for our own time. In Part I, various streams of socialism are reviewed, and Marxism is located within the wider historical current of socialism. In Part II, the theoretical foundations of socialism are reconsidered by examining Marx's own economic theories, the controversy over socialist economic calculability, and the recent debate on market socialism. Part III treats the realities and the failure of the Soviet type of 'socialism'. Anomalies in the Soviet Union, crisis, Perestroika, and dissolution are reviewed. The analysis of the Eastern European revolutions and of the economic reforms in China follows in the final chapter 7.

Socialism is indeed a huge issue and it has been discussed from many different standpoints. As well as political economy, studies in philosophy, social thought, political science, sociology, feminism and ecology have frequently related to the topic of socialism. Since, however, political economy has played a central role in Marxism, and was employed to create a deterministic economism in the Soviet type of socialism, a contemporary reconsideration of political economy for socialism certainly has an important role to play in preparing sounder foundations for socialism. This volume intends to contribute to this task and to serve as a contemporary introduction to political economy for socialism.

The author's position on political economy is critical of conventional, Soviet-type Marxist theories, and, as a corollary, non-dogmatic. Nevertheless, the author has employed as far as possible Marx's original thought and theories at the level of contemporary economic studies. Consequently, this work adopts a different perspective from that of some socialist economists who argue in favour of (market) socialism and oppose the Austrian critique, but frequently on grounds provided by the very Austrian economic theories themselves. In this respect, this volume does not pretend to be comprehensive, but wishes to present readers with some suggestions for the future, and aims at analysing the crisis of socialism, which is the major problem of our age, from the standpoint of Marxist political economy.

Part I

Ideas

Socialism, generally speaking, comprises three overlapping concepts; socialist ideas, socialist movements, and social systems based upon socialist ideas. Ideas and movements for socialism have historically contained various strands. We will briefly review these ideas and movements in this Part of the work.

1 Origins of Socialism

FORMATION OF VARIOUS CONCEPTS OF SOCIALISM

According to M. Beer,[1] the term 'socialism' first appeared in November 1827 in the *Co-Operative Magazine*, an organ of the Association of London Co-operative Unions, and became generally used in the 1830s. It is, therefore, not so old a term. It was initially used in the context of the growing co-operative union movement under the influence of R. Owen (1771–1857), and meant co-operative reformism as opposed to individualism. However, the term was soon also applied to the ideas of utopian socialists such as C.H. de R. Saint-Simon (1760–1825) and F.M.C. Fourier (1772–1837), who were the heirs to many of the ideals of the French Revolution. The term 'socialism' then came further to connote a wide range of ideas and movements which intended to bring about an ideal society and to liberate people from poverty and oppression on the basis of the co-operative principle and against the individualistic, competitive principle of bourgeois society. Besides co-operative and utopian socialism, other kinds of ideas of socialism appeared almost at the same time. For instance, romantic socialism, represented by J.C.L. Simonde de Sismondi (1773–1842), asserted that the return to a patriarchal peasant farming life would restore a harmonious and stable economic order.

Anarchism was professed by, among others, W. Godwin (1756–1836), P.J. Proudhon (1809–65), and M.A. Bakunin (1814–76), as a strand of early socialism. In order to bring about a communal society anarchism laid stress on the natural, spontaneous free will of individual persons and opposed authoritarian political power and governments which control people from above. These principles were also applied by anarchism to the structure of social movements themselves, and it was argued that such movements had no need for centralised, permanent organisation. Proudhon has also been characterised as a bourgeois socialist for he intended to improve the economic position of workers mainly through administrative reform within bourgeois social relations. Sometimes, but not always anarchists, such as these under the influence of Bakunin, had recourse to direct destructive behaviour and terrorism, especially after the 1880s.

In the period of social upheaval in the Continent of Europe from the

July Revolution in 1830 to the February Revolution in 1848, the term *communisme* came into use, along with socialism, in France and other European countries. The term signified the intention to strive for *commune*, a society of association based on *communauté* (community of property), by abolishing class distinctions and the system of private property. The aims of communism largely overlapped with those of socialism and, in particular, of utopian socialism. In the 1840s the communists, as compared to the socialists, aimed at more thoroughly common property ownership, and their outlook was thought of as more revolutionary, militant and directed toward a strong organisation.

K. Marx (1818–83) and F. Engels (1820–95) did not call themselves socialist in their youth. The international workers organisation which they joined was given the name The Communist League in its founding congress in June 1847. In its second congress in November 1847, Marx and Engels were asked to write a manifesto for the League. The result was *the Manifesto of the Communist Party*,[2] published in February 1848 and already in broad circulation during the February Revolution. This famous small book declared that the task of workers of all nations was to unite for self-emancipation and the realisation of classless communism. It was based on the authors' new world view, i.e. historical materialism, which viewed human history, including bourgeois society, as a long, continuous process of class struggles.

In order to provide scientific grounds for this kind of social thought and for such assertions, the economic law of motion of modern society, i.e., the basic mechanism of the economic life of the bourgeoisie and the proletariat as the subject of the revolutionary workers' movement, had to be systematically clarified. For this purpose, critiques of and solutions for the theoretical defects of the classical economists, such as A. Smith (1723–90) and D. Ricardo (1772–1823), who viewed the capitalist market economy as a natural harmonious order of liberty, were indispensable. Starting in the 1850s, Marx concentrated on this work during the latter half of his life. The resultant three-volume work, *Capital* (I, 1867, II, 1885, III, 1894)[3] revolutionised the principles of political economy by theoretically analysing the historical character of the capitalist economy. The theory of production of surplus value, in particular, which showed how surplus value as the social source of profit, interest, and ground rent is extracted from the surplus labour of wage workers, was epoch-making in scientifically clarifying the economic basis of class relations in a capitalist society. Together with historical materialism, this theory is often seen as a decisive moment in the development of socialism from utopian socialism to scientific socialism.

The above view is presented by F. Engels in *Socialism: Utopian and Scientific* (1882),[4] but, to be more precise, socialism or communism as social thought and social movements, should be distinguished from Marxist political economy as an objective social science. While socialism contains political ideology and value-judgements, Marxist political economy as a social science must attempt to establish an objective recognition of the world, according thoroughly with facts and logic. Historical materialism is a powerful Marxist world-view based upon socialist ideological thought, but it cannot in itself be a social science. Marxist political economy has historical materialism and socialist ideology as its guiding forces, especially in setting the problem of clarifying the historically specific character of capitalist economy and its intrinsic contradictions. The objective scientific recognition of the capitalist economy to be found in Marxist political economy always serves to strengthen the foundations of historical materialism and the grounds for socialist assertions. In this regard, it is accurate to define Marxism as scientific socialism even though not directly a science. Despite the close relationship between them, we should not confuse the relatively independent role of political economy as an objective social science with that of socialist ideology, or of historical materialism.

By themselves neither Marxist ideology nor historical materialism can guarantee that political economy will arrive at a correct recognition of objective reality. When political economy is treated as ideology then Marxist political economy cannot maintain the freedom to pursue the objective truth, and tends either to be rejected politically in the capitalist world, or to become dogmatically sterile in the socialist countries. One cause of the failure of the Soviet type of socialism was actually the enforced sterility of political economy treated as part of the national ideology, used to justify the existing political leadership, and not allowed the freedom to pursue critical objective researches of the existing economic order. For the future of socialism we have to endeavour to restore a sound and fruitful relationship between socialism and political economy as a social science. In any case, it is clear that Marx's work in political economy helped socialism to develop from a mere movement of enlightenment based on utopian thought into scientific socialism based on the objective foundation of the self-emancipation of the united wage-workers. The term socialism came to be used broadly, and to include Marxist communism, about the time Marx completed *Capital*.

Social Democracy was widely identified with socialism in this respect. For example, the Social Democratic Labour Party was founded by the Gotha congress in 1875, and was renamed the German Social Democratic Party in 1890. This party contained extensive workers' organisations, and grew as an important political force under the influence of Marxism. It played a central role in the activities of the Second International (Workers' Association), which was founded in 1889 by representatives of workers from 20 countries. Through its activities, the concept of socialism, or Social Democracy, no longer confronted Marxist communism but rather included it. Other socialist ideas and movements, however, were not totally eclipsed by the powerful growth and influence of Marxism. For instance, Fabianism, which intended to achieve gradual socialist reforms, also formed an influential social movement, especially in the UK. Social Democracy also encouraged the growth and increased the influence of the revisionist wing of Marxism, such as the current of E. Bernstein (1850–1932).[5]

Different views appeared also from within Marxism concerning the way of organising the workers' party, as well as the strategy and tactics for social revolution. Especially important in this context were the issues of how theoretically to analyse parliamentary democracy, and how to confront the imminent danger of world war. The centre line, represented by, among others, K. Kautsky (1854–1938),[6] formed the mainstream of the Second International, criticised revisionism and defended Marx's theories. However, the centre failed to maintain its position against the imperialist war, and as a result caused the collapse of the Second International on the eve of the First World War. Among the left-wing Marxists who opposed the centre line, R. Luxemburg (1871–1919) emphasised the importance of mass movements and general strikes.

V.I. Lenin (1870–1924), by contrast, led the Bolsheviks in the Russian Social Democratic Party with the strategy of turning the War into a revolutionary civil war under the guidance of a strictly disciplined vanguard party. The Bolsheviks achieved victory in the Russian Revolution of 1917 by promoting the political and social rule of council organisations (soviets) comprising workers, peasants and soldiers. The Bolsheviks were renamed the Russian Communist Party in 1918, and founded the Comintern (Communist International or Third International) in 1919. After the death of Lenin, Stalin consolidated Soviet society by concentrating authority and power in the hands of the party and state bureaucracy. The Soviet Union behaved as the orthodox leader of communist movements all over the world, and tended to propagate its own organisational principles, revolutionary tactics, and road to the construction of a socialist economy as the uniquely correct model for other countries. There remained, however, various Marxist positions which were more or less critical of Soviet-type communism, as well as various socialist positions outside Marxism. Against the backdrop of the failure of the Soviet type of social system, the increased energy and heightened potential of Euro-communism, Euro-socialism, and the new left in advanced capitalist countries, are particularly noteworthy. Through today's deep crisis of socialism we have been given a good opportunity to reconsider the potential and the original strength of the socialist tradition from a broader point of view, liberated from the Soviet interpretation of Marxism.

COMMUNIST IDEAS AS NATURAL RIGHT

The various types of social thought which became the strands of modern socialism or communism actually emerged in ancient times and have run through human history (often underground). These ideas have powerfully influenced people's minds, and from time to time caused fierce struggles. They originated in the deep anger and pain precipitates by the meanness and stupidity of action motivated by self-interest. They were also due to the unfairness of various social orders in which the majority of people were oppressed and lived in poverty and misery. From the pain and anger caused by the existing social order several strands of thought naturally sprang up, idealising and longing for a communal harmonious social life of free people. M. Beer's *History of British Socialism* (1940) starts with presenting such currents of thought from the time of the ancients, and far preceding modern socialism.

For example, in the 5th century BC Plato asked in his *Dialogues on the State* what is evil, and replied that it is wealth and poverty. For wealth brings forth extravagance and laziness, while poverty brings forth meanness and immorality. Therefore, in the ideal just state those in the position of politicians, who represent the virtue of reason and intelligence, and those in the position of warriors, who represent courage and vigour, should have neither private property nor family so as to concentrate on state affairs without self-interest. Thus, Plato asserted that communism of consumption should be imposed on these two social groups. In the later Roman age, remarkable ideas emerged in poems by Virgil and Horace, as well as in the Stoic philosophy of Seneca, full of admiration for communal life and the natural right. Such conditions were to be found among people in a pure and incorrupt natural order before the birth of private property.

Since Christianity was initially born as a religion of the lowly and hungry, it also contained communistic sentiments such as those in 'Blessed be ye poor, for yours is the Kingdom of God', and actually idealised communistic religious life by regarding self-interest as a hindrance to salvation. In the Medieval age, Fathers of Christian churches like H. Isidor (560–636) in Seville, Alexander of Hales (?1175–1245), or Stoic philosophers like William of Wykeham (1324–1404) maintained that the natural right of people in a natural order of things consisted of a fair egalitarian communal life without distinctions of wealth or private property. They often contrasted such an ideal natural order to the existing social order after the birth of private property in order to show the corruption and degradation of human beings.

This sort of tradition of pre-modern communist ideas actually exerted considerable influence on the leaders of peasant revolts starting at the end of the Medieval age. We see such examples in J. Ball (?–1381) and T. Müntzer (?1490–1525). J. Ball led a peasant revolt influenced by the communist thought of J. Wicliff (?1324–84), a pioneer of British religious reformation, and was executed for his pains. T. Müntzer guided a revolt of peasants and lower class citizens by radicalising the doctrines of M. Luther (1483–1546) and J. Hus (?1369–1415), and was also executed. The communistic strain in Christianity, which strives for actual salvation of oppressed peasants and the lower strata of the population, has been inherited and revived by liberation theology in the third world countries.

Similar ideas of human brotherhood and sisterhood in the face of God appeared in many forms of religion other than Christianity. According to such ideas, people are naturally born equal as brothers and sisters and should not be discriminated against on the basis of property or social class. For the oppressed lower strata of the population, salvation from unfair existing social discrimination is assured in life after death. Sometimes the ideas were applied to this world and promoted social reform movements in order to bring about a fair communal life on earth. Radical peasants' revolts were in many cases sustained by such religious beliefs.

In Japan, the radical and long-lasting peasant revolt *Ikko Ikki*, was organised in many regions of the country by the *Jodo-shinshu* Buddhist sect for about a century after the late 15th century. In the feudal Edo period (1603–1867), especially in its later years, many peasants' revolts occurred often similarly encouraged by Buddhist religious belief.[7] Such revolts led Shoeki Ando (?1703–62)[8] to contribute to original communistic thought by criticising Buddhism and Confucianism. He wanted to abolish discrimination and oppression and to realise a natural communal life with common property, labour and equality for all people, based on a materialist view of nature and the human activity of production (direct cultivation in particular).

These pre-modern communistic thoughts mostly idealised a communal egalitarian life without discrimination and oppression, and presented this state of affairs as the human natural order. From this point of view, private property and self-interest, together with the oppressive social relations between the ruling and the ruled, were criticised as the unnatural source of human degradation and corruption. Therefore, natural law and a natural human right were conceived as having existed in a natural egalitarian and free society with communal property.

These pre-modern ideas of natural law are clearly different from the modern concept of natural law to be found in the Enlightenment. In the latter the bourgeois right of private property was positively affirmed in the theory of property rights based on labour and opposed to feudal or absolutist arbitrary rule and levies. If we treat the various modern socialist ideas, which assert the realisation of a natural human right in a co-operative society, as successors to the pre-modern concept of natural law, then we have to admit the existence of two separate strands to the concept of natural law in the modern age.

On what grounds could the pre-modern concept of natural law advocate an ideal communal society without ruling classes and private property? Oral tradition about primitive communist societies in the old pre-historic ages, and inference based on evidence from peripheral primitive communal societies, probably served as the grounds for radical critiques of corruption and misery in existing societies. At the same time, in religious ideas could be found a fundamental sense of egalitarian humanism, even if in an alienated form. This sense of egalitarianism might also have relied upon the factual observation that human ability across the social classes is broadly equal, and this even before 'the concept of human equality acquired the permanence of a fixed popular opinion' (*Capital* I, p. 152) in modern society. Although the pre-modern concept of natural law seems old-fashioned, especially from a modern bourgeois point of view, it cannot be simply replaced by the modern Enlightenment concept of natural law. To criticise the alienation and devastation of humanity and Nature caused by modern capitalist market economy, and to overcome it in thought, we often find ourselves obliged to return, consciously or unconsciously, to the pre-modern strain. We then have to reconsider the meaning of a fundamental natural human right, and to re-examine the social norms in the relations between human beings and Nature, as well as among people.

One problem for the social concept of natural law is that it has not been possible to encounter a purely natural order of things since the very beginning of human history, as human beings have consciously re-formed Nature and their own social relations through work. However, the actual original order of remote pre-historic societies does not matter much. What matters are points of view from which to criticise existing social corruption and oppression as an unnatural, disfigured social order. Such points of view also necessarily call for the realisation in the future of a basic human right and fundamental natural norms in social life. Pre-modern concepts of natural law emerged from such foundations, and in many cases appeared in religious revelations and doctrines, literary works, or philosophical thought. In general, they did not demonstrate reasonable ways of realising the ideal communistic society, but tended to conceive of such a society as a glorious, if remote, past order which was already difficult to reach on earth. We should recall their significance, however, as a deep and far-reaching source of modern socialism in the face of the restrengthened modern bourgeois ideology of natural law in the line of neo-liberalism.

UTOPIAN SOCIALISM

In modern times, communism and socialism were based on the insecurity and anger caused by the socioeconomic disasters and devastation associated with a capitalist market economy. At the same time they came to rely more on rational concepts and plans for a new social and economic order, rather than on religious revelation, or the philosophical glorification of an imaginary past. However, socialism before Marx was not based on scientific studies of the economic mechanism of modern bourgeois society, the latter treated as an obstacle to be overcome. Early socialism offered mostly ideological cricism of the misery caused to the mass of people by the development of industrial society, and presented alternative ideal social orders in an utopian way. Utopian socialists generally expected that the main agents who would realise the alternative ideal society would be upper class people moved by persuasion. This was an additional utopian feature of early modern socialism.

T. More (1478–1535) initiated such early modern socialist thought. Despite growing up in the family of a cardinal and becoming a great politician and jurist, he presented a prototype of modern utopian socialism in his *Utopia* (1516).[9] The first Part of *Utopia* sharply criticised actual

British social conditions. The fate of working people was seen as more miserable than that of beasts of burden. Money and vanity were the source of all evil. Through the enclosure of cultivated fields, docile sheep were eating up peasants and farmland. In the second Part, the book relates the story of the king and philosopher Utopus who conquered the Abarakusa peninsula and constructed an utopia on the basis of communism and education. There were 54 provinces, each of which consisted of 6000 families or farms. A family or farm had about 40 members and two slaves. Provincial councils and a federal council, the members of which were to be elected, dealt with public affairs. Agriculture was seen as the social basis of this utopia. A certain proportion of the population shifted annually between agricultural and urban activities. Working time was six hours a day and wealth was publicly owned. People were monogamous and lived simply, not knowing luxury. Slaves were convicted persons who in other countries would have been executed, or poor immigrants from abroad who were allowed to leave the utopia at any time.

More's critique and his concept of utopia are still relevant and appealing in our society after almost five centuries. In Japan, a model of most advanced contemporary capitalism, the much increased price of land in central metropolitan areas is driving inhabitants away, turning the land over to business use. Business is eating people. Compared to the notoriously long working hours with pronounced fatigue for workers in contemporary Japan, a system of six hours work a day still seems a shining ideal. A shift system between the urban and rural population, and a decentralised political system which attaches importance to provincial councils, are also appealing.

More included a suggestive and interesting debate in his story of utopia. In the debate, More himself asks if communism would not eliminate the incentive of private gain as motivation for industry, make people idle, and result in general poverty. A communist, Raphael, replies to this and states that More's doubts derive from the social system based on private property, and that the mentality of people in utopia would become atuned to the communist social system of life. In the contemporary arguments on the transformation of the Soviet type of socialism into a capitalist market economy, we often see simple repetitions of More's rhetorical question in this debate. Human beings have made only very little progress on this question.

At the dawn of the modern age absolutist imperial rule promoted the birth of capitalism and the formation of the modern nation state, ruling over people based on an estate system and supported by the theory of the divine right of kings. Kings concentrated political power, could command the life and property of citizens, and were not afraid of abusing their power. More was actually executed by King Henry VIII, when he refused to recognise the King's divorce and supremacy over church and state.

As the social power of the bourgeoisie grew, however, so did demands for a bourgeois revolution to abolish absolutist imperial rule. The Puritan Revolution (1649) and the Glorious Revolution (1688) in Britain pioneered such revolutions. J. Locke (1632–1704) presented the logical grounds for justification of such a revolution in his *Two Treatises of Civil Government* (1690).[10] His work exercised great influence on the later American Declaration of Independence (1776) and on the French Revolution (1789–1804).

According to Locke, all people are created equal by God, and have inalienable natural rights of life, liberty and property. Government is formed by people's agreement to assure them of these fundamental rights (state theory of social contract). Therefore, making a revolution to abolish and change a government opposed to this basic task is one of the people's fundamental rights. In support of his view, Locke argued that the grounds for the right to private property derived from the theory of property right by labour, i.e. the legitimacy of private property acquired by the owner's own labour. This theory was fundamental in turning the concept of natural law into a classic expression of the bourgeois right of private property. We can certainly dispute, however, whether the theory of property right based on labour properly legitimates private property in land, or unearned income such as interest, ground rent, profit, and inheritance. In this context, it should also be recalled that the slogan of French Revolution was 'liberté, egalité, fraternité', and that the American Declaration of Independence proclaimed the people's fundamental right to life, liberty and pursuit of happiness. These expressions of the spirit of bourgeois revolution did not intend consciously to oppose the right to private property, but still showed some hesitation in exactly how this right should be located.

While bourgeois revolutions were overthrowing various absolutist regulations, creating social conditions conducive to the growth of a free capitalist market economy, they all had recourse to the concept of universal and fundamental human rights to liberty and equality. The concept of human rights, on the one hand, realised formal freedom and provided an equal footing for commodity owners to trade in the market. However, on the other hand, it had wider and interesting implications because it already implied the overcoming of the limitations of the capitalist market economy. When people were liberated from the bondage of pre-modern communal societies and participated in a market economy as formally free individuals on an equal footing with each other, the social demand for more substantial liberty and equality (egalité) also emerged. In this sense, one source of the concept of socialism, separate from the pre-modern communal concept of communism, was the idea of freedom and equality, even if not substantial, to be found in a market economy.

Though the French Revolution of 1789 is generally regarded as a typical bourgeois revolution, it had a rather complex character. As the Revolution proceeded from the overthrow of the absolutist ancien regime and the establishment of constitutional monarchy, to the moderate republican Girondist regime, and further to the radical republican Jacobin dictatorship which executed King Louis XVI in 1793, it assumed the character of a radical social change based on the middle and lower classes of people. The framework for a capitalist bourgeois order was then already radically overcome. The Jacobins led by M.F. de Robespierre (1758–94) redistributed farmland completely and equally among peasants, strictly taxed speculative gains made by property holders, and attempted to realise substantial equality in economic life by means of a controlled economy.

Although Jacobin radical social reform was short-lived and ended with the denunciation of Robespierre, his execution by the opposition groups and the restoration of moderate republicanism, it showed that the bourgeois revolution had the potential to surpass market freedom and equality based on bourgeois property rights, and to demand more substantial liberty, equality and fraternity for the people. The failure of the Jacobin experiment seems even to have anticipated that of the Soviet type of society in a small pioneering way. Though both were tragic, it is clear that the former already contained some tendency toward socialism.

The social thinking and experimenting aiming at the liberation of the people and in ferment during the French Revolution, actually led to the formation of a capitalist socioeconomic order under Napoleon's imperial rule, and under the subsequent rule of the restored Bourbons. Nevertheless, utopian socialists such as Saint-Simon and Fourier in France, inherited the radical aspect of the bourgeois revolution. They sought solutions for the poverty of workers and for economic malaise, such as overproduction, in the new industrial society. Saint-Simon was born into a noble family tracing its descent directly to Charlemagne. He joined a volunteer army to fight in the American Revolution, and he supported the Jacobins in the French Revolution. He then tried to apply natural sciences such as biology and physics to sociology, and, in his *Catéchisme Politique des Industriels* (1823–4) and *Nouveau Christianisme* (1825),[11] drew up the following perspective. The progress of organic social formations started historically with the primitive age of idolatry, passed through the age of polytheism corresponding to the slave system, and the age of Christianity corresponding to the feudal system of social estates, and then, after the 15th century, entered the age of crisis when scientists and industrialists appeared with a new scientific world-view. Though the French Revolution intended to push forward this progress, it failed as it fell into a chaotic anarchical situation.

The failure, Saint-Simon thought, must be made good by the creation of a society of association where 'all men become brothers'. This society should be based on co-operation among industrialists and scholars representing the sciences. In such a society, parasitic living would be excluded and labour would be an obligation which falls on all members of society. In return, all persons would be guaranteed equal opportunities, as well as the distribution of income according to their ability and contribution to society. National plans would be made for production in agriculture and manufacture, and national borders would be gradually abolished so as to realise universal peace.

Saint-Simon's schemes present a attractive idea of association, to be realised on the foundation of the growth of industrial society. From this idea Saint-Simonism was formed by B.P. Enfantin (1796–1864) and others after the beginning of the 1830s, and even took the form of a religious movement. A. Comte (1798–1857), the founder of sociology, was also among Saint-Simon's the disciples. In Saint-Simon's socialism, however, the social subjects who would realise the new ideal co-operative society were not precisely identified. Class antagonism between capitalists and workers was ignored. While capitalists and workers were bundled together as industrialists, it was in practice assumed that leadership would be undertaken by industrial capitalists. Thus, it was hoped that appeals for a change in the ideas of industrial capitalists would bring about a society of association as an 'industrial system'.

This way of thinking in a sense anticipated the contemporary citizens' movements which demand that capitalist firms play a cultural and social role in achieving desirable socio-economic and ecological conditions, as well as in protecting and improving the health of people. Its significance and potential must not be neglected, but it is surely utopian to expect that only a change in the ideas of capitalist firms, or their managers, is sufficient to create a new society based on association.

Fourier also represents some typical characteristics of the early French socialism of this period. He was born in a wealthy merchant family and enhanced his level of culture by self-education while active in business. He was deprived of his property in the French Revolution, and was disillusioned by its social consequences. He then drew a precise plan for an ideal future society in *Le Nouveau Monde Industriel et Sociétaire* (1822),[12] among other works. According to Fourier, human history comprised four stages; the age of Eden, the primitive age, the savage age, and the age of civilisation. In the age of civilisation poverty was derived from superfluity itself. An alternative social order of harmony should thus be founded. In the harmonious society, four twelfths of annual social income would be distributed to capital, five twelfths to labour, and three twelfths to talent. The proportion accorded to labour would increase as society made progress.

The basic unit of this association society would be called a phalanx comprising a population of 1600–1700 living together in a huge collective house – like the Palais Royal – called phalanstère. In a phalanx, mechanised agriculture and manufacturing would be combined, and rural life would be amalgamated with urban life. In the life of association, people's natural desires would be directed to creative activity. Powerful workers corps would be organised locally, nationally, and internationally. We can see how precise Fourier's ideas were in his detailed plan of a phalanstère, as well as in the following daily schedule for a person living there:

The daily schedule for Lucas in June
at 3:30 Getting up, preparation.
at 4:00 Participation in a group for a stable.
at 5:00 – in a gardeners' group.
at 7:00 Breakfast.
at 7:30 – in a mowers' group.
at 9:30 – in a vegetable gardeners' group under a tent.
at 11:00 – in a series on cow sheds.
at 1:00 Lunch.
at 2:00 – in a series on forestry.
at 4:00 – in a manufacturing group.
at 6:00 – in a series on irrigation.
at 8:00 To the Exchange of sentiments.
at 8:30 Dinner.
at 9:00 – in amusing intercourse.
at 10:00 Going to bed.

Fourier's conception contains attractive and profound suggestions, such as the overcoming of the separation of manufacturing and agriculture, as well as of towns and villages, the solution of the problem of disfigured single-talented personality caused by the division of labour, a proper size for the society of association relying upon direct democracy, decentralised autonomous life of association, and a collective house for these purposes. These suggestions have been succeeded by later socialist ideas, or by attempts to construct new harmonious villages. The daily schedule, however, seems hard to keep, as it demands 14 1/2 hours of work a day and leaves just 5 1/2 hours for sleep. Fourier argued that the schedule would not make people exhausted, as a large proportion of the working time is devoted to agricultural operations with a variety of activities in healthy conditions. Nevertheless, the schedule probably reflected the generally tough work conditions immediately after the Industrial Revolution. Although the healthy environment and the variety of activities are attractive features, the schedule is still severe. More's conception of 6 hours of work a day is more appealing since it leaves enough time for activities independent of work, especially in Japan where hard and long work hours occasion not a few karoshi cases (overwork to death).

Fourier believed that his precise blueprint for the phalanstère is the best social system, and personally led a well-regulated, punctual life in Lyon. To the end of his life he waited every day punctually from noon onwards for a charitable benefactor who would appreciate his blueprint, and would not worry about being called a lunatic of the Palais Royal. It was all in vain. While presenting a radical conception for a new society of association, Fourier was opposed to revolutionary struggle and to class struggle. We see another typical characteristic of utopian socialism in this regard too.

Another early socialist, Simonde de Sismondi was born in the family of a wealthy pastor into Geneva, became a banker, and faced difficult times during the French Revolution. He found himself, together with his father, in self-exile in England and Italy where he practised farming. After returning to Geneva in 1800, he became associated with romantics admiring the society of the past at the salon of Madame de Stael, and published *Nouveaux Principes d'Economie Politique* (1819), among other works.[13]

In that book, Sismondi emphasised the inevitability of production far exceeding consumption in a modern industrial society, and the resultant poverty and *calamité* (disaster) for people. According to him, this was because, on the one hand, capital accumulation reduced consumers' demand by substituting machinery for labourers and pauperising peasants, and, on the other, it increased the supply of products regardless of the level of consumer demand. In contrast to T.R. Malthus (1766–1834), Sismondi ascribed overproduction and poverty not to natural law, but to the increasing introduction of machinery in the process of capital accumulation. In this respect, his under-consumption theory was more influential than Malthus' theories in forming Marx's crisis theory. It presented a sharp critique of an inherent difficulty of the capitalist economy. Sismondi's proposed solution for the disaster of overproduction was different from either Malthus or Marx. He argued for a return to a patriarchal peasant farming system where an ideal natural balance between production, income and population would be easily tenable. This perspective was clearly influenced by the romanticism of Sismondi's day, also to be found in broader fields such as literature. It characterised Sismondi as a founder of romantic socialism.

While utopian socialism dreamt of a harmonious ideal society to be realised in the future, romantic socialism, in contrast, idealised a past patriarchal peasant farming, and aimed at restoring it as the basic unit of a society of association. Later, Russian *Narodniks*, whom Lenin opposed and criticised at the beginning of his political career, made romantic socialism an actually existing social movement. Romantic socialist ideas seem to revive frequently as part of the ecological thought and movements in our day. We cannot easily disregard the attractions of utopian and romantic socialism both in their critiques of capitalist economy and in their naive but moving conceptions of a more desirable society.

2 Modern Socialism

Unlike pre-modern communism, utopian and romantic socialism presented a modern critique of the capitalist economy, and contained elements of the modern conception of socialism. However, since they were sustained by nebulous utopian ideas and by the idealised image of a past agricultural society, they could not specify the actual agents of the socialist transformation of an industrial capitalist society. Therefore they could not for long remain the mainstream of modern socialism.

OWENISM

R. Owen is generally cited as a representative utopian socialist in Britain. Indeed his attitude showed a clear aspect of utopian socialism since he drew up plans for an ideal co-operative society and perpetually appealed to capitalist managers, politicians, and even to Queen Victoria, to further the realisation of his ideas. His activities, however, had a further aspect, if partial and unsuccessful: pioneering practice in the co-operative and the trade union movements. This aspect was probably rooted in the British tradition of practicality which is not limited to social thought and movements. At any rate, it actually made Owen more than a mere utopian thinker in the socialist tradition.

Owen was born in 1771, the son of a Welsh saddler and ironmonger, and was educated at a village school. He left home at 10 years of age to become a draper's apprentice in Stanford, moved to Manchester in the middle of industrial revolution, and became a capitalist manager at the early age of 18. He then achieved the position of joint manager of a cotton-spinning factory in Lanarkshire, southern Scotland. There he experimented with new methods of factory management during the first quarter of the nineteenth century. The lessons he drew were summarised in his *A New View of Society* (1813–14).[1]

In Owen's opinion, the character of a person is decisively formed by the circumstances under which that person grows up and works. Therefore, an improvement of such circumstances always serves to reform the human character. This view led Owen to reduce working hours in his factory at New Lanark to 10 a day, down from 14–16 a day. He also provided a public nursery, a school, a home for the aged, and a mutual aid association shop. Owen intended to take good care of the workers as 'living machines'. The result was remarkable: workers stopped heavy drinking, friction among them was reduced, diligence increased, and Owen's factory could raise profits despite the shortened working hours. Thus, believing in the beneficial effect of reason and education, Owen appealed to capitalist managers, politicians and the government to make general this way of treating workers and so improve society. In 1824, Owen built a colony called New Harmony in Indiana, USA, spending £30,000 for the purchase of land alone, and moved there together with 900 other people. He intended to bring to realisation a model of a society of association in which private property and self-interest were to be denied. This attempt in New Harmony turned out to be a failure, and Owen returned to Britain in 1829.

Owen's views were adopted by the London Co-operative Union movement, founded in 1824, influenced in the Grand National Consolidated Trades Union (GNCTU), formed in 1834 with the aim of shortening the working hours, and were also influential in the rising Chartist movement of 1836–48. On occasion Owen played a leading role in these movements. One of his initiatives in the co-operative movement was to found in 1832 the National Equitable Labour Exchange in London and attempt to put in practice the theory of labour-money, put forth by such Ricardian socialists as W. Thompson (1775–1833) and J. Gray (1798–1850). Members of the co-operative unions were given a certificate of labour, i.e., labour-money, in exchange for their products and according to the labour-time necessary to produce the latter. They could then obtain any product in the Exchange by using the certificate. Equal exchange of labour among the products of the co-operative members was, thus, to be realised through labour-money, leaving no room for unequal exchange, or the exploitation of labour.[2]

Owen and his followers believed that social evils and unfairness could be corrected by improving the human character. They thought that the harmonious environment of a society of co-operation (communistic society) was necessary for this purpose. In trying to achieve this, however, they consistently opposed the use of violence by the masses of the people, including strikes and all class war in general. They relied on the goodwill of wealthy upper class persons and statesmen, as well as on democratic gradualism, to realise an ideal society for the people. They maintained this position even during the period of the upsurge of Chartism. This aspect of Owenism has often been cited by Marxists as one of its utopian limitations. However, Owenism's influence repeatedly reappears and its positive role should not be neglected when one considers the essential tasks of trade unions and co-operatives and wishes for a fuller growth for these organisations, especially in the advanced capitalist countries. It is also interesting to note that the idea of labour-money, or a sort of certificate of labour, is frequently revived and put to use in local co-operative activities, such as mutual help for housework, or the nursing of children and the aged at home.

Chartism focused on the People's Charter of 1837 and demanded the democratisation of the British Parliament. In particular, the Chartists demanded universal suffrage for men and the removal of the requirement of a minimum level of personal assets before one could be a candidate for Parliament. As a mass movement of revolt, Chartism was influenced by Owen's thought, but it also went beyond Owen's limitations by fostering a wide range of political and union activities by the organised workers themselves. Chartism contained the first revolutionary demands and actual activity by the working masses to reform British society on the grounds of labour and socialism. Through the experience of Chartism, socialism became rooted in Western societies as a popular and democratic tradition. While its radical revolutionary side was inherited by Marxism, its influential gradualist reforming side has also remained as a powerful tradition in Britain and other capitalist countries. For instance, J.S. Mill (1806–73) argued in his *Principles of Political Economy*, written in 1848 and used as the standard textbook of economics before A. Marshall (1842–1924) published his *Principles of Economics* in 1890, that 'the laws and conditions of the production of wealth partake of the character of physical truth', whereas the distribution of wealth is 'a matter of human institution only'.[3] These contrasting opinions, although certainly eclectic, reflect Mill's sympathy with the aim of co-operative socialism, considered 'good sense' in those days, for a more equitable distribution.

FABIANISM

The Fabian Society was founded in 1884. The title came from the Roman general Fabius who had a strategy of gradually, patiently fighting back against the invasion by the Carthaginians led by Hannibal. The Society attached importance to learning and to 'principles of penetration', i.e. to the transformation of people's minds through education. The Fabians undertook activity aiming at achieving socialism in a gradual manner. They intended to reconstruct the tradition of Owenism and

Chartism as democratic socialism. They were opposed to centralised bureaucracy, and adopted the strategy of realising socialism gradually through educational and political movements. In their practical strategy, the Fabians were quite different from the more naive and non-political Owenism, as well as from the more revolutionary Marxism. The dramatist and commentator G.B. Shaw (1856–1950), and the sociologists Beatrice Webb (1858–1943) and Sidney J. Webb (1859–1947), among others, supported such Fabian activities.

Fabianism made use of D. Ricardo's theory of differential ground rent, inherited by J.S. Mill, in order to demand the abolition of private landed property as a source of unearned income. Extending this point of view, the Fabians aimed at bringing under social control profit and interest as unearned private income, so as to bring about a liberal and fair society based on labour. In this regard, they were also influenced by the theoretical power of Marx's political economy. It is also noteworthy that, in the line of J.S. Mill and his collaborator Harriet Taylor, they earnestly took up the issue of women's liberation and became one of the sources of modern feminism. The ideas and activities of the Fabian Society served as a pillar for the British Labour Party, and the leading Fabian S. Webb became a Labour party Cabinet minister in the 1920s. Generally speaking, socialism tended to resort either to utopian persuasion of capitalist managers and politicians, or to radical revolutionary struggle by political parties and the mass movement. By contrast, Fabianism presented a strategy of realising socialism through cumulative social reforms, to be effected gradually by daily activity within the existing political system of a democratic society. Against the revolutionary and militant socialist route, Fabianism opened up the alternative route of adapting socialism to popular democratic daily activity.

As we see in *Fabian Essays in Socialism* (1889), edited by Bernard Shaw, the intention of the Fabians was clearly not to remain within the framework of bourgeois democracy, but to move toward the realisation of the ideals of socialism.[4] This intention has become a regular undercurrent in the British Labour Party, and also in Labour Parties or Socialist Parties in other capitalist countries. As revolutionary Marxism has often argued, there is certainly a danger that Fabianism, by merely demanding everyday social reforms and partial revisions of the capitalist economy, may not go beyond social democracy and may end up as a complement to the capitalist system. The root of this danger lies in the theoretical insufficiency of Fabianism's critical analysis of the capitalist economy. For example, since the source of ground rent, profit and interest as unearned income was not analytically related by the

Fabians to surplus-labour produced by workers in the capitalist production, social justice tended to be seen as realisable through the redistribution of income by taxes and welfare policies. The task of socialism finally to overcome the capitalist market economy itself, and to liberate workers from alienated and subordinated labour in the process of capitalist production, tended to disappear from the Fabian perspective and movement.

Nevertheless, Fabian socialism, aiming at a fair and liberal socialist society by means of democratic reforms, is certainly a strategic alternative which ought to be reassessed by Marxism as the latter struggles systematically to overcome capitalism by employing a more thorough theoretical analysis of the capitalist economy. The argument that Marx's thought and theories are incompatible with Fabian democratic gradualist strategies, and that Marxism should always be linked to Leninist militant revolutionary party strategies, is too narrow an interpretation of Marxism and does not make the most of the rich potential of Marxism for our age.

MARXISM

Marx and Engels

K. Marx, in co-operation with F. Engels, founded scientific socialism, or Marxism, as one strand among many within the broad current of modern socialism. Marxism served to strengthen modern socialism by overcoming the weaknesses its other strands. Because of this, large numbers of workers and intellectuals were attracted to Marxism in our century, and Marxism became a powerful force in making ours a century of revolutions. However, we have to review the characteristics of Marxism in order to understand its success as well as the defects and the resultant failure of Soviet-type societies.

Social thought aiming at socialism or communism had generally provided three types of foundations for its assertions. Firstly, human history was reviewed and summed up from the standpoint of a presumed original, or natural, state of human social life. The possibility of realising a co-operative and harmonious future society was sought in such historical arguments. The question of how to read history is always intimately connected with one's position on how to solve contemporary social problems. Pre-modern communist concepts, which idealised the natural order of human society in the remote ancient age, or Saint-Simon's and Fourier's socialism which criticised the crises and the poverty in the midst of plenty in the modern industrial age, all tried to sum up past human history with a view to drawing conclusions about the future. Secondly, various communist and socialist concepts were grounded on critical observation and examination of oppression, poverty and discrimination against working people in the existing social order. Finding solutions for such pressing problems for the mass of people was even thought of as a morally important social task. Thirdly, utopian plans for a desirable future society which would relieve and liberate working people were drawn in frequently quite precise terms.

By contrast, Marxism is characterised by its efforts, and conspicuous achievement in several works, to provide scientific foundations for declaiming in favour of communism or socialism. Hence it deserves to be called scientific socialism. There are four interrelated characteristics of Marxism in this respect. Firstly, Marx and Engels undertook an unprecedently profound and accurate study of history and of social science (particularly political economy), reconstructed various preceding philosophical world-views, and presented a grand and persuasive summation of world history in historical materialism.[5] As we shall see later, the one-sided and stereotyped interpretation and application of historical materialism, so common among 'orthodox' Marxists, have now come under thorough review. Even the revision, not to mention the deconstruction, of historical materialism is now being attempted by Marxists. However, historical materialism, which sums up human history up to and including bourgeois society as the evolution of class societies driven by the dialectical relation between productive powers and the relations of production, remains deeply informative and persuasive. We do not as yet possess a comparable alternative. One strength of Marxist socialism is evidently the possession of such a powerful summary view of human history.

Second, Marx was able systematically to clarify the principles of motion of capitalist economy with all its historical specificities and inherent contradictions. This he achieved in his main work *Capital* through a strenuously critical study of political economy, and by following the 'guiding thread' of historical materialism. On the one hand, Marx reformed the basic principles of political economy by overcoming the narrow bourgeois ideological framework of classical political economy which assumed that capitalism was the natural order of things. Principles of political economy as a socio–historical science were thus established, to serve as a theoretical standard for understanding and analysing economic oppression, exploitation, and the contradictions of the capitalist economy. This enabled Marx totally and scientifically elucidate the character of capitalism, as well as the plausibility of capitalism's total transformation, demanded by modern socialism. The objective foundations for a socialist movement were, thus, theoretically established.

The appropriateness of Marxist economic theories as frame of reference for the critical analysis of the capitalist economy is not at all impaired by the failure of Soviet-type societies. This leads us to expect with certainty the re-appearance of the socialist hope that capitalism would be overcome. However, we should also endeavour to solve the problems remaining in *Capital*, and to reconsider the problematic interpretations of Marx's theoretical system in the light of the crisis of socialism in our age. We would lose sight of Marx's original intention to ground socialism on the objective study of social science if we neglected the scientific re-examination of *Capital* itself, and dogmatically accepted the book's theories or the applications of the latter by leading Marxists.

Thirdly, on the basis of historical materialism and the political economy of *Capital*, Marxism expects the united working class to act as the subject of history, and to realise its own self-emancipation in socialism. Marxism does not believe that socialism relies on the moral actions of capitalists, or the ruling politicians to effect social reform and to bring salvation. However, as was shown by Marx's and Engels' own activities, Marxism also attaches importance to the role of intellectuals and of workers' political parties, in making workers conscious of international developments and of the scientific foundation of their struggles for self-emancipation.

Fourthly, in contrast to the precise plans of a future society drawn by utopian socialists, Marx's works do not contain any concrete and detailed systematic plans for a future society, with the exception of certain suggestions for the co-operative society beyond capitalism. It must be assumed that for Marx the principles of socialism were to be understood through (or in opposition to) the principles of the capitalist economy. It also presumably follows that more detailed and precise plans of a future society must be determined by historically concrete conditions and by the subjective decisions of people. Such plans could not be properly generated through the basic theories of political economy alone. Scientific socialism should not indeed over-generalise about the future, nor assert as desirable what objective scientific theories and analyses cannot yet directly show as scientific truth. In any case, lack of concrete plans for a future society is often regarded as a defect of Marxism. It has actually proved a source of confusing confrontations among Marxists in the course of development of the socialist movement, as well as in the process of constructing a socialist economy in post-revolutionary societies. However, this absence also gives us room in the present crisis of socialism to reconsider the plausibility of various alternatives, which can replace the Soviet type of society for the future.

Marxism after Marx

The controversy on revisionism took place in the Marxist current after the death of Marx and Engels. E. Bernstein (1850–1932), who was once regarded as one of most the promising Marxist theorists, opened the way for revisionist assertion by refuting the relevance of Marx's economic theories to late 19th century capitalism. This was especially so for Marx's theory of the polarisation of society into a smaller and smaller number of capitalists and a larger and larger number of increasingly impoverished workers.[6] In Bernstein's opinion the first half of the Erfurt Programme (1891) of the German Social Democratic Party, which employed Marx's theory of the polarisation of society and 'the law of impoverishment of workers', no longer matched the actual development of capitalism. The growth of joint-stock companies counteracted the centralisation of property, small producers and firms were able to survive and even proliferated in some sectors, especially agriculture. Moreover, the development of the means of transportation and communication, as well as the growth of credit and cartel systems, increased the flexibility of the capitalist economy and its ability to prevent acute economic crises. Thus, the expectation of a radical socialist revolution fostered by 'the law of impoverishment of workers' in the process of the polarisation of society and through increasingly severe crises, was untenable and wrong. Therefore, argued Bernstein, the first half of the Erfurt Programme had lost its basis, as had Marx's doctrine. The German Social Democratic Party should abandon both of these, and should confine its tasks to the latter half of the Programme, i.e. to the achievement of democratic and gradual reforms.

Bernstein's argument represented the first, and typical, strand of revisionism within Marxism. Similar arguments have been repeated since then at various times and places. They seem to be powerfully reviving at the moment against the backdrop of the failure of Soviet-type 'orthodox' Marxism. There are two major theoretical problems with Bernstein's argument. First, Bernstein's rejection of Marx's basic theories as outdated was based on a rather over-hasty matching of these theories against the actual features of late 19th century German capitalism. Bernstein should have instead explained these novel features of capitalism on the basis of Marx's theory. By not doing so he exhibited confusion between the level of research into the basic principles of capitalist economy, as that is found in *Capital*, and the level of research of more concrete studies into the changing stages or periods of capitalist development, or the level of research into the different features of the various types of a capitalist country. Secondly, Bernstein's interpretation of Marx's theory of the polarisation of capitalist society and 'the law of impoverishment' of workers, found in the Manifesto of the Communist Party, as the major element of Marx's economic theory is much too narrow. Bernstein neglected the richer theoretical content of *Capital*. Following the methodology of K. Uno, the basic principles of the capitalist economy should be examined in their purest form by omitting the theory of the polarisation of society, which assumes the existence of non-capitalist producers still to be proletarianised. The actual process of proletarianisation with the attendant impoverishment of workers, observed in many third world countries, must be analysed at a more concrete level of research.[7]

These two problems were not satisfactorily dealt with either by K. Kautsky (1854–1938) in his reply to Bernstein,[8] or by later Soviet 'orthodox' Marxism. They have remained a source of further confusion among Marxists. For example, although Kautsky presented a most comprehensive critique of Bernstein's assertions by persuasively pointing out the latter's superficial interpretation of Marx's theories, he did not succeed in locating the actual roots of Bernstein's revisionism in the changed conditions of capitalist development. Instead, Kautsky insisted on demonstrating that the tendential polarisation of society fully held throughout the late 19th century German capitalist development. Even though Kautsky initiated an important Marxist field of study in *The Agrarian Question* (1899), he was apt to emphasize only the *de facto* proletarianisation of peasant farmers, and could not explain why a large peasant class should remain in late developing capitalist countries such as Germany, and unlike Britain. Neither could Kautsky explain how important was the social alliance of the working class and the peasantry in such cases.[9]

G.V. Plekhanov (1857–1918) and R. Luxemburg (1871–1919) joined Kautsky in countering Bernstein's revisionism. Plekhanov attacked mainly Bernstein's misunderstanding or misinterpretation of historical materialism. Luxemburg argued in *Sozialreform oder Revolution* (1899) that social reform and social revolution were inextricably linked for the German Social Democratic Party, since social reform was the means and social revolution was the aim of the Party.[10] In practice, however, the German Social Democratic Party and other parties of the Second International which was theoretically led by Kautsky, increased their political ability to effect economic reforms through parliament on the basis of the growth of trade unions. In fact these parties could be thought of as on a Fabian road to socialism through parliament democracy. The analysis of the complex structure of social classes, including the remaining peasantry, became an important political issue for them in order to expand their political support. While Bernstein's revisionism represented in fact a direct importation of Fabianism into Marxism which negated Marx's basic theory, Kautsky's reply simply maintained the relevance of the basic positions of Marxism and restated the final goal of socialism. In the controversy, the strategic possibility under certain historical conditions in the advanced capitalist countries of following Fabian gradual democratic reforms, but based on Marx's thought and theories, was not sufficiently investigated.

After the controversy on revisionism, in which Kautsky seemed to win majority support among Marxists, the debate of how to define imperialism became an increasingly acute problem for Marxism as the First World War came closer. Kautsky, once again by sticking to Marx's basic theory of capitalism, made light of the concrete historical and political importance of imperialism. He defined the latter as merely one of the favoured policies of industrial and finance capital as they sought to expand trade with agricultural areas.[11] As a result, Kautsky and the mainstream of the Second International could not offer an effective theoretical basis for socialists and workers to resist and revolt when faced with the crisis of the imperialist World War. The Second International collapsed when it failed to oppose war budgets in the name of defending the fatherland of each national group of workers.

Against Kautsky, Lenin made clear in *Imperialism* (1917) the historically concrete necessary character of imperialism resulting from the growth of monopoly capital in the major countries, which divided and re-divided the colonial territories across the world.[12] The World War, therefore, was an imperialist war as far as all sides were concerned, and had to be opposed and turned into a revolutionary civil war. On these grounds, Lenin and the Bolsheviks, operating under the strict discipline of the vanguard party principle (democratic centralism under which discipline was generally applied in a top-down, army-like fashion) led the Russian Revolution of 1917 to success and to the development of Soviet society thereafter.

Although Lenin could with good reason brand Kautsky a renegade, the possible ways of using Marx's thought and theories in opposing the imperialist war and in developing strategies for the success of the socialist revolution were not limited to the Bolshevik vanguard party. Outside Russia the left wing of the Second International, above all R. Luxemburg,[13] tried to organise mass revolts by more democratic general strikes in their opposition to the First World War and during the German revolution after the War. Luxemburg was concerned with the lack of democratic participation by the mass of working people under the rule of Lenin's vanguard party, and openly criticised this aspect of the Russian Revolution. Luxemburg's critical point of view is worth remembering and re-assessing given the failure of oppressive Soviet communism. The social revolutions in Poland, Luxemburg's country of origin, and in other Eastern European countries in 1989, were evidence of the actual possibility of social revolution through democratic mass revolt, as Luxemburg wished. These revolutions, however, took place in a historically different context and in possibly the reverse direction from the one Luxemburg had in mind.

A. Gramsci (1891–1937), a founding member of the Italian Communist Party, and other Western Marxists who promoted Euro-communism, also opposed the methods of command used by the Leninist vanguard party and by the Stalinist bureaucracy. They attempted to make the best of Marx's thought and theories in forming a popular front against fascism and in developing a democratic socialist movement. They attached importance to the democratic traditions, the existing political mechanisms of Western societies, and the organic role of intellectuals.[14]

The renaissance of Marxism in the Western countries since the 1960s unfolded on the basis not only of criticism of the capitalist social system, but also by keeping a certain critical distance from Leninist–Stalinist Marxism. The majority of contemporary Western Marxists aspire to social reforms through the democratic movement of workers and citizens. However, it is probably the case that the Leninist vanguard party still has a strategic role to play and some significance in the revolutionary liberation struggles of third world countries with severely oppressive political systems or military governments. At any rate, it is safe to state that Marxists across the world do not any longer accept that Marxism–Leninism, or any other alternative line, is the universally correct and unique strategic route for Marxism.

For the future of socialism, Marx's original thought and theories should be re-considered and deepened in order to make various alternative strategies more easily conceivable, in accordance with the concrete historical conditions of each society. The present crisis of socialism gives us a good opportunity to rethink Marx's thought and theories.

Part II
Theories

3 Marx's Socialism

Marx's socialism is called 'scientific'. Early socialists generally tended to condemn the oppression of working people in modern society on moral grounds, and to draw emphatic plans for an ideal future society. Marx criticised the utopian nature of these plans, and strove to consolidate the theoretical grounds for socialism. This he did, first, by developing an accurate summary of human history in the formula of historical materialism, and secondly, by systematically clarifying the economic laws of motion of modern capitalist society. Marxism was thus formed as a type of socialism grounded upon historical materialism and political economy. In this respect it can well be characterised as scientific socialism and contrasted with the preceding utopian socialism.

It follows that the foundations of Marx's socialism have to be understood and re-examined by paying special attention to the content of historical materialism and to Marx's economic theories. The economic theories of *Capital* systematically clarify the historically specific character and the intrinsic contradictions of the capitalist economy, and so persuasively demonstrate that it is possible to realise socialism by overcoming capitalism. Nevertheless, the main task of these theories remains to form an objective recognition of the capitalist economy as a historical formation which can be transformed. Political assertions and political movements which aim at ending the history of class societies, including capitalism, and which wish to form a society of co-operation as an association of free persons, must be sustained by practical and historical materialism in addition to the scientific objective recognition provided by political economy.

Thus, Marx's political economy and historical materialism have relatively independent roles in establishing the foundations of socialism. At the same time they are mutually related in a dialectical way. Their relation used to be explained in the following simplistic and one-sided way: Marx's dialectical materialism was obtained by reversing Hegel's idealist dialectic; historical materialism was formed when dialectical materialism was applied to human history; Marxist political economy was developed by applying historical materialism to a capitalist economy. In this type of interpretation, often encountered among Marxian theorists of the second and third International, dialectical materialism and historical materialism were treated as if they were metaphysical truth, and not in need of scientific evidence.[1] At the same time, Marxist political economy tended to be regarded as a class-biased science, and was confused with ideology. As a result, it was hard for Marxist political economy to establish objectively scientific grounds for socialism.

The tasks of Marxist political economy go beyond the narrow limitations of classical and neo-classical economics, both of which treat the capitalist market economy as a natural and harmonious order. The broader tasks of Marxist economics include the elucidation of the historically specific character of the capitalist economy, and these tasks are determined under the guidance of historical materialism. Setting the tasks of Marxist political economy in this manner certainly deepens the latter's theoretical insight into the socio–historical character of the market economy and capitalism. The political implications for socialism, which can with justification be suggested by such theoretical insights, have to be derived from the system of objective recognition of the capitalist economy based on facts and logic, and always bearing in mind that political economy is not an ideology but a social science. If there is error or incompleteness in Marxist political economy, it certainly has to be corrected in a scientific way on the basis of facts and logic.

At the same time, the content of historical materialism, and the perspective of socialism, have to be deepened and extended in line with the progress in the theoretical study of the capitalist economy. However, this task was not sufficiently and consciously taken up either by Marx or his followers. In the case of Marx, historical materialism was formed in the process of joint work with F. Engels resulting in *The German Ideology* (1845–6, in *Marx–Engels Collected Works* (*MECW*), 5). It was summarily formulated in the Preface to *A Critique of Political Economy* (1859). Marx did not particularly re-examine the content of historical materialism after forming his own system of political economy in *Capital*. This does not necessarily mean that Marx believed every part of his formula of historical materialism to be the undeniable scientific truth. At any rate, in view of the considerable progress of Marxist economics it is remarkable that there has not been any comparable and related re-examination of historical materialism. This might be one of the reasons why many Marxists have tended to treat historical materialism as metaphysical absolute truth, a fact which became especially clear in the process of fossilisation of 'orthodox', Soviet-type Marxism.

In the current deep crisis of socialism, the grounds for Marxism have to be re-examined broadly, including historical materialism. Furthermore, we must reconsider the question of which elements Marx did adopt from preceding theories of socialism and which fresh points he added to those as a result of forming the economic theories of *Capital*. Finally, how can the perspective of materialist socialism be further expanded by the theoretical study of the problems left unsolved in *Capital*? Let us approach these issues in this chapter by tracing the formation of Marx's thought and of his theories of political economy.

HISTORICAL MATERIALISM

Historical materialism was formed apparently before Marx began to formulate his own system of political economy. This fact tended to be interpreted as meaning that Marx's economic theories were a direct application of historical materialism and relied totally on materialist socialism. However, it is possible to detect the influence of Marx's economic studies on the way in which he summed up human history in the formula of historical materialism. Marx constantly seeks supporting evidence for his view of human history in political economy, unlike other major world-views of history.[2] It should be borne in mind, however, that this type of evidence derives from the specific study of capitalism, and its validity for other human societies must be demonstrated by a thorough study of history itself.

Before Marx's birth and during his youth, G.W.F. Hegel (1770–1831) had formed a grand and erudite system of philosophy which explained dialectically the phenomena of the human spirit, external nature, world history, and the existing social structure, as the logical development of the contradictions occuring in the process of the self-revelation of the absolute spirit. This was the zenith of German idealist philosophy. The absolute spirit in Hegel was a driving and creative subject, much like a rationalised Christian god. Subsequently, L.A. Feuerbach (1804–72) was influential in the left wing of Hegel's followers, and developed the critique of Christianity which was dominant in Western societies. Feuerbach asserted that the essence of the Christian god is the external idealisation of common supreme human feelings (such as fraternity or love) in the alienated image of godhood. He thus turned Hegel's idealist philosophy into humanistic materialism. In this view, god was not a creator, but a creation of the human mind, akin to fantasy. The conclusion was that human life should be liberated from such religious fetishism. Young Marx was deeply influenced by this kind of thinking. However, Marx soon became aware that Feuerbach's humanism still saw human beings abstractly as natural beings and without considering the socially and historically concrete conditions of practical human activity. To Marx it seemed that men and women living in a class society were not only spiritually alienated from their essential activity, but actually from their own labour and its results.

Marx reached this point of view in the course of his critique of Hegel's philosophy of law. In opposition to Hegel, Marx thought that existing legal relations and forms of state neither had autonomous life of their own, nor were they the result of the self-development of the absolute spirit. They were, instead, rooted in the order of human material life relations, which Hegel called 'a bourgeois society'. Marx began to study political economy systematically, and to examine the anatomy of bourgeois society, including the specific form of alienated labour.

On the basis of such critical consideration of Hegel and Feuerbach, and before he actually started full-scale work on political economy in London, Marx summed up his own view of the essence of human beings, society, and history, in historical materialism. The latter provided a perspective for socialism far exceeding the essential limitations of past human history, including bourgeois society. Historical materialism, the general result of his early investigations, 'which, once won, served as a guiding thread' for his succeeding studies, was briefly formulated in the Preface to *A Critique of Political Economy* (1859). I shall quote from it by dividing the essential part of the text into three paragraphs concerning, (1) the structure of social formations, (2) the logic of revolutionary changes of these formations and, (3) the summation of human history.

> (1) In the social production of their life, men enter into definite relations that are indispensable and independent of their will, relations of production which correspond to a definite stage of development of their productive forces. The sum total of these relations of production constitutes the economic structure of society, the real foundation, on which rises a legal and political superstructure and to which correspond definite forms of social consciousness. It is not the consciousness of men that determines their being, but, on the contrary, their social being that determines their consciousness.
> (2) At a certain stage of their development, the material productive forces of society come in conflict with the existing relations of production, or – what is but a legal expression for the same thing – with the property relations within which they have been at work hitherto. From forms of development of the productive forces these relations turn into their fetters. Then begins an epoch of social revolution. With the change of the economic foundations the entire im-

mense superstructure is more or less rapidly transformed. In considering such transformations a distinction should always be made between the material transformation of the economic conditions of production, which can be determined with the precision of natural science, and the legal, political, religious, aesthetic, or philosophic – in short, ideological – forms in which men become conscious of this conflict and fight it out.

(3) In broad outlines Asiatic, ancient, feudal, and modern bourgeois modes of production can be designated as progressive epochs in the economic formation of society. The bourgeois relations of production are the last antagonistic form of the social process of production – antagonistic not in the sense of individual antagonism, but one arising from the social conditions of life of the individual; at the same time the productive forces developing in the womb of bourgeois society create the material conditions for the solution of that antagonism. This social formation brings, therefore, the prehistory of human society to a close.[3]

This pithy summation of human history intended to provide a fundamental perspective of the development of human societies, by utilising the studies of history available at the time. This view was also formed through the economic study of bourgeois society, and was intended to be used as 'a guiding thread' for the further full-scale study of political economy. Indeed, historical materialism tends to base its view of human history on the study of the characteristics of capitalist society, as these are elucidated by political economy, rather than on the evenly-weighted study of the entire history of past societies.

A capitalist society, basically maintains and develops the material conditions of human life completely by means of a commodity economy, independently of political and religious social relations. Thus, in a capitalist society, the economic relations of material life, which are the foundation of social life, have a distinctly autonomous logic of motion and a structure independent of the other dimensions of social life. Consequently, so long as the various aspects of social life must organically relate to each other, the forms and most of the content of social consciousness, as well as the legal and political superstructure, must basically correspond to, and be regulated by, the motion and constitution of the economic base of capitalist society.

Neither this distinction, nor the relations of regulation between the economic base and the social, political and ideological superstructure, are so clearly discernible in pre-capitalist societies. In these societies, base and superstructure organically penetrated each other in a multitude of ways. The further back we go into the ancient epochs the more undifferentiated the two were. However, if one's interest in the analysis of such societies is prompted by the economic study of capitalism itself and, specifically, by the intention of using the results for the deeper study of capitalism, one still has to ask how the forms of political and ideological life corresponded to the special economic forms of material life and served to maintain the relations of production. The content of historical materialism suggests such questions from the point of view of the study of capitalist society.

At the same time, Marx's understanding of capitalism was guided and made more profound by his view that capitalism was not a natural and ultimate social order, but a historically specific set of social relations, signifying the last phase of the pre-history of human society. This pre-history was a period of antagonistic class societies. In this regard, Marx's treatment of capitalism was guided by a vision of a liberated world transcending class society. Thus, through Marx's critical study of the preceding political economy, historical materialism was grounded on the economic anatomy of bourgeois society, and presented a novel perspective for the whole of human history.

Most critiques of historical materialism fail to understand, much less negate, these fundamental elements of Marx's method. For instance, one type of critique of historical materialism which concentrates on the distinction between base and superstructure of societies, has frequently cast doubt on the relevance of this distinction for pre-capitalist primitive societies, by referring to historical studies produced by economic anthropologists. It should be admitted that the formula of historical materialism is not scientific truth but, rather, a hypothetical frame of reference for the analysis of the historical development of human societies, and it should not be applied mechanically. The motion of the economic base cannot be completely autonomous, and the role of the superstructure is not always simply passive, even though the latter is, in the last instance, conditioned by the former. Nevertheless, in the case of capitalism, the relative autonomy of the economic base of society and the resultant distinctive relation between the motion of the base and that of superstructure are clearly evident. It should be stressed again that Marx's historical materialism was formed, and given methodological foundations, through the study of capitalist society in particular.

What can we then make of Marx's proposition that 'in broad outlines Asiatic, ancient, feudal, and modern bourgeois modes of production can be designated as progressive epochs in the economic formation of society'? Is is not the case that its over-simplified, Euro-centric, linear view of history reflects the limitations of historical study in Marx's time? The proposition makes, for instance, no reference to the existence of pre-historic primitive communist societies, nor to the growth of various communal societies in different parts of the world. This inadequacy has to be remedied in order to broaden historical materialism. However, in so far as the entire development of multifarious historical societies has finally been integrated into one modern world history driven by capitalist development in a few leading countries, Marx's opinion that socialism would transcend the prehistory of human class societies (this pre-history ending with capitalist bourgeois society) maintains a certain persuasiveness as a world-view of history.

Another important point in the formula of historical materialism is that Marx defined the productive forces, neither Hegel's absolute spirit nor Feuerbach's natural human being, as the driving subject of dialectical inference. In the base of societies, definite relations of production are formed corresponding to a definite stage of development of the productive forces. In the process of development of the productive forces the existing relations of production, together with their legal expression in the property relations, turn from forms conducive to the development of the productive forces into forms fettering them, and thus begins an epoch of social revolution. This view, on the one hand, critically opposed the romantic current of socialism which produced a critique of capitalism, but also idealised past patriarchal farming societies or even very primitive human societies. On the other hand, this view rejected the idealist view of history which identified the cause of historical development with the development of the absolute spirit or human ideas. In doing so, historical materialism attempted to grasp the material basis for the progress of human societies.

The interaction of the productive forces and the relations of production can generally be thought of as the driving force of the material life of human societies. In particular, the entire process of the birth, growth, and maturity of capitalism has been a historical transformation which corresponds to the development of the material forces of production. However, the direction, speed, ecological and human dimension of the forces of production have all been much influenced, limited, and disfigured by the dominant capitalist relations of production. Thus, the actual formation of specifically capitalist relations of production was decisive in promoting rapid industrialisation, in clear contrast to the feudal age. The formation of monopolistic organisation among capitals, on the other hand, has tended to hinder industrial innovation. The global, as well as local, destruction of the ecological environment has frequently recurred in the process of the capitalist development of productive forces. The development of the productive forces, thus, cannot be a neutral independent factor determining the appropriate relations of production. The transition from capitalism to socialism cannot occur simply as a result of the growth of the productive forces. Construction of a sound socialist society cannot adopt and uninterruptedly promote all productive forces developed under capitalism.

In this regard too, the formula of historical materialism should not be metaphysically taken as absolute truth, but should be applied and extended flexibly. Unlike the absolute spirit in Hegel's dialectical view of history, the development of the productive forces should not be interpreted as a transcendental, unbending driving force of history. In view of the frequent ecological crises of our age, we have to make clear that the range of alternative paths for the development of the productive forces has been widened, at least in the contemporary stage of capitalist history. The advantage of (sound) socialism over capitalism is to enlarge the possibility of selecting more humane and ecologically acceptable industrial technologies.

Studies of the capitalist economy are essential to extend and supplement historical materialism in all the above-mentioned directions. However, Marx and Engels presented their arguments for socialism by directly applying the original historical materialism in *The Communist Manifesto*.

SOCIALISM IN THE COMMUNIST MANIFESTO

The Communist Manifesto (1848) consists of four sections; 'Bourgeois and Proletarians', 'Proletarians and Communists', 'Socialist and Communist Literature', and 'Position of the Communists in Relation to the Various Existing Opposition Parties'. The first two sections positively present Marx's and Engels' view of socialism, and we will summarise the main points below.

To begin with, 'the history of all hitherto existing society is the history of class struggles'.[4] In older societies, class struggles were fought within a complicated arrangement of society comprising various orders, a manifold gradation of social rank. In modern bourgeois society, however, the struggles become simplified into the class antagonism between the two great hostile camps: the bourgeoisie and the proletariat. The formation of such a bourgeois society was the result of the breakdown of feudal society, which took place when the feudal relations of production became no longer compatible with the growing productive forces.

Modern productive forces, in turn, begin to come into conflict with bourgeois property relations, while the latter foster the rapid, almost magical, growth of the former. This is shown in the recurrence of commercial crises which imperil the existence of the bourgeois order, each time more seriously. The development of modern industry and machinery, the growing competition among capitalists, and commercial crises, make the livelihood of workers more and more precarious and impoverished. At the same time, the workers become concentrated into greater masses, begin to form trade unions against the bourgeoisie in order to keep wages up, and begin to struggle in association with each other. Though in substance international, the form of the struggle is initially national, directed against the national bourgeoisie. With the development of modern industry, the bourgeoisie produces 'its own grave-diggers. Its fall and the victory of the proletariat are equally inevitable'.

In the second section, *The Communist Manifesto* deals with questions typically addressed to communists, and argues that the task of communists is always to try to represent the interest of the proletariat as a whole. The section summarises the aims of working class revolution as follows:

> the first step in the revolution by the working class is to raise the proletariat to the position of ruling class, to win the battle of democracy. The proletariat will use its political supremacy to wrest, by degrees, all capital from the bourgeoisie, to centralise all means of production into the hands of the State, i.e., of the proletariat organized as the ruling class; and to increase the total of productive forces as rapidly as possible (*MECW*, 6, p. 504).

In the beginning this is to be effected only 'by means of despotic inroads on the right of property, and on the conditions of bourgeois production' (ibid.). The measures taken to achieve these aims will differ in different countries, but the following ones will be generally applicable in the most advanced countries; (1) abolition of property in land; (2) a heavily progressive income tax; (3) abolition of the right of inheritance; (4) confiscation of the property of emigrants and rebels; (5) centralisation of credit in the hands of the State; (6) centralisation of the means of communication and transport in the hands of the State; (7) extension of factories owned by the State, and the improvement of the soil in accordance with a common plan; (8) equal liability of all to labour and establishment of an industrial army, especially for agriculture; (9) combination of agriculture with manufacturing industries, and gradual abolition of the distinction between town and country; (10) free education for all children in public schools, and linking of education to industrial production, etc. (*MECW*, 6, p. 505).

Furthermore, when, in the course of the development of communist society, class distinctions disappear, 'the public power will lose its political character'. While national differences are daily vanishing owing to the world market, the hostility of one nation to another will come to an end, in proportion as the antagonism between classes within the nation vanishes. In an associational society which replaces old class societies, 'the free development of each is the condition for the free development of all' (*MECW*, 6, p. 506).

To read *The Communist Manifesto* is enormously appealing, even after the fall of the Soviet Union and the Eastern European 'communist' countries. Several of the declarations of the socialists are strikingly fresh even today; the call for a thoroughly democratic and egalitarian social order enabling the free development of each individual in association with others; the demand to combine agriculture with manufacturing in order to effect a more even and harmonious regional development of the economy; the internationalist attitude representing the universal common interests of working people; the authors' genius to identify the revolutionary role and ability of the proletariat. It seems quite natural that this small book has been so influential in attracting so many people across the world to the ideas of socialism.

Despite all this, *The Communist Manifesto* has left us with certain problems. Above all, its fundamental critical analysis of capitalism and its basic view of socialism were still directly based upon the application of the formula of historical materialism and, being a rough sketch, several weaknesses and problems remain. According to *The Communist Manifesto*'s analysis, the development of the productive forces was definitely the historical driving force which dissolved the feudal relations of production, the latter having been fetters to the former. Subsequently, in modern society the development of the forces of production has contradicted the bourgeois relations of production, a fact exemplified in the recurrence of commercial crises, it has polarised society into the richer and richer bourgeoisie and the poorer and poorer proletariat, and has, thus, made the proletarian revolution inevitable. The development of the productive forces will be further accelerated in a post-revolutionary society by the proletariat organised as the ruling class.

Thus, the entire process of the birth, growth, and decline of capitalism was conceived in one fell swoop as the changes in the relations of production resulting from the development of the productive forces. The inevitability of the proletarian revolution was asserted in the same context, and the social changes in post-revolutionary society were treated as realisable on the basis of the further accelerated growth of the productive forces. The development of the productive forces was clearly regarded as the driving agent causing changes in the social relations of production.

On the other hand, *The Communist Manifesto* presented a view of history based on class struggle, and emphasised the role of the bourgeoisie in dissolving feudal, society and forming modern industries and the world market. It also stressed the role of the proletariat, fighting in unison against its own impoverishment so as to realise a society of association. The subject of the dialectical transformations in history appears to be the changing ruling and ruled classes, rather than the development of the productive forces as a bare natural process. Later, in *Capital*, the bourgeoisie was defined as 'capital personified' (I, p. 739), and the subject of Marx's dialectic further became capital itself. Thus, Marx's reversal of Hegel's idealistic dialectic into a rational materialist one involved three steps in switching the subject of the dialectic: from the absolute spirit to the development of the productive forces, to the changing social classes, to capital itself.

The topics which Marx dealt with while discussing the subject of dialectical change were quite different, and so these steps may not have been immediately inconsistent. However, by carefully reconsidering these steps, as well as the manner of development of the productive forces in the light of the analysis of the motion of capital, we can clarify the role which the proletarian revolution can be expected to play. We can then avoid crude economism, which tends to believe that the mere quantitative expansion of the productive forces would solve all the socioeconomic problems of socialist society. *The Communist Manifesto*, being a rough sketch, could not go into these arguments in sufficient depth. The bourgeoisie and the proletariat, in so far as they both promoted the further growth of the productive forces, were supposed to push human history forward by dissolving the preceding social order. In this regard, the roles and positions of the two major classes in a capitalist society were conceived within the framework of the formula of historical materialism.

Nevertheless, there is a crucial problem left unsolved here, namely, how to understand the inevitability of the proletarian revolution as a result of the growth of modern productive forces. Marx and Engels seem to assume that as the accumulation and centralisation of wealth in the hands of a smaller and smaller number of capitalists proceeds, the poverty of the proletariat increases even more rapidly and the working class is forced to revolt and revolutionise the social system. Also related to this view, the historical changes in the form and scale of ownership of the means of production, which take place as productive forces grow, were seen as the focal point in the polarisation of bourgeois society into a declining number of richer and richer capitalists and an increasing number of poorer and poorer workers. Centralisation of the means of production was also seen as a precondition for their nationalisation by the proletariat. 'Orthodox' Soviet-type Marxism has long attempted to defend these points, in particular, (1) the inevitability of socialism due to the tendency toward the impoverishment of the proletariat, and (2) the nationalisation of the means of production as the main road to socialism.

Point (1) above has become hard to defend in an unsophisticated manner as real wages of workers in the advanced capitalist countries have tended to increase more or less since the late 19th century. Indeed, as Marx made clear in *Capital*, the production of relative surplus-value through an increase in productivity could still be achieved even allowing for a certain rise in real wages, if there was a reduction of the unit labour-value of the means of consumption. During the so-called Fordist regime of accumulation of the 1950s and 1960s which was accompanied by high economic growth, real wages rose more or less parallel to the growth of productivity in advanced capitalist countries. Thus, the attempt of orthodox Marxists to defend point (1) has seemed unconvincing to non-orthodox Marxists and to workers in the advanced countries, not to mention non-Marxists.[5] Point (2), on the other hand, was an ideological source of statism in Soviet orthodoxy. We have to examine how far these points were based on Marx's own theoretical work after the 1850s, including his life-work *Capital*.

In 1872, five years after the publication of the first volume of *Capital*, Marx wrote with Engels a Preface to a new German edition of *The Communist Manifesto*, in which they argued that 'the general principles laid down in this *Manifesto* are, on the whole, as correct as ever'. Among the notes made for the improvement of some details, the two following points seem important.

Firstly,

> the practical application of the principles will depend, as the *Manifesto* itself states, everywhere and at all times, on the historical con-

ditions for the time being existing, and for that reason, no special stress is laid on the revolutionary measures proposed at the end of Section II.

We can actually see that of the previously stated demands contained within *The Manifesto*, items (2), the progressive income tax, (5), the centralisation of credit, (6), the centralisation of the means of communication and transport, (7), factory ownership by the State, as well as the first half of (10), public schooling, all have to some extent been realised within the advanced capitalist countries by our own time. The demands to be achieved by socialist methods must indeed differ according to the historically concrete circumstances which also relate to national diversity.

Secondly, Marx and Engels noted that the lessons from the historical experience of the Paris Commune of 1871 must also be learnt:

> One thing especially was proved by the Commune, viz., that 'the working class cannot simply lay hold of the ready-made State machinery, and wield it for its own purposes'.

While Marx and Engels asserted the need to centralise all instruments of production in the hands of the State, they also added here that the bureaucratic institutions of the State themselves should be a target of communal social restructuring. This point leads us further to the famous passage in Marx's *Critique of the Gotha Programme* (1875), which argued that

> Between capitalist and communist society lies the period of the revolutionary transformation of the one into the other. Corresponding to this is also a political transition period in which the state can be nothing but the revolutionary dictatorship of the proletariat.[6]

The notion of the dictatorship of proletariat was combined with Lenin's theory of the vanguard party, and was used to legitimate the dominant position of the communist party bureaucrats as a coherent social order, especially after the Stalin regime was established. This was far from Marx's original notion. It is natural to interpret Marx's idea as a relatively short period of revolutionary dictatorship by the proletariat, completed by the communal restructuring of the inherited State machinery. Marx basically expected that public power would lose its political character, and that working people would win full democracy.

This expectation was later further developed as the notion of the death of the State, for example, in Engels' *Anti-Duhring* (1878).[7] The centralisation of the means of production in the hands of the State was not meant to prevent the weakening of the political power of the State. The notion of the dictatorship of the proletariat in Marx was not at all compatible with the creation of Stalinist statism which lasted for generations. The notion of dictatorship rather belongs to 'the practical application of the principles' which 'will depend on the historical conditions for the time being existing', and was advanced under the powerful impression made on Marx by the Paris Commune. The communal restructuring of the State machinery, including the decentralisation of State power, may possibly be achieved more democratically in advanced countries today.

In any case, the points which were freshly added by Marx and Engels in 1872 are mostly practical and political, and represent in particular the development of their theory of the State after the historical experience of the Paris Commune. It is rather curious that Marx did not discuss the theoretical implications for the principles of socialism deriving from his major work on political economy. Marx might have assumed that the priority for him was to complete the theoretical system of *Capital*, or that *Capital*'s contributions to the ideals of socialism could be easily understood by readers. At any rate, since Marx did not elaborate on the relationship between *The Manifesto* and *Capital*, the latter has tended to be read simply as a straightforward extension of the former, without inconsistencies or additional considerations for socialism. However, the broad and profound theoretical system of *Capital* not only presents a critical understanding of the motion of a capitalist economy, but also suggests a wealth of insights into the principles of political economy for socialism. Let us try to summarise some of the most important theoretical points in this regard.

THE LABOUR THEORY OF VALUE AND SOCIALISM

The Forms and the Substance of Value

One point on which Marx's political economy is fundamentally superior to Ricardo's is in theoretically recognising the historically specific character of the capitalist economy. This point is significant even as far as the basic theory of value is concerned. In addition to the distinction between use-value and value as the two factors of the commodity, the concept of value itself is structurally doubled in *Capital* into the forms and the substance of value.

The forms of value spring from historically specific social relations among commodities to be exchanged, and develop into the money form, or the price form, of commodities, as well as into the capital form. As Marx noted,

> it is one of the chief failings of classical political economy that it has never succeeded ... in discovering the form of value which in fact turns value into exchange-value (I, p. 174).

This defect is closely related to the fact that classical political economy neglects the historically specific character of a commodity economy and of capitalism.

Connected with this recognition, Marx also made clear that the labour process is

> the universal condition for the metabolic interaction between man and nature, the everlasting nature-imposed condition of human existence, and it is therefore independent of every form of that existence, or rather it is common to all forms of society in which human beings live (I, p. 290).

In the long history of human societies, the labour process and the resultant labour products have frequently and generally been unrelated to the forms of value. Labour-time embodied in useful products did not constitute the substance of value so long as the products were not commodities, as in the case of the own-consumption of the peasants' produce, or corn-rent paid to the feudal lord (I, p. 131). Only when the products were given a commodity form and were subsumed under the form of value did the labour-time embodied in them become the substance of value. Only through the capitalist process of production will all products take a commodity form as a social necessity, which inevitably makes the labour-time embodied in them the substance of value.

The twin conception (the forms and the substance) of value reflects the heterogeneous origins of the forms of value and of the labour process. As Marx points out,

> the exchange of commodities begins where communities have their boundaries, at their points of contact with other communities, or with members of the latter (I, p. 182),

whereas the labour process was performed endogenously within communities of varied social order. The forms of value in a commodity economy, such as the price form, essentially originate in exogenous economic relations arising between societies, and therefore assume the external quantitative form more or less independently of the endogenous quantitative relations of the social labour process arising within societies.

One implication of this recognition for socialism is clear: so long as the forms of value are originally exogenous, and relatively independent of the endogenous social labour process, then these forms can be removed so as to bring about a society of association at a higher level of development of history. Thus, Marx could theoretically prescribe for such a society a social system of distribution of means of consumption and allocation of means of production directly by labour-time. In the famous section on 'The Fetishism of the Commodity and its Secret' in *Capital*, Marx assumes, 'only for the sake of parallel with the production of commodities, that the share of each individual producer in the means of subsistence is determined by his labour-time' in a society of association, and continues:

> Labour-time would in that case play a double part. Its apportionment in accordance with a definite plan maintains the correct proportion between the different functions of labour and the various needs of the associations. On the other hand, labour-time also serves as a measure of the part taken by each individual in the common labour, and his share in the part of the total product destined for individual consumption. The social relations of individual producers, both towards their labour and the products of their labour, are here transparent in their simplicity, in production as well as in distribution (I, p. 172).

By contrast, A. Smith believed that commodity exchange originates in the intrinsic human propensity 'to truck, barter, and exchange one thing for another'.[8] According to Smith, commodity exchange causes the division of labour, and thus gives rise to a market economy as the natural order of things. Were this true, a planned economy based on association would be an unnatural prospect and contrary to fundamental human propensities. However, this view is not correct, as human societies in the pre-capitalist period had long been organised basically without commodity exchange, and in certain cases developed a social division of labour, as in the caste system of the primitive Indian com-

Marx's Socialism

munity. Marx's theory of value forms contains a profound critique of this view of classical political economy, and suggests the possibility of realising a socialist society of association.

Units of Economic Accounting

In the Soviet type of socialist society, which was based on Marx's political economy, the social relations of workers towards their labour and labour products were not actually made 'transparent', and a kind of (quasi-)price form, as well as (quasi-)money such as the rouble, were used continuously. Why was that the case?

One reason was the technical difficulty of calculating the labour-time embodied in a product unit, including not only the direct labour input of the final process of production, but also the indirect labour-time transferred from the consumed means of production. If we assume homogeneous labour across industries and a single product for each industry, then it can be theoretically shown that the labour-time embodied in the products is determined as the solution to a set of simultaneous equations representing the technological system of reproduction. Assume, for instance, n industrial sectors in society. To produce one unit of the ith product, a_{ij} units of the jth product and l_i hours of direct labour are technically necessary. Let the total of direct and indirect labour embodied in one unit of the ith product be t_i hours. Then, we have n simultaneous linear equations with n unknown t_i,

$$
\begin{aligned}
a_{11}t_1 + a_{12}t_2 + \ldots + a_{1n}t_n + l_1 &= t_1 \\
a_{21}t_1 + a_{22}t_2 + \ldots + a_{2n}t_n + l_2 &= t_2 \\
&\ldots \\
a_{n1}t_1 + a_{n2}t_2 + \ldots + a_{nn}t_n + l_n &= t_n
\end{aligned}
\tag{3.1}
$$

The n unknown t_i can be determined in terms of a_{ij} and l_i, the latter representing the technical conditions of production. We shall discuss why l_i can be treated as homogeneous in the next section. The allocation of labour-time to an individual product in the joint products produced by an industry can be conventionally determined by considering the relative strength of social demand, or need, for each product.[9] However, products in a modern society are actually so numerous that calculating the labour-time t_i embodied in each product by solving hundreds of thousands of simultaneous equations was practically impossible, given the level of Soviet computing technology. As computers progress it will become easier to calculate t_i, especially if we limit the number of unknowns to a certain range of strategically important products.

In the Soviet type of planned economy officially fixed prices were in any case generally used, as well as physical input–output data and the planned distribution of products and services. In their function, these officially fixed prices were not subject to the anarchical movement of demand and supply, and were quite different from prices in a market economy. If the price form and money appear in principle only within the anarchical free market economy, officially fixed prices in the Soviet Union were only quasi-prices, and money was, at most, quasi-money. Nevertheless, they were also different from units of account of labour-time, and the labour-time in each product was not actually measured.

Prices in the Soviet Union initially followed the pattern of prices of the pre-First World War period, and were subsequently officially altered from time to time on the cost-plus principle. Thus, if the price system of the Soviet type of economy failed after a certain period, this failure should not be identified with the failure of Marx's prescription for the application of the labour theory of value to socialism. At the same time, we also have to admit that the system of officially fixed prices actually worked over several decades in achieving relatively rapid economic growth. We rather have to ask theoretically how was it possible for it to work for as long as it did. We should bear this point in mind and return to it as the exposition proceeds.

Apart from the difficulty of calculating the labour-time in each product, there is another possible reason for using prices in a planned economy, even if officially fixed. Namely, even if labour-time is practically measurable, it could not serve as a measure of the growth of the disposable quantity of products. If we assume a given number of workers with given annual hours of labour, it follows that there cannot be any growth or change in the net social product in terms of labour-time. Furthermore, a common objective physical measure of different use-values does not exist; aggregation of steel, televisions, and T-shirts in terms of kilograms or tons does not make sense. Measures of quantitative growth of the national product, such as the economic growth rate, make clear sense only when the composition of the national product is assumed to maintain the same internal proportions. In this theoretically clear case, the growth rate of the real net national product (NNP) in terms of constant prices signifies nothing other than the growth rate of the total product of a nation.

However, a change in the composition of the total product, other things being equal, could also appear as a change in the growth rate of the net national product, if constant prices were used. If, for instance, a change in the composition increased the weight of products with relatively high value added per worker, then it would appear as if the real net national product had grown. However, in so far as the use-value of the products whose quantity was relatively increased is not commensurable with that of the products whose quantity was relatively reduced, the theoretical meaning of this case is not clear. To state that the 'increased' products have use-value greater than the 'decreased' products as is evidenced by indices based on their constant (deflated real) prices, is simply an expedient assumption used to facilitate economic accounting of national production. There are no strong theoretical foundations for use-value commensurability. Similar problems inevitably emerge when new products are created and incorporated into the national accounts. Production of new products is expediently regarded as production of weighted amounts of some similar old products.

In the same manner, officially fixed prices can serve to construct real (deflated) aggregate indicators measuring, if somewhat conventionally, the growth of the national economy. The smaller the change in the composition of the national product, the more accurate and the clearer the meaning of such macroeconomic accounting. In the same expedient sense, official prices can measure changes in the distribution of products to workers, firms, the State, or different regions. For instance, if the composition of consumer products obtained by a worker remains the same, an increase in real monetary income clearly signifies that the products distributed for individual consumption have been physically so much increased. If the composition of the social product can be treated as constant, then a change in monetary distribution among workers, firms, the State, or regions can be assumed approximately to represent a change in the distribution of the national product among them. In undertaking this measuring function, officially fixed prices would be no less useful than market prices reduced to base year fixity.

If we assume that social prices (s-prices) are set directly proportional to the labour-time embodied in each product, it follows that they would decline in inverse proportion to the growth of labour productivity over time. Then, the real national product at constant prices would certainly increase per worker, or per given amount of annual social labour–time, especially if the composition of the national product remained constant. This exemplifies the necessity of possessing some unit of economic accounting for the total product independent of labour-time, even if it is a more or less conventional one. It should be stressed that officially fixed prices can serve for this purpose just as well as do prices in a market economy.

Quasi-market or Full-market Pricing?

Although officially fixed s-prices in a planned economy may be thought of as a sort of price form, and that implies certain functions of s-money, they must also be distinguished from the price form, or the money form, of commodity value in a market economy. Reform of actually existing official prices in order to allow them to function more like the price form in a market economy was repeatedly proposed by Eastern European socialist reform movements. The utilisation of a freer market price system and the profit motive was, on the one hand, urged in order to increase individual motivation, and rationality in allocation of resources and labour, more in accord with social needs. On the other hand, it was assumed that the market price system would serve as an effective means of reducing centralised State power, and of increasing the autonomy of local economies, firms, or industries, with more self-management for workers. Although this type of reform was experimented with rather successfuly in Yugoslavia, and then began to be introduced in other Eastern European countries, the reform movements after 1989 generally went beyond this idea, toward a full-scale market economy and down the road to capitalism. In China, the experiment of a socialist market economy is still going on with a certain success in securing a high rate of economic growth.

The problem remains, however, whether it is possible to use a market price system in a socialist society with public ownership of the major means of production and a certain degree of planning. If Marx's proposition that 'only the products of mutually independent acts of labour, performed in isolation, can confront each other as commodities' (I, p. 132) is strictly true, the use of the market price system in such a planned society is conceptually impermissible, and can even be seen as sheer revisionism, eventually leading to complete individualistic privatisation. However, Marx's proposition is not consistent with his own recognition of the exogenous origin of commodity exchange, and cannot be true. Indeed, the economic forms to be found in a commodity economy, including the market price form, can be understood without reference to the specific relations of production behind them. This corresponds to the historical fact that a commodity economy could develop to certain degree through contact between various pre-capitalist societies.

From the theoretical recognition of the exogenous character of the economic forms of commodity economy, such as money prices, capital, profit and so forth, we can appreciate the possibility not only of removing these forms from the social labour process in the future, but also of flexibly utilising them as an adjustment mechanism for allocating products and labour among associational regional societies or co-operative firms, based on the public ownership of the means of production. In the latter case, free or very cheap distribution of certain goods and services such as basic education and medical services, officially fixed pricing for basic goods and services such as energy and housing, and market pricing according to changes in the balance of demand and supply for other goods and services, can be selectively combined and the combinations altered by democratic social decision.

In such a combination there cannot be fully consistent market pricing as the costs of production of goods bearing market prices must contain some of the costs of certain means of production with controlled fixed prices, as well as socially controlled s-wages. Market prices can also be easily subjected to zoning control, with their highest and lowest levels determined by social agreement. In these respects, market prices in a socialist economy may generally have the character of quasi-market prices, or a sort of s-prices. They can appear and function in transactions between the State (or the central planning board), and firms or individual workers, but they would have increased significance when transactions among firms and workers are undertaken horizontally and not through the State. It has to be one of the most important items on the economic agenda to determine in a democratic way which goods and services should be transacted with s-market prices, which should be handled with officially fixed prices, even though altered from time to time, and which should be distributed free or very cheaply.

For any combination, the social distribution and allocation of labour-time should be made as transparent as possible, starting from the assessment of the economic relations among the strategically important goods and services. In the *Critique of the Gotha Programme*, Marx assumes that the individual producer

> receives a certificate from society that he has furnished such and such an amount of labour (after deducting his labour for the common funds), and with this certificate he draws from the social stock of means of consumption as much as the same amount of labour costs,

and then says that 'here obviously the same principle prevails as that which regulate the exchange of commodities, as far as this is exchange of equal values' (*MECW*, 24, p. 86). Similarly, Marx states that the allocation of labour-time to various needs to be satisfied, which is observable even for Robinson Crusoe on his island, contains 'all the essential determinants of value' (I, p. 170). When these propositions, together with Marx's conception of the law of value as equal exchange of labour-time, are applied to a socialist economy, it should be expected that the exchange relations among individual workers, collective producers (firms), and a central social organisation would be based on the equal exchange of labour-time. Thus normal prices would presumably be proportional to labour-time embodied in each product.

Under what conditions would prices would become directly proportional to labour-time embodied in products? One possible condition is that workers receive the whole of fresh labour-time through a socialist form of wages (let us designate this form as s-wages), leaving no surplus to firms as a whole. Then the common funds of society should be drawn from workers and not firms, and the expansion of firms would in general be realisable only through the use of such common funds. Let us call this a full s-wage model of socialism, as s-wages here represent both necessary labour-time v and surplus labour-time s, or the substance of value added in a capitalist economy.

In so far as workers obtain only the equivalent of v, however, fully equal exchange of labour-time among various products is not necessary in order to maintain industrial reproduction. Given the total amount of labour-time embodied in a unit of the ith product, $t_i = c_i + v_i + s_i$, the equivalents of indirect labour c_i, and of the necessary labour-time v_i must be recouped through exchange with society to enable the reproduction of the ith product. However, the equivalent of surplus labour s_i need not be recouped entirely, and a basic freedom exists in socially dealing with it. In my view, the substantial content of the law of value allows the unequal exchange of labour-time embodied in products over a range equal to s_i. Thus, the prices of production (i.e. cost price plus average profit), or the normal market prices gravitating around prices of production, are to be seen not as the revision, but as the concrete form of realisation of the law of value.[10]

In a socialist economy, for industries or firms to continue to exist the equivalent of $(c_i + v_i)$ must be recouped in the exchange of products, through some price form, some certificate, or rationing. Furthermore, it is important to note that in a socialist economy the fundamental social freedom in handling the equivalent of s_i is considerably larger than in a capitalist economy, because this equivalent need not be subject to the application of the equalisation of the profit rate.

As the portion of necessary labour-time distributed in the form of free (or cheap) communal consumption, or rationed cheaply, increases, money wages may represent a smaller and smaller portion of labour-time necessary to reproduce labour-power over the generations in a certain type of socialist economy. Therefore, in such a socialist economy, so far as common funds are drawn from industrial firms and not from individual workers, the determination of prices in terms of money may systematically underestimate costs as regards wages. As a result, the mark-up over cost in such socialist economies can be, in practice, overestimated and subject to more flexible manipulation than average profit in capitalism. Thus, when s-prices are given to products in such a socialist economy, either officially fixed or in accord with fluctuating demand and supply in a market, they can be more flexible and operational over a wider range than in the case of competitive prices of production in capitalism. This flexible and broad operational potential of the s-prices system could be one reason why officially fixed prices in the Soviet type of economy were able to function for decades despite the much condemned distortions from the view of equilibrium market prices, or prices of production.

An Egalitarian Theory of Labour and Work Motivation

Socialism, including Marxism, basically stands for an egalitarian view of human beings. However, there remains a issue which may contradict this view in the application of Marx's labour theory of value to socialism: the problem of skilled or complex labour.

In defining 'the value-forming substance', Marx states that the value-forming labour must be of an average or a socially necessary labour-time, and continues,

> Socially necessary labour-time is the labour-time required to produce any use-value under the conditions of production normal for a given society and with the average degree of skill and intensity of labour prevalent in that society (I, p. 129).

In the case of the same useful labour producing the same product, it is easy to compare the degree of skill and intensity of labour by the achieved amount of work during a given length of time. The modern conditions of production, using machinery, tend to equalise the result of labour after a relatively short period of training, and generally make workers interchangeable.

When different kinds of useful labour are compared, skilled labour is called complex labour. It is difficult to measure the degree of skill and intensity of labour among different kinds of useful labour since the results of work, i.e., the different sorts of products, are physically incommensurable. Marx's resolution, reducing complex into simple labour, does not present us with an actual and unambiguous social basis for calculation, and is rather problematic:

> More complex labour counts only as intensified, or rather multiplied simple labour, so that a smaller quantity of complex labour is considered equal to a larger quantity of simple labour. Experience shows that this reduction is constantly being made. A commodity may be the outcome of the most complicated labour, but through its value it is posited as equal to the product of simple labour, hence it represents only a specific quantity of simple labour. The various proportions in which diffferent kinds of labour are reduced to simple labour as their unit of measurement are established by a social process that goes on behind the backs of the producers; these proportions therefore appear to the producers to have been handed down by tradition (I, p. 135).

Consequently, when Marx in the *Critique of the Gotha Programme* contemplated the distribution of the means of consumption through labour certificates in the lower phase of communist society, he recognised 'an unequal right for unequal labour' according to 'unequal individual endowment and thus productive capacity of the workers as natural privileges', since society was still being 'encumbered by a bourgeois limitation' (*MECW*, 24, p. 86). However, in the case of complex labour, the degree of skill, and the mental and physical productive capacity of workers is impossible to make commensurate in their products. It is objectively impossible to define how much more labour a certain type of skilled worker can do in a given time in comparison with an unskilled worker, so long as the different use-values produced by them are not commensurable.

We can also note here that modern automated machinery and equipment, as well as a raised level of general education, have increased the interchangeability among working people across industries and jobs, and decreased the importance of hard to acquire skill, as far as the basic economic activities are concerned. Along with this strong tendency, however, two other conspicuous tendencies are discernible in contemporary capitalism.

One of them is a 'bureaucratic form' of labour management. This form of management grades segmented jobs into various formalistic ranks and categories, and treats the expenditure of labour of workers, who have basically similar human ability, according to their job ranking. In the typical conception of American labour management, each worker is attached to a segmented job in a company, rarely to be promoted to a higher rank. If the worker wants a better job, the worker has to exit and try to find the better job in another company. Motivation to remain continuously employed in the same job is provided by job security depending on the length of service (the longer the career, the less the risk of being laid-off), as well as by a general increase in real wages, roughly in proportion to the increase in productivity, as seen during the post-Second World War 'Fordist' period lasting until the 1960s. By contrast, under Japanese labour management of regular workers in a big business, each worker expects to be promoted sooner or later to the upper, more responsible ranks, through training on the job and mostly in order of seniority. Although the increase in real wages tends to lag behind productivity in Japan, the motivation to work, as well as a loyal attitude toward the company, is secured by life-long employment combined with the seniority promotion system. Despite these differences, both the American and the Japanese way of labour management have in common the bureaucratic formal ranking of various job categories.

Related to this is the tendency to assume that the expenditure of labour by workers with higher skill, or of a higher rank, is specifically intensified labour, and contains more simple labour expended over a given period of time. This is related to the assumption that educated or trained skilled labour-power must be paid more in order to guarantee the reproduction of such special labour-power. It is true that in a pure capitalist market system the educational or training costs of skilled labour-power form a part of the value of such labour-power, which has to be recouped in order to make possible the continuous supply of necessary skill over the generations on the basis of the family system. It is ironic, however, that such reproduction of the value of skilled labour-power in a free market system tends to create an immobile social stratum, somewhat similar to the old feudal Estates, and inherited over the generations through the family. Although such an effect of the value of labour-power is actually discernible, the value of labour-power itself, or the necessary labour-time to reproduce it, must theoretically be independent from its use-value, or the expenditure of labour in production, in the Ricardo–Marx tradition. A rise or a fall of wages, or the value of labour-power, therefore does not affect value produced, or value added, by a given number of workers, given the length of the working day, but affects adversely the profit share and the profit rate.

If in a socialist society all the costs of education and training for socially necessary skill are expended publicly from social common funds rather than privately, a higher reward need not be given to skilled workers in order to secure their generational reproduction. Even then skilled labour would not be instantly interchangeable with general simple labour. However, should we acknowledge from this fact that the expenditure of skilled labour is more intense, and provides more labour in a given time than simple labour, particularly if we take out of consideration the special costs of education and training?

As regards the degree of mental stress or physical fatigue, very wide differences exist, even within the category of interchangeable simple labour. Still, as similar expenditure of fundamentally the same human ability to work, various useful labours can be seen as homogeneous abstract human labour, simply measured by labour-time. In the case of skilled workers with specialised education and training, such workers may usually work with less competition and more satisfaction deriving from their achievements as specialists, thus frequently with less fatigue. There is generally no objective reason to believe that such workers expend more labour in a given time than unskilled workers. If we contemplate for a moment the reason why we can recognise the character of abstract human labour within the different useful concrete forms of labour, it is clear that we can apply the same reasoning to the issue of complex labour. We can recognise in complex or skilled labour the mobilisation of a broadly common human ability to work in a wide variety of ways, equally as in simple labour in its different concrete forms.

Marx's conception that in the lower phase of communism there would be unequal rights to society's produce deriving from the unequal individual capacity to labour could even be used to legitimate as a natural order of things the contemporary bourgeois technique of labour management by segmenting workers. Likewise for the market method of reproducing skilled labour-power through a higher personal income for such labour-power. The conception, however, cannot be supported by an objective reality of skilled workers actually providing more labour in a given time compared to unskilled ones. In Soviet-type societies there had been attempts to legitimate the various degrees of privilege in the economic life of State and Party bureaucrats by seeking recourse to Marx's concept of an unequal bourgeois right to produce arising from unequal capacity to labour. Thus, the issue should be critically reconsidered from the standpoint of the basic theoretical problem of skilled labour. Indeed, any attempt to assess the amount of labour expended in various complex activities could easily become arbitrary, and the estimates could be inflated on political grounds, since there is hardly an objective measure for this amount either theoretically or practically.

From our point of view, a fundamentally equal right arising from the expenditure of an universal human capacity to labour should be generally recognised from the initial phase of communist or socialist society. Unequal distribution of the means of consumption can be introduced through some socially agreed arrangements. This distribution, however, should vary according to need (for instance, the number of family members to be supported), or according as motivation and work incentives have to be provided. The existence and the degree of unequal distribution should be decided in a democratic way. The decision should be based on the recognition that a given labour-time of any concrete form, type and level of skill, contributes equally to society.

The aims which Marx set for the higher phase of communism, such as 'to each according to his needs', or distribution according to need, as well as the resolution of the antithesis between mental and physical labour, should be incorporated, as far as possible, in the tasks of the lower phase of communism or socialism. In the Soviet type of society, the realisation of the higher phase of communism was assumed to be too far away to be practicable, and the 'bourgeois right' of an unequal right arising from unequal capacity to labour, based on Marx's conception of the lower phase of communism, was employed to legitimate the privileged life of the State and Party bureaucrats. Although Marx's theory of skilled or complex labour leaves room for such a confusing conception, we can already be certain that there are no theoretical grounds in political economy for such legitimacy.

ON THE DIVISION OF LABOUR

It is instructive to reconsider today the differences between A. Smith and Marx on the division of labour. A. Smith believed in the positive impact which the division of labour would have on labour productivity and the wealth of nations. Beginning with the famous example of the division of labour in the manufacture of pins, Smith emphasised the positive effect of the division of labour, not just in the workplace but also on a social scale. At the same time, he assumed that the origin of the division of labour was in the human natural propensity to exchange, and exchange would result in harmony in a market economy.

Against Smith, Marx presented a theoretical view based on the external origin of commodity exchange. At the same time he sharply distinguished between the character of the division of labour in manufacture and in society in general. Marx's argument was;

> The planned and regulated a priori system on which the division of labour is implemented within the workshop becomes, in the division of labour within society, an a posteriori necessity imposed by nature, controlling the unregulated caprice of the producers, and perceptible in the fluctuations of the barometer of market prices (I, p. 476).

> If, in the society where the capitalist mode of production prevails, anarchy in the social division of labour and despotism in the manufacturing division of labour mutually condition each other, we find, on the contrary, in those earlier forms of society, on the one hand, a specimen of the organisation of the labour of society in accordance with as approved and authoritative plan, on the other hand, the entire exclusion of division of labour in the workshop or, at the least, its development on a minute scale, sporadically and accidentally (I, p. 477).

It is clear that Marx was superior to Smith in his historical recognition here. He expected socialism to overcome both 'anarchy in the social division of labour and despotism in the manufacturing division of labour' in a capitalist society. The irony is that in the Soviet type of allegedly Marxist countries, considerable growth in the division of labour in the workshop was achieved by excluding anarchy in the social division of labour, but was also accompanied by a despotic 'authoritarian plan', both in the workshop and in society at large. This result seems to me far removed from Marx's expectation that a society based on association would realise the emancipation of human beings from the evils of the division of labour under capitalism.

A fundamental evil of the division of labour in the workshop had been pointed out already by Smith, although somewhat inconsistently with his preconception of harmony in a market economy, and interestingly followed up by Marx. According to Smith;

In the progress of the division of labour, the employment of the far greater part of those who live by labour, comes confined to a few very simple operations; frequently to one or two. But the understanding of the greater part of men are necessarily formed by their ordinary employments. The man whose whole life is spent in performing a few operations, of which the effects too are, perhaps, always the same, or very nearly the same, has no occasion to exert his understanding, or to exercise his invention to in finding out expedients for removing difficulties which never occur. He naturally loses, therefore, the habit of such exertion, and generally becomes as stupid and ignorant as it is possible for a human creature to become... The uniformity of his stationary life naturally corrupts the courage of his mind... It corrupts even the activity of his body, and renders him incapable of exerting his strength with vigor and perseverance, in any other employment than that to which he has been bred.[11]

Marx directly adopted Smith's sharp insight into the deleterious effect of the manufacturing division of labour, and stated;

Manufacture with division of labour converts the worker into a crippled monstrosity by furthering his particular skill as in a forcing-house, through the suppression of a whole world of productive drives and inclinations, just as in the states of La Plata they butcher a whole beast for the sake of his hide or his tallow (I, p. 481).

Some crippling of body and mind is inseparable even from the division of labour in society as a whole. However, since manufacture carries this separation of branches of labour much further, and also, by its peculiar division, attacks the individual at the very roots of his life, it is the first system to provide the materials and the impetus for industrial pathology (I, p. 484).

These evils of manufacture prior to the Industrial Revolution were not at all overcome by the introduction of machinery, as capitalist factories employing machinery were also based upon the division of labour at the workshop. 'The separation of the intellectual faculties of the production process from manual labour' (I, p. 548) was further completed there.

Factory work exhausts the nervous system to the uttermost; ... it does away with the many-sided play of the muscles, and confiscates every atom of freedom both in bodily and in intellectual activity (I, 548).

The Taylor system, which was based on behavioural studies of working activity for more effective labour management, was then easily pursued. The Fordist bureaucratic management of division of labour in large factories developed further along the same track, and intensified the alienation of human labour. Even contemporary ME information technologies, which promote automation not only in factories but also in offices and in the service industries, are used by capitalist management in order to intensify labour in narrowly limited work operations, despite the fact that such technologies could potentially broaden the intellectual faculties of the individual.

Smith was also concerned with the possibly deleterious effect of the division of labour on national defence since this division corrupted the vigour of men. He hoped that the spread of primary education would solve this problem. It is clear by now that the elevation of the general level of education is not a sufficient solution, though valuable in itself, and not only as far as the problem of national defence is concerned. Even from the view of capitalist management, not to mention the socialist standpoint, the tendential corruption of the intellectual and bodily vigour of workers, or the loss of motivation due to tedious and monotonous work, is an onerous problem. The threat of unemployment, competitive pressure from surplus workers from rural agricultural areas and abroad, the development of 'scientific' labour management such as Taylorism, Fordism, and of a bureaucratic management system, have all been employed repeatedly to confront this problem. It is interesting to note that the introduction of ME automation systems did not eliminate the problem, but rather raised the significance of strenuous, careful human intervention in order to reduce the failure rate in products and strengthen competitive power in the market. Though the Japanese style of management with job rotation, team work, learning by doing, and flexible organisation within the firm, works relatively better in this regard, it still leaves a lot of hardship for workers and is far from resolving the evils of the division of labour.

It is thus definitely worth remembering that the solution of the evils of the division of labour has been an indispensable ideal of socialism. The solution need not follow the dream of the young Marx and Engels that in communist society people would 'hunt in the morning, fish in the afternoon, rear cattle in the evening, criticize after dinner, just as I have a mind, without ever becoming hunter, fisherman, shepherd, or critic.'[12] Alteration of work need not be so frequent but, if wanted, it may be made possible in the course of a life's career. The most important aspect to be resolved would be the antithesis between mental and physical labour. In order to do so, it should be attempted at the earliest stage of socialist society to increase worker participation at various levels of decision-making, to facilitate life-long education and training, to realise a shorter working day, and to develop cultural life. Through such efforts, the emancipation of women from various forms of the division of labour, which have long subjugated them to men in both social and personal life, will also be realised more easily.

The Soviet type of society was strikingly different from Marx's vision of communism emancipating the full faculties of working people by solving the evils of the division of labour in capitalism. Although it improved the general and higher education system, this achievement was not put to much use in order to increase the positive and democratic participation of working people in decision-making at any level. Under strictly authoritarian forms of organisation of the division of labour, both in the workshop and in society at large, the mental faculties of working people, and eventually their positive motivation to work well, were narrowly limited and gradually crippled.

An unfortunate theoretical source of poor guidance on this issue came from the one nation, one factory concept of socialism, employed by Kautsky and Lenin.[13] As Marx's approval of this concept is not at all clear, that may have come from a misreading of Marx.[14] For instance, in *The Poverty of Philosophy* (1846–7) Marx seems to suggest this concept when he states:

> Society as a whole has this in common with the interior of a workshop, that it too has its division of labour. If one took as a model the division of labour in a modern workshop, in order to apply it to a whole society, the society best organised for the production of wealth would undoubtedly be that which had a single chief employer, distributing tasks to the different members of the community according to previously fixed rule. But this is by no means the case. While inside the modern workshop the division of labour is meticulously regulated by the authority of the employer, modern society has no other rule, no other authority for distribution of labour than free competition.[15]

Against Proudon's ahistorical and abstract treatment of the division of labour, Marx argued that the social character of the division of labour had historically changed. Marx criticised the division of labour in a modern capitalist society by pointing out that, 'authority in the workshop and authority in society, in relation to the division of labour, are in inverse ratio to each other.' (*MECW*, 6, p. 185). Given that he looked forward to the 'overall development of individuals', it must have been far from his ideal to organise the whole of society in the authoritarian way of the capitalist workshop.

Likewise, we have to re-read carefully the following statement by Marx in *Capital*:

> The same bourgeois consciousness which celebrates the division of labour in the workshop, the lifelong annexation of the worker to a partial operation, and complete subjection to capital, as an organisation that increases it productive power, denounces with equal vigour every conscious attempt to control and regulate the process of production socially, as an inroad upon such sacred things as the rights of property, freedom and the self-determining 'genius' of the individual capitalist. It is very characteristic that the enthusiastic apologists of the factory system have nothing more damning to urge against a general organization of labour in society than that it would turn the whole of society into a factory (I, p. 477).

It is clear in this context that 'turning the whole of society into a factory', as in the one nation one factory concept, was not Marx's ideal, but, rather, a poor image of socialism constructed by capitalist apologists. This image should definitely be distinguished from Marx's own concept of socialism as an associational 'general organisation of labour in society'. After the failure of Soviet socialism, one challenging and apparent task for the future of socialism is to find a way of overcoming the evils of the division of labour so as to restore and fully to develop the essential human nature. Demands for democratic humanistic socialism, decentralisation, and workers' self-management are certainly necessary for the future of socialism.

THE FUNCTIONS OF SURPLUS LABOUR

Can Surplus Labour be Eliminated?

Engels declared in *Anti-Dühring* that

> two great discoveries, the materialist concept of history and the revelation of the secret of capitalist production through surplus-value, we owe to Marx. With these discoveries Socialism became a science (*MECW*, 25, p. 27).

Marxist socialism, despite being based on Marxist political economy which is an objective social science and therefore qualifying for the appellation scientific, remains a set of political positions. Marxist socialism, therefore, should not be directly identified as a science. Nor is the materialist conception of history directly a science, though it remains a scientific view of world history in so far as it is based on political economy. We now have to pursue further the point that theoretical revelation of the secret of capitalist production through the analysis of surplus-value actually established the grounds for socialism.

Marx clearly revealed the mechanism of production of surplus-value. In his theory, capital duly pays the value of labour-power to wage-workers enabling them to purchase necessary means of consumption which contain the socially necessary labour-time for the reproduction of labour-power. The use-value of labour-power, meanwhile, is labour to be expended during the whole of the working day, and includes both necessary labour-time and surplus labour-time. The labour theory of value of the classical school could not explain why capitalists could obtain surplus labour in the form of profit (and rent) from wage-workers, when capitalists paid the value of labour. The discovery of the distinction between the value and the use-value of the special commodity labour-power was decisive in order to overcome this shortcoming of classical political economy. This discovery is certainly related to the key aspect of Marx's theory namely, the clarification of the historically specific nature of the capitalist commodity economy. In doing so, Marx also made clear that the capitalist production of surplus-value is only a special form of the exploitation of the surplus labour of the direct workers in the various social formations of class society.

Upon these scientific grounds, Marxist socialism could assert its aim of eliminating exploitation and class society by revolutionising the capitalist economic order. Marx's theory of surplus-value elucidates the plausibility and the historical meaning of such a revolution, as well as the essential role of working people in realising it. What, then, does it really mean to abolish the capitalist production of surplus-value and to end exploitation?

There are two possible positions on this point. First, with the abolition of the production of surplus-value and of exploitation, workers would obtain the whole of their labour-time, and there would be no surplus labour. This position inherits one aspect of Ricardian socialist theory namely, labour's claim to the whole of the product of labour. However, this claim would not be realised through fair exchange based on the labour-value contained in products, and so this position differs from Ricardian socialist theory. It is clear that workers would not usually consume the whole of the product of labour privately. Some of this product will certainly be used socially in order to enable the expansion of reproduction and to make possible various forms of social consumption. However, since all such social uses are to the workers' own present and future benefit, labour-time allotted to such social use should not be regarded as surplus labour distinct from necessary labour.

Secondly, although the antagonism between necessary labour and surplus labour will disappear in a socialist society, there will still exist a distinction between surplus labour and necessary labour. Marx clearly expressed this position in *Capital* in the following way.

> Surplus labour in some form must always remain, as labour beyond the extent of given needs. It is just that in the capitalist, as in the slave system, etc., it has an antagonistic form and its obverse side is pure idleness on the part of one section of society. A certain quantum of surplus labour is required as insurance against accidents and for the progressive extension of the reproduction process that is needed to keep pace with the development of needs and progress of population (III, p. 958; see also p. 1016).

In the *Critique of the Gotha Programme* Marx discussed in more detail how to divide 'the co-operative proceeds of labour', or the total social product.

> From this must now be deducted: First, cover for replacement of the means of production used up. Secondly, additional portion for expansion of production. Thirdly, reserve or insurance funds to provide against accidents, disturbances caused by natural factors, etc . . . There remains the other part of the total product, intended to serve as means of consumption. Before this is divided among the individuals, there has to be deducted again from it: First, the general costs of administration not directly appertaining to production. This part will, from the outset, be very considerably restricted in comparison with present-day society . . . Secondly, that which is intended for the common satisfaction of needs, such as schools, health services, etc. From the outset this part grows considerably in comparison with present-day society and it grows in proportion as the new society develops. Thirdly, funds for those unable to work, etc., in short, for what is included under so-called official poor relief today (*MECW*, pp. 84–5).

Although Marx assumes that through the use of labour certificates in the lower phase of communist society 'the same amount of labour which he [an individual producer] has given to society in one form he receives back in another' (*MECW*, p. 568), the amount of labour which an individual worker receives after deducting all these portions from the social product will be roughly the same as necessary labour in present-day capitalist society. If the means of consumption which are consumed socially and in common grow considerably, then the labour-time received and consumed individually would clearly become less than the whole of the necessary labour-time. Necessary labour-time is conceptually the labour-time required to reproduce labour-power over the generations, and therefore it should also contain the labour-time necessary to meet consumption needs which are social rather than individual, for example, free schooling, medical services and so on. This component must then be excluded from surplus labour.

Thus, there is good reason to assume with Marx that the distinction between surplus labour and necessary labour will remain in a socialist society. However, as the social function of surplus labour will radically change in a truly co-operative society, the meaning of this distinction will become quite different from that in class societies. In its functions, surplus labour will not confront but rather complement necessary labour. Since the expansion in the means of production, the common insurance funds against accidents and so forth, into which surplus labour will flow, will be the workers' own property and not any more alien to them, the entire labour-time and its product will belong directly or indirectly to the workers themselves. In this regard, the two seemingly separate positions regarding the existence of surplus labour in a socialist society may not be so far apart in their substantial meaning.

As a corollary, considerable flexibility will exist in co-operatively and democratically determining the quantitative division between necessary labour and surplus labour, or between necessary labour individually consumed and necessary labour socially consumed. Similarly, there will be democratically determined flexibility in the allocation of social funds (containing both surplus and necessary labour) among various purposes such as the expansion of reproduction, insurance, communal consumption in the forms of education, training, medical care, social welfare for aged and disabled, housing, and so on. One failure of the Soviet type of socialism, with its highly centralised authoritarian form of economic planning, was the lack of such co-operative democratic decision-making in dealing with social funds. This eventually caused a general sense of alienation of workers, and ruined the socialist ethic of positive participation in social life. As we shall see in Chapter 5, this social distortion in Soviet-type society was one source of the Marxist critiques which define those societies as class societies. It is essential for the future of socialism to devise democratic social mechanisms and organisations enabling working people to participate in decision-making, determining both the degree of surplus labour and the proportions in which the social funds are put to various uses.

The Functions of Profit

Even though surplus labour will remain in a socialist society, its capitalist forms of profit, interest, and ground rent accruing as private income, will disappear. Certain aspects of their substantial functions, however, have to be carefully studied and built into the socialist economic order.

Indicator of Economic Growth

Both profit and the profit rate serve as indicators of macroeconomic growth. When technological conditions of reproduction are given, the general rate of profit is usually inversely proportional to the real wage rate. Similarly, the rate of expansion of production in a socialist economy is, in general, inversely related to individual and communal final consumption as a proportion of the annual social product, given technological conditions. It is a critically important economic issue for an associational socialist society to plan democratically the rate of expansion of production, its total amount, and the main components of the social surplus product. In the case in which the economic plan is expressed in terms of prices, whether representing directly proportional labour-time embodied or not, then the issue in its formal expression will be similar to planning a general rate of profit and a wage rate.

Guide to Allocation

A further function of both profit and the profit rate in a capitalist market economy is to adjust the allocation of resources and labour across industries according to changes in social demand. In a lower phase of communism or socialism, in which 'the human metabolism with nature' must be performed 'in a rational way', 'with the least expenditure of energy' still within 'the realm of necessity'(III, p. 959), adjusting the supply of goods and services in accordance with social needs must remain as an important problem.

As regards goods and services to be used for the common satisfaction of needs, such as childcare, schooling, and health services, it must be desirable for a socialist society to supply those free of charge, or cheaply, by employing social common funds essentially as a part of the necessary labour-time of workers. On the one hand, the need for such services can be forecast with a certain probability, and free provision will probably not increase this need substantially. On the other hand, supplying these services free of charge, or cheaply, is desirable so as to guarantee equal basic conditions for human life. Given these qualifications, a society can agree to spare a certain part of the common funds in meeting these needs, social arrangements for which, to some extent, already exist in not a few capitalist countries. The profit principle of the capitalist market economy should be disregarded in these areas.

It is worth carefully considering whether a socialist society should extract the common funds to be used for these, as well as other, social purposes, from individual income by using a sort of personal income tax, or from firms by using a sort of corporation tax. If only the latter was used, and as the supply of free, or cheap, goods and services would increase in a socialist society, the nominal stipend distributed to working people in money (which for convenience we call socialist wages or s-wages), would become a smaller part of the total cost necessary to reproduce labour-power. Then, *ceteris paribus*, the cost of production for firms would become correspondingly reduced, enabling firms to increase the surplus beyond cost in terms of money (we may call it socialist profit or s-profit). Given the lack of competition equalising the rates of profit among socialised firms, this would obscure the necessary adjustment between social needs and conditions of supply. Conversely, the room for flexible manipulation of prices, either officially fixed or determined by individual firms, would be correspondingly widened.

In order to avoid the arbitrary (political) manipulation of prices, and to make as clear as possible the necessary adjustment of prices according to social needs and real costs, the funds for social common consumption should probably be levied on individual income, and not on s-profit. Ideologically this would also serve to strengthen the perception of working people that they have a right to participate in social decision-making.

It is interesting to consider further a full s-wage model, as suggested on p. 52, distributing to individual workers the whole of the social annual net income, i.e., the result of both surplus and necessary labour expressed in terms of money (s-wages). Then, the necessary funds for expanded reproduction, insurance for accidents, and so on, must also be levied on workers. There will be no s-profit on average for firms. S-prices covering costs in this model must, in principle, become directly proportional to labour-time embodied in each product. This method may be the easiest way of ascertaining the amount of labour-time embodied in products (t_i in (3.1)) through the price mechanism. I cannot see any fundamental reason why this model cannot be realised in a socialist society, though the model may not be popular due to the lack of flexible independence on the part of individual industries and firms.

In so far as surplus beyond cost, or s-profit, is allowed to accrue to individual firms, accurate and honest accounting in a generally applicable measure, such as in units of s-money, is certainly indispensable. Money, even as labour certificates, would be used by people to allocate their income among desirable goods and services, or by firms in order to maintain their operations. We can think of this through the metaphor of democratic voting with the use of money. Real consumers' sovereignty should be widened in socialism by organising and transmitting to producers the consumers' demand for high quality and adequate variety of products. In order to reduce the risk of bureaucratic control from above rationing should be avoided, except when good social reasons for its introduction have been democratically established.

Even with officially fixed prices the changes in social needs must be reflected in the motion of s-profit, as the changes alter the efficiency of turnover of invested funds (s-capital). For industries and firms with increasing s-profit due to increased social need for their product, more funds for expanded production must be obtained from a part of s-profit, as well as from credit. If there is rationing of the necessary means of production, the flexible adjustment of the distributed quantities must also be undertaken according to the movement of s-profit. In the case in which the prices of products are subject to determination by individual firms, reflecting the balance between social demand and supply, then the function of the s-profit rate will become closer to that of the profit rate in a capitalist economy.

However, even with such market prices, several differences still exist between socialism and capitalism. One such is that the s-profit basically belongs to the people as a whole, and not to capitalists or managers of firms. A substantial portion of it can thus be levied by society, although some part of it can also be retained by firms. In the case of the Chinese socialist commodity economy of the late 1980s, for instance, 55 percent of s-profit of firms is usually delivered to the State, and of the amount retained within the firms, 40 percent is used for the expansion of production, 20 percent for research and development, 20 percent for bonuses, and 20 percent for welfare of workers in the firms.

In any case, the function of profit in guiding the reallocation of resources and labour according to changes in social needs can be realised even without capitalist private profit and the competitive law of the equalisation of the rate of profit in a free market, through the different types of price systems and the various rules governing the use of the s-profit in socialist economies. A centrally planned economy based on rationing can be maintained relatively easily so long as both social needs and technologies do not change much, as seen in the Soviet economy, but would tend to face difficulties in adjusting flexibly to changes in needs and technologies.

However, a planned supply, even if not necessarily a system of rationing from above, will be more plausible in the future as ordering systems and the monitoring of the needs of consumers by means of electronic information systems are now being developed by both capitalist firms and co-operative movements. The development of more flexible ways of producing variable multiple models of products through computer technologies will also help in this respect.

Stimulus to Innovation

A third function of profit or surplus value in Marx's economics is to promote technological innovation. A capitalist who has managed to introduce an exceptionally superior technological method of production in comparison to the dominant method in an industry, can reduce the labour-time, and the cost necessary to produce one unit of the product, whilst being able to sell the product with a social value estimated on the basis of the general conditions of production in the industry. Although the extra surplus value, or extra profit, obtained will eventually disappear with the gradual diffusion of the method of production across the particular industry, its existence tends to impart a powerful drive to technological innovation in a capitalist economy. An analogous course of acquisition and disappearance of extra profit occurs in the process of innovative introduction and diffusion of new types of products. As to the source of extra surplus-value, Marx's conception that 'the exceptionally productive labour acts as intensified labour' (I, p. 145) is dubious, because workers with the same intensity of labour cease to generate extra surplus value after the generalisation of the new technology. The source of extra surplus value must therefore lie in the redistribution of the social surplus labour through the price mechanism.[16]

The capitalist private form of extra surplus value or extra profit should disappear in a socialist economy. However, its substantial function of improving the methods of production through the use of a part of social surplus labour must remain as an aspect of the general economic norms common to all human societies, and must consciously be adopted by a socialist society in one way or another, in so far as a socialist society is to achieve its reproduction 'with the least expenditure of energy' in a dynamic way within 'a realm of necessity'.

A part of the social surplus should be socially expended on research and development (R & D) projects of a large social scale. Indeed, it will be an advantage of socialism relative to capitalism to be able more easily to organise large-scale R & D operations nationally and internationally, without being restricted by the narrow capitalist view of profit. Soft energy paths, or technologies suitable to the conservation of the natural environment, for instance, can be systematically developed. Given definite purpose and motivation, socialised R & D would be successful, as was rather unfortunately exemplified by Soviet (and US) military industrial development.

However, especially in a developed consumer society, such large-scale socialised R & D would not be enough. In order to stimulate innovation leading to new methods of production, as well as to new types or models of products, at least two or three rival or competing institutions for R & D would probably be necessary in each industry. Competition among them need not necessarily be based on pecuniary motivation alone. These institutions should be located next door to actual workplaces in order to facilitate experimental production, as in most R & D sections of capitalist firms. A certain portion of the social funds should be allocated to such R & D activities to allow them flexible access to necessary resources and means of production. In view of the efficiency of military R & D in the Soviet Union, there seems no reason why such arrangements cannot be developed in a more decentralised competitive way aiming at improving the people's livelihood in a planned economy. In the case of new products, careful monitoring is certainly necessary to estimate whether and how much they are acceptable to society.

A more difficult problem for a planned economy is the actual application of new methods of production, and new types of products, because this requires unavoidable changes in the necessary combination of inputs and outputs across industries. The more successful R & D activities become in facilitating changes in the products and methods of industries, the more important this problem will be. The problem contains at least two separate issues; (a) how to achieve flexible reallocation of resources necessary for new method of production, or for new types of products, and (b) how to secure motivation and incentive for managers and workers to introduce the new methods of production, or the new types of products.

It is clear that the absence of arrangements for solving these issues and facilitating dynamic industrial innovation was one of the major defects of the Soviet type of centrally planned bureaucratic economy. The oft-repeated critiques of the lack of innovative dynamism in the Soviet type of centrally planned economy by Hayek and the Austrian neo-liberal economists, must have had some justification in this respect. However, the solution of this defect need not be found only in a free capitalist market. There are several ways to achieve a solution under different forms of socialism.

So long as socialist economies aim at planned allocation of at least some important resources under whatever form of socioeconomic order, the development of computer information technologies can be the material basis for easing the severity of the allocation problem. In addition, a certain amount of slack in stocks of means of production and productive capacity in each industry has to be allowed for in order to adjust supply flexibly to changes in economic plan. We should note that flexible adjustment of supply according to changing social demand in a capitalist economy is also realised partly by the existence of such slack in stocks and capacity.

As for the problem of lack of motivation and incentives for innovation, the Soviet type of highly concentrated enterprises, often monopolistically supplying their products to the whole country under a highly centralised bureaucratic system, was an important factor in causing the problem. Such a system might have worked during the catching up process of industrialisation, especially on the basis of relatively stable technical methods of production, but tackling the question of material motivation and incentives for innovative changes in the methods of production and types of products remains a serious problem within a social order similar to the Soviet one. However, even under a planned economy we may conceive of the following arrangements employing socialist price systems.

There should be many firms or enterprises in each industry so as to foster rivalry and to avoid monopolistic laxity. Property in the means of production should be public. If an associational firm in such an economy can obtain a certain portion of extra surplus, or extra s-profit, by reducing the cost of production, or by creating new products, this will give a strong spur to innovation for both managers and workers even under a system of officially fixed prices. The s-price for a new product in the planned economy must be officially determined by comparing the product's use-value to that of some comparable existing product. It should be determined so that an extra s-profit is afforded to the producer. Such pricing will last for a period of time during which the new method of production, or the new product, will spread across the economy. Subsequent to this, the cost of production would again determine price. Switching away from the old product must be promoted in the meanwhile.

One necessary condition is that firms should be able flexibly to alter the means of production employed, and should be able to determine what products to supply, even if prices are officially fixed. Such flexibility is possible to some extent in a quantitatively planned economy, as flexible changes in the social plan become plausible with the development of computer technology, and given some reserve stocks of resources. Flexibility and an incentive system for firms is surely also possible in a decentralised system of a quasi-market in goods and services.

If a fluctuating market price system is employed in a market socialism, the extra s-profit will be more clearly obtainable for firms through innovation. One basic difference of such extra s-profit from capitalist extra profit would be that it will not be acquired by the private owners of capital assets, but it will primarily belong to associational firms. This would remain so even if a part of the profit were distributed among the workers of the firm as an incentive bonus, and another part of it accrued to the State or to society. In the case of Chinese management by contract for state firms, 55 percent of s-profit generally accrues to the State. There is an argument that the incentives to managers for potential innovation is not income but the increase in private wealth resulting from successful innovation. This argument is not well founded theoretically, and can be empirically refuted by seeing how directors and managers in Japanese firms strive for innovation and 'rationalisation' despite often having few shares in their company. Similarly, managers by contract in Chinese state firms are now strenuously motivated.

The Substance of Ground Rent

In a capitalist economy, extra profit which is due to superior conditions of production deriving from natural advantages of land open to monopoly exploitation compared to marginal necessary land is transformed into differential rent. Marx's concept of its substance as 'a false social value' (III, p. 799) produced by capitalist competition is not clear. In my view, discussed elsewhere,[17] the substance of differential rent is nothing but a transfer of social surplus labour through the competitive capitalist price mechanism.

Despite its similarity with extra profit deriving from technologically superior methods of production, extra profit transformed into differential rent does not have a socialist function in the promotion of productivity or, indeed, any role whatsoever rooted in the general economic norms common to all human societies. For a society which is organised as a conscious association working according to a plan, Marx assumes that 'Society would not purchase this product [of land – M.I.] at 2 1/2 times the actual labour-time contained in it; the basis for a class of landowners would thereby disappear (III, p. 799). It is indeed conceivable that in a planned economy a certain kind of land product, say wheat, would be estimated in terms of actual labour-time contained in it, and that its producers as a whole would receive from society the equivalent labour-time in a certificate, or in the money form. In such a case, if agricultural farms are separately organised under different conditions of land, the equivalent of the actual labour costs of production must be given to each individual farm, without regard to the different amount of product per unit of cost. In terms of labour-time or prices, this means that farms with worse land than average would appear subsidised, and those with better land would appear levied. Contrariwise, if the average equivalent per unit of product was paid to each unit of product, the farms with better land than average would acquire extra s-profit, whereas the farms with worse land would not recoup the real costs, and might become unable to continue production without subsidy.

If an officially fixed price of an agricultural product is determined so as to guarantee the real production costs of farms with marginal necessary land, then extra s-profit would naturally accrue to all other farms with better land, and this has to be levied for society's benefit. The same is true when an equilibrium price is determined at a similar level under market socialism. Abolition of both the landowner class and differential rent paid to landowners does not rid a socialist society of these economic problems.

It is not certain how accurately the Soviet type of socialism managed to theorise, assess, and handle the problems relating to different conditions of land. Such problems may have been a source of regional inequalities, eventually causing ethnic conflicts, permanent dissatisfaction of farmers, and a tendency toward the deterioration of agriculture in the Soviet Union. Individual acquisition of extra s-profit by better (located) land in market socialism, without paying either differential rent or similar levies to the State, would help explain the rapid emergence of very wealthy farmers (families with 10,000 yuan) in the suburbs of big cities of China.

One practical problem lies with distinguishing between the result of improved methods of production and the result of utilising better land, especially because the differential conditions of land change with alterations in the methods of production. Therefore, the estimation of structural differentials of conditions of land tends to be delayed. However, in order to build a fair economic order for the whole of the working people, we have to bear in mind that in a socialist society these difficult issues have to be resolved in a practical way.

In a capitalist society, the landowners' right to reject utilisation of land can increase the price of land products beyond the prices of production even for marginal necessary land, and can bring about an extra profit accruing as absolute rent. The quantitative limit to such an increase in price is, in my view, theoretically given by the possible additional investment on the existing leaseholds of better soil types.[18] With the abolition of the landowner class, an associational society can certainly use land freely without paying any rent to landowners. If, however, in a socialist society prices, either officially fixed or determined in a quasi-market, are employed, the utilisation of land for farms, industrial firms, and individual houses must be carefully planned or guided. Rent-free utilisation of land in a planned economy may cause unfair and uneven bureaucratic distribution of desirable sites of land among economic agents. Distribution through a quasi-market would often result in a confusing patchwork of land use. Practically planned zoning would be necessary, in any case. Furthermore, society can use absolute s-rent, as well as quasi-differential s-rent to reduce inequalities in housing sites, and to guide the location of investment. Being exempt from the limitation of functions of absolute rent in a capitalist economy, s-rent may serve in this sense as a new type of policy device to guide regional economic development.

The Role of Credit and Interest

Marx made clear that money serves not only as means of circulation of commodities, but also as the absolute form of value when it functions as hoarding, means of payment, and world money. Further, in his theory of the turnover of capital, it was shown that hoarding of idle money, such as depreciation funds for fixed capital, reserves for accumulation, reserves to meet price fluctuations, and reserves for the continuation of the production process in the period of circulation, must be repeatedly formed. A basic function of the capitalist credit system in the forms of commercial credit and bank credit is the utilisation of these idle funds so as to increase the efficiency of the motion of capital both in the expansion of production and in the adjustment of imbalances across industries. In this context, interest is the redistribution of a part of surplus-value among industrial or commercial capital. However, there is another line of argument in *Capital*, following the classical school, which treats interest as the accrual of a part of profit to a moneyed capitalist class separate from industrial capitalists.[19]

It is a characteristic of Marx's work not to possess a strong theory determining the general rate of interest, unlike his theory regarding the general rate of profit. The rate of interest was seen by Marx as determined by the balance between social demand and supply of money capital, usually varying between zero and the general rate of profit.

At first sight, credit and interest would disappear as moneyed capitalists and the monetary market mechanism were eliminated, especially in a planned socialist economy. However, even with labour certificates, or *s*-money, in a planned economy, individual firms would store reserve funds for the expansion of operations, depreciation of durable means of production, and to meet unforeseen changes in economic and other conditions. Marx noted that those items, among others, have to be deducted from the total social product before the latter is distributed among individual producers. Marx's notion regarding the whole society must also be applicable to individual firms in so far as these firms are to continue their operations with a certain degree of autonomy. Individual workers may also store some of their income in the form of labour certificates, or *s*-money, for future use, such as holiday tours, setting up home, insurance for reduced income by illness or old age.

Such storage of funds may more or less be balanced with the fresh use of stored funds, as Marx assumed in his reproduction schema. The balance, however, cannot be exact in the short run, particularly with respect to each industry, and normally there would be a surplus left, such as saving out of personal income, reserves formed by firms or industries to meet accidental shocks to the economic mechanism, and funds similarly accumulated out of *s*-profit. By employing this balance of idle funds a socialist credit mechanism can be constructed.

In a planned economy with perfect rationing of all goods and services there can be no room for credit, but there can for certain functions of the public debt. If the State borrows idle funds through public banks or in the form of bonds, and operates directly or indirectly (say by over-issuing of s-money) to reduce the real value of s-money, or labour certificates then the stored idle funds would gradually lose their value, as in the case of inflation in a market economy. Particularly when the real rate of interest is negative, such State debt will function as an additional hidden levy on firms and people.

If, besides rationing, some part of the means of production can be directly transacted among firms, then inter-firm credit employing bills for labour certificates, or s-money, will emerge. The firms which receive such bills and do not have sufficient idle funds to continue operations, will exchange the bill with labour certificates, or s-money, at the public banks where various idle funds would be deposited. Some firms may ask banks for loans when additional expansion of production or capacity is desired to meet social demands. Individual persons could also sometimes borrow in order to make their expenditure more flexible and their outgoings more even. Through such a credit mechanism, the mutual utilisation of idle funds will facilitate the more flexible reallocation of economic resources in accord with spontaneously changing social needs. The expansion of credit itself could be made flexible by anticipating the return payment of funds in the future.

The rate of interest to be paid by borrowers could be determined by a central planning board as a strategically important price for loanable funds; or it could be given a range within which it can move reflecting the general balance of supply and demand of credit; or it could, finally, be set allowed to move freely without any direct limits imposed on it. Even if the interest rate moves freely or within a range, it can be much influenced by the public banks and the central planning board, as well as by the operations of the public debt. Here again, not just the nominal but the real rate of interest matters. Usually the real rate of interest should be positive to promote saving for social accumulation, and to restrict reckless borrowing. The rate of interest would regulate the pace of accumulation or expansion of firms, as firms would depend on loans only when their marginal surplus, or s-profit, obtainable by additional expansion of operation was expected to exceed the rate of interest. Thus, the operationality of the rate of interest will be a powerful instrument for macroeconomic policy in any socialist economy which allows individual firms more or less independent decision-making.

The role of credit and interest must therefore be bigger as a quasi-market, or even a real market, are increasingly incorporated in the socialist economy. Credit need not be regarded as an anti-socialist, or a plain capitalistic money-making mechanism. It can positively serve to promote more flexible and efficient economic adjustment of production and consumption. The rate of interest can also provide a powerful policy device 'softly' (i.e., not by direct order) to control the pace of economic growth in a socialist economy, just as monetary policy aims at doing in a capitalist economy. The functioning of credit can be made rational and fair, different from the capitalistic use of credit for speculative profit-making which often causes bubbles and their collapse. In a socialist economy, interest can no longer be an economic foundation for a moneyed capitalist class, but it will represent a just redistribution of economic surplus among associational firms, the State and individuals, and it will have the rational function of facilitating the utilisation of idle funds.

HOW TO SECURE DYNAMIC FLEXIBILITY

Crisis Theories and Models of Socialism

The purpose of Marxist crisis theories is to reveal the fundamental contradictions of capitalism, as well as their concrete appearance. Consequently, these theories have substantially influenced the nature of the socialist solution of capitalist contradictions.

Marx himself left the theory of crisis unfinished, and held, somewhat inconsistently, four variants of such a theory. These could be further classified into two major types: excess capital theories and excess commodities theories. For instance, in the third part of vol. III of *Capital*, Marx attempts to show that excessive capital accumulation causes a fall in the rate of profit, due to either the tendency of the organic composition of capital (c/v) to rise, or to labour shortage inducing a sudden rise in wages. The fall in the profit rate endangers capitalist accumulation and generates crises (III, p. 350, pp. 360–8). In this type of theory, over-supply of commodities in the market appears as a result of the over-accumulation of capital, the latter being expressed as a fall in the profit rate. However, Marx also states in the same part of *Capital* that,

> The conditions for immediate exploitation and for the realisation of that exploitation are not identical... The former is restricted only

by the society's productive forces, the latter by the proportionality between the different branches of production and by the society's power of consumption (III, p. 352, see also Part Five, p. 615).

In this type of excess commodities theory, over-production of commodities beyond effective demand due to either the anarchical disproportionality of production across various branches, or the narrowly restricted consumption of the masses, is conceived as the ultimate reason of crises as well as of the fall in the profit rate.

The Japanese Uno school has attempted to complete the labour shortage variant of the excess capital theory of crisis, in order to provide a basic theory of typical regular business cycles and crises. According to this school, the basic contradiction in the capitalist economy lies in the difficulty of treating the human ability to labour as a commodity. The contradiction is manifested in the outbreak of a sharp overall crisis due to the over-accumulation of capital relative to the labouring population. The theory is grounded on the capitalist law of population namely, the periodic re-absorption and re-formation of the industrial reserve army (or the relative surplus population) in the process of capital accumulation. The inevitability of sharp crisis is demonstrated concretely through the workings of the credit system. When the labour shortage pushes up wages thereby reducing the rate of profit, there occurs a credit crunch accompanied by an increase in the rate of interest, which ends the boom period. This variant of crisis theory, unlike others, can easily show that prosperity and depression are cyclically repeated through crisis, thus forming regular business cycles. The capitalist economic law of motion contains both self-destruction and the innovative restructuring of its process of accumulation.

By contrast, 'orthodox' Marxian theories of crisis, often in an one-sided manner, took over the excess commodities theory and tended to emphasise the destructive effect of the imbalance between supply and demand. In this type of theory, the basic contradiction of capitalism was seen to lie in the anarchical relation between the branches of production, as well as in the narrowly limited consumption of the masses. This view was combined with the formula of historical materialism as, for instance, when Engels stated that 'In these crises, the contradiction between social production and capitalist appropriation ends in a violent explosion'.[20] Lenin echoed this when he defined the capitalist contradiction as one 'between the social character of production and the private character of appropriation'.[21]

The kind of socialism patterned on this type of orthodox theory would naturally assume that the nationalisation of the means of production and central planning would be the most effective solution to the contradictions of capitalism. Nationalisation would be the surest device for eliminating private capitalistic appropriation, central planning and nationalised production would end capitalism's anarchic disproportionality, and the elimination of unemployment with rising real incomes of workers in the planned economy would remove the problem of underconsumption. In addition, such theories stress that Marxism, unlike anarchism, assumes a revolution in the nature of the State, so that the new proletarian State could be used as a central organiser of economic planning, especially in the first lower phase of communism. This conception was reinforced in the Soviet type of societies by assuming that Marx's ideal socialism in which the State withers and disappears, can be realised only in a higher phase of communism, and was not really achievable in the foreseeable future.

This type of centrally planned economy, coupled with statism, contains the danger of bureaucratic control of the whole of society, and the suppression of democratic participation from below. The danger was actually realised in Soviet-type societies. The proletarian dictatorship turned into the dictatorship of State and Party bureaucrats over the workers. Despite being a social formation different from capitalism, this society recreated the oppressed and alienated position of workers. The self-emancipation of workers, and their elevation into real masters of society through the abolition of the commodity form of labour-power was not achieved. While the importance of this fundamental task of socialism can be easily appreciated from the point of view of the labour shortage variant of crisis theory, it tended to be neglected by 'orthodox' Marxism due to the latter's inclination toward the disequilibrium and the under-consumption variants of crisis theory. At the same time, the possibility of decentralisation of economic decision-making and a rise in the spontaneity of activity by various economic agents, were made light of by such 'orthodox' Marxism.

A Socialist Form of the Industrial Reserve Army

A centrally planned economy with full employment will have difficulty in adjusting the supply of goods and services to changes in social needs. If workers have a positive right to their jobs, the potential of the economy for flexible adjustment will become quite small. It would be hard to meet an increase in social demand for some consumption goods by a corresponding increase in supply. Relative shortages of some means of production would also be hard to resolve rapidly. Bottlenecks or partial shortages of some means of production would create idle capacity and leave workers redundant in many workplaces, thus tending to spread further the phenomena of the economy of shortage.[22]

In a capitalist economy, the dynamic adjustment of imbalances between the demand and supply of commodities is ordinarily performed through the additional allocation of resources for expansion via the market mechanism. The elasticity of this process of expansion is basically secured by the existence of an industrial reserve army of working population, available for mobilisation in additional employment in any branch of production. Therefore, a capitalist economy becomes inflexible and maladjusted when the bulk of the industrial reserve army is absorbed through the overaccumulation of capital toward the end of the prosperity period. As a result, in the last phase of prosperity in typical business cycles, disproportionality with much speculative trading spreads and leads to a crisis.

The successful removal of unemployment by a socialist planned economy would present industries in need of expansion with the structural difficulty of inflexibility of the labour supply. As a corollary, structural disproportionality would tend to emerge, accompanied by the phenomena of shortage. In order to resolve this difficulty, the flexible utilisation of the social surplus in the form of extra stocks of means of production, the mobilisation of idle funds, and the elastic alteration of the planned pace of expansion of industries, would all be necessary, though not sufficient. In addition to those steps, a socialist form of the industrial reserve army of working population should be created, both in planned and in market socialism.[23] This socialist form of the reserve army will certainly be different from capitalist unemployment, being a kind of arranged leave or sabbatical from work, with a guarantee of sufficient income, the possibility of more studying or extra training, as well as a guarantee of work in the near future. Together with this arrangement, a social consensus among workers to change their jobs across industries and regions, say, every five years, would be desirable so as to maintain the flow of workers from surplus to deficit manpower areas.

In all these arrangements, the workers' positive attitude towards their own mobility would be imperative to a flexible and dynamic socialist economy. Information about available jobs, and workplaces with attractive work conditions should be accessible to all workers. The mobility of workers must become a reality through voluntary applications to move, and not by authoritarian orders from above, nor by the enforcement of the capitalist market mechanism. Though the incentive to change jobs will be more in the nature of acquiring new experiences, some material incentives, functioning as an expedient quasi-market device, would also be offered in the case of necessary but unpopular jobs. Limiting the unpopular jobs should certainly be continually striven for through the improvement of technology.

A problem for a society with a high mobility of labour is maintaining family life and allowing parents time to look after their children. Transfer to a new workplace in the same area would generally be more convenient for workers. At the same time, however, the tendency to migrate, already rising in the capitalist world, would be further facilitated in a socialist economy by fewer working days per annum, public childcare facilities, and special arrangements for inter-regional transport for families which choose to separate. Only when the flexible mobility of workers is ensured will the adjustment of the allocation of resources across industries and technological change in industrial methods of production, become easily conceivable within each firm and within whole industries.

CONCLUSION

From what we have argued it follows that the concrete mechanisms of a socialist economy likely to exist in the foreseeable future need not be theoretically specified in an universal and unique manner. A completely planned economy can be theoretically formulated with a certain consistency. If some sort of spontaneous dynamic flexibility is to be incorporated into the economy, however, the mechanism of a socialist economic system would become more or less indeterminate. In particular, various combinations of plan, quasi-market arrangements, and a market for the allocation of goods and services, can be designed. The functions of economic agents, such as the State, local governments, firms, co-operative unions, local communities, families, and individuals can also be diverse. Diversity can also apply to the forms of property ownership or to property rights. Although in a socialist economy the main means of production and natural resources, including land, must basically be publicly owned, this need not signify the State ownership of all these resources. The mode of distribution of property rights to different social economic agents would determine the very pattern of a socialist economy. Given the diversity in several aspects of the socioeconomic order of socialism, the role of associational democratic decision-making and workers' participation in this process, will be correspondingly decisive.

For such democratic decision-making, it is imperative to learn from the historical lessons of the Soviet type of economy, both positive and negative. At the same time, the basic theories of the capitalist economy, such as those in *Capital*, not only present us with what is to be overcome and abandoned, but also elucidate capitalism's substantial capacity for flexible adjustment and growth in accordance with changing social demands. Replacing the latter is a challenge which has to be met with conscious socialist mechanisms. Although the basic theories of the political economy of capitalism cannot be substituted by a similarly complete and concrete model of socialist economic mechanisms, these theories still serve as a solid frame of reference for the consideration of what should be accomplished under variegated social arrangements in socialism. A capitalist market with all its functions is really worth imitating in its positive and rational aspects for socialist ends with socialistically constructed mechanisms, but in a broader sense than O. Lange's type of market socialism, which we shall examine in Chapter 4.

4 Market Economy and Socialism

After the fall of Soviet central planning, the transition to a market economy has been regarded as the main alternative strategy for the economic restructuring of those societies. China is also restructuring its economy toward a socialist market economy, though politically the Chinese Communist Party still holds power. Does this restructuring of socialist economies mean that, after all, it is impossible for a socialist planned economy to exist without relying on a market? Can a socialist economy form a rational and dynamic economic system which would replace and surpass the market economy? The issue of how to understand the relationship between the market and socialism, has reappeared as a crucial theoretical problem for the future of socialism.

The important theoretical issues were already presented in the so-called socialist economic calculation debate which started in the 1920s.[1] In that debate, and following N.G. Pierson's (1839–1909) critique of the socialist economy, L. von Mises (1881–1973), F.A. Hayek (1899–1993), M. Weber (1864–1920) and others argued that no basis for economic calculation to achieve the rational distribution of limited resources and capital can obtain in a centrally planned economy without market prices. Against these theorists, counter-arguments were presented by, among others, F.M. Taylor, H.D. Dickinson, O. Lange, M. Dobb (1900–76), and P.M. Sweezy (1910–).

Almost half a century later the theoretical issues of that debate have resurfaced, and their political implications are being reconsidered in examining the failure of centrally planned economies. A series of studies have been produced, and a vibrant debate has re-emerged on market economy and socialism. Let us first review and re-assess the contemporary significance of the socialist economic caluculation debate, and subsequently consider the recent debate on market and socialism.

THEORETICAL CRITIQUES OF A SOCIALIST ECONOMY

Most of the representative theoretical critiques of socialist economic planning can be found in F.A. Hayek (ed.), *Collectivist Economic*

84   *Theories*

Planning (1935). Faced with the Marxist assertion that under socialism the market pricing mechanism should be replaced by conscious communal physical planning, or by using labour time as the measure for distributing the means of production and consumption, these critiques deny that rational collectivist economic planning can exist.

It is worth noting in advance, and so as to avoid confusion, that there can exist several theoretically different types of prices in socialist economies, as we have seen in the previous chapter. This is so even if all these prices are accounted, say, in terms of rubles or yuan. For instance, we can theoretically conceive of, (1) prices directly proportional to labour-time embodied in goods; (2) prices structurally related to labour-time in a certain way, such as prices of production in Marxist economics; (3) prices determined on the basis of social technological cost conditions, exemplified by equilibrium prices in Sraffian theory; (4) equilibrium prices equating demand and supply in the market, such as those in general equilibrium theory; (5) fluctuating market prices reflecting the anarchical movement of demand and supply in the market.

In a socialist economy with public ownership of the means of production and associational planning all such prices may have, in one way or another, the nature of quasi-prices or s-prices, the latter being different from prices in a free market economy. Type (1) can approximate Marx's concept of labour certificate in their substantial function. Types (2), (3), (4) may generally coincide as regards reproducible goods and services in a static economy, if the equalisation of rates of profit with a given level of real wages is also assumed for a market economy. For the case of the Soviet type of socialist economy, type (3), or prices determined by costs without strict equalisation of the profit rate, would be the concept closest to officially fixed prices. The critiques of collectivist economic planning are based, for the most part, on neoclassical price theory which stresses the balance between demand and supply. This theoretical foundation leads the critiques to assert the indispensability of the pricing mechanism to a rational economic system.

Pierson

N.G. Pierson's (1839–1909) paper 'The Problem of Value in the Socialist Society' (1902), thought of by Hayek as 'the first important contribution to the modern discussion of the economic aspects of socialism' (*H*, p. 27),[2] argues that there is a serious error in the widespread view that value phenomena will disappear in a socialist society, to be replaced by merely technical problems. Pierson offers the following two reasons.

First, international trade between socialist countries in which means of production are nationalised, would necessarily depend upon prices reflecting demand and supply, and must be settled by money payment. If the amount of labour embodied in products is to be used as a measure of exchange, the degree of diligence and efficiency must be disregarded, and as a result an hour of work by a 'coolie' (unskilled native labourer) in China would be treated unduly as equivalent to an hour of labour by a skilled worker in an advanced country. A country may arbitrarily acquire more of the goods of other countries by using less fertile land or a less efficient method of production.

Second, within a socialist country, estimation of the distribution of social net income would become problematic. Such estimation by labour-time would treat all the different kinds of work as equivalent to each other, and the right to a higher income resulting from a higher ability would be negated. Even among the goods which are produced by the same amount of labour, certain goods in higher demand due to their quality or utility would also be thought of as more valuable. Exchange of goods, or exchange values, must naturally emerge thereupon.

Since the point on international trade was scarcely pursued in the rest of the analyses, let us comment on it here. So far as socialist countries are independent, they can trade internationally with prices which are determined by the balance between the demand and supply of goods in the international market. Economic relations with capitalist countries, if they exist, must be based on international market prices. Consequently, the planned domestic economies of socialist countries have to be protected from the effect of the anarchic fluctuations of the world market. Therefore, socialist countries need a degree of social control over international trade. If economic planning is decentralised, the local communities would undertake such social control of trade to a certain extent. However, at the very least, the control of the macroeconomic balance of international payments, together with the national control of the supply of money and credit, must be one of the responsibilities of the central planning agency of a socialist country. The costs and benefits of international trade should in any case be socialised.

On what grounds, however, can we argue that international trade with prices determined in a free international market is most rational and fair? Pierson seems to have believed in the absolute rationality and fairness of neo-classical price theory, as well as that the workings of the free market bring about such rationality and fairness. In reality, however, one of the major factors for the deepening underdevelopment and poverty in many third world countries which achieved political independence after the Second World War, is rooted in the very exploitative working of prices in the world market, rather than in international political oppression.[3] Finally, is there not a sense of discrimination and prejudice in Pierson's view of the inequality between the labour of a Chinese 'coolie' and of a skilled worker in an advanced country? Theoretically this point is related to the treatment of skilled or complex labour, discussed in Chapter 3 (pp. 53–7).

Terms of trade between socialist countries may deliberately be adjusted so as to exclude the exploitative function of trade due to differential industrial competitive power, and rather independently of the anarchical determination of prices in the international market. Such terms of trade may further be operated in order to promote independent economic growth in under-developed countries. Together with socialist co-operative development aid, this would be an important advantageous aspect of socialism, applicable internationally. Although this ideal was not realised by COMECON (the Council for Mutual Economic Assistance) under Soviet hegemony, purchases by the Soviet and China of sugar from Cuba at prices above the level of the world market exemplify a more general possibility.

Pierson's argument that a country would arbitrarily acquire more of the goods of other countries by using less fertile land or less efficient methods of production in the case of trade based on labour is also incorrect. A country which purposely uses less fertile land or less efficient methods of production would have fewer products for domestic consumption, and could not obtain more of foreign goods by the same amount of labour, even if the smaller amount of domestic products could be exchanged with the same physical amount of foreign goods. Pierson may have incorrectly surmised that the change in the terms of trade in favour of the country with less efficient production would imply an increased physical volume of consumption by this country, which does not at all follow.

Von Mises

Pierson's second reason was restated and extended by L.von Mises (1881–1973). In his famous article 'Economic Calculation in the Socialist Commonwealth' (1920), von Mises assumed that 'Under socialism all the means of production are the property of community' (*H*, p. 89), and continued as follows: 'It is characteristic of socialism that the distribution of consumption-goods must be independent of the question of production and its economic conditions' (*H*, p. 90). The basis for distribution can thus be variously chosen. However, we can assume a simple principle, namely, that all members of society are treated alike and receive the same bundle of coupons redeemable within a certain period against a definite quantity of certain specified goods. Then, all persons would dispose of some goods allotted to them in order to acquire other desired things in exchange. There must be 'room for the use of a universal medium of exchange – that is, of Money' (*H*, p. 92). Such exchange in terms of money will be narrowly limited to consumption goods, and will not be extended to production goods which will all be publicly owned.

The administration will observe the market conditions of exchange and attempt to adjust supply according to demand. However, if the citizens are to have the right of choice, say, between cigars or cigarettes, demand and supply of some goods will not be equal, and either cigars or cigarettes will pile up in the distribution office. A simple solution for this problem would be to adopt 'the standpoint of the labour theory of value', which entitles the citizens to receive the product of one hour's labour for every hour's work, less the amount (or tax) aimed at communal use. 'Yet such a manner of regulating distribution would be unworkable, since labour is not a uniform and homogeneous quantity' (*H*, p. 94). Besides, there remains the problem of how to evaluate the cost of materials. Mises recognises that 'Monetary calculation has its limits' (*H*, p. 98). It can not embrace 'extra-economic' factors such as beauty of a neighbourhood, the health, happiness, and the honour of individuals or nations. Nevertheless, within the limits of economic life, 'monetary calculation fulfills all the requirements of economic calculation' (*H*, p. 101). Calculation of value in terms of money cannot be rationally performed without goods of a higher order, i.e. means of production, being included in the ambit of exchange. Yet, with public ownership of the means of production in a socialist commonwealth, which 'finds it impossible to use money as an expression of the price of the factors of production (including labour), money can play no role in economic calculation' (*H*, p. 108): the administration cannot make the proper calculations in order to find out the least expensive method of achieving its ends. In the static state of the economy we can dispense with economic calculation, but as the static state is impossible in real life, 'we have the spectacle of a socialist economic order floundering in the ocean of possible and conceivable economic combinations without the compass of economic calculation . . .

There is only groping in the dark. Socialism is the abolition of rational economy' (*H*, p. 110).

What can be said regarding the applicability of labour to the value computations of a socialist community? From von Mises' point of view, two major defects exist. First, 'It leaves the employment of material factors of production out of account'. When a unit of the raw material *a* is produced by an hour's labour,

> 2 units of *a* and 8 hours' labour are used in the production of *P*, and one unit of *a* and 9 hours' labour in the production of *Q*. In terms of labour *P* and *Q* are equivalent, but in value terms *P* is more valuable than *Q*. The former is false, and only the latter corresponds to the nature and purpose of calculation (H, p. 113).

Secondly, differences in the qualities of labour are ignored: the proportion of substitution of complex by simple labour is not clear, and may be arbitrary.

Closely related to these problems of economic calculation,

> the exclusion of free initiative and individual responsibility, on which the success of private enterprise depend, constitutes the most serious menace to socialist economic organisation (*H*, p. 116).

Socialist undertakings lack internal pressure to restructure and improve production, cannot be adjusted to the changing conditions of demand, and thus become 'a dead limb in the economic organism' (*H*, p. 118). Although Marxist leaders assert the superiority of a socialist system because of its greater rationality, this cannot be true from the point of view of economic rationality. 'What is happening under the rule of Lenin and Trotsky is merely destruction and annihilation' (*H*, p. 125).

This last comment by von Mises obviously, and mistakenly, ascribed the economic crisis in the Soviet Union in the early 1920s to the essential character of the centrally planned economy, whereas that crisis was due to the civil war and foreign military intervention immediately after the revolution. Von Mises failed to foresee the possibility of continuous economic growth for the Soviet economy, which took place and lasted from the 1930s to the 1960s. However, with the fall of Soviet collectivist economic planning, von Mises' theoretical critique of the socialist economy has regained its significance. His central point was that in a socialist economy in which the means of production are publicly owned and not exchanged through the market, the economic values of the factors of production cannot be calculated. Therefore, it is impossible rationally to find the lowest cost among the various methods of production. Although their theoretical connection with this point is somewhat ambiguous, von Mises' further points regarding the absence of free initiative for innovation and the difficulty of adjusting to the changing conditions of demand in a centrally planned socialist economy, are also quite important.

Throughout his critique, von Mises repeatedly returns to the possibility of using labour as a unit of economic computation instead of prices determined in a market. His denial of labour as a possible measure follows his teacher's, E. von Böhm-Bawerk, critique of Marx's value theory.[4] The value controversy, which appears so remote from this issue, is, rather unexpectedly, profoundly related to the controversy on socialism. Of the two defects of measuring in terms of labour mentioned by von Mises, we have already discussed the second, namely, the assessment of the differential quality of labour which is equivalent to the problem of estimating skilled or complex labour. If this problem is theoretically separated from the problem of how to treat the labour cost necessary to educate and reproduce skilled labour-power, it becomes the problem of reducing various useful concrete labour into homogeneous abstract human labour, which, as we have seen in Chapter 3, is a soluble problem.

To criticise the labour theory of value von Mises assumes a time preference theory of interest with reference to investment in raw materials, similar to that of Böhm-Bawerk, so that he naturally conceives that commodity P with a larger input of raw material than Q will also have a higher value. Marx's theory of prices of production based on the labour theory of value, can also show that P would be more expensive than Q in terms of prices of production, given a general rate of profit across industries. At any rate, von Mises' critique here implicitly presupposes the existence of an average rate of interest, or profit on investment, as well as evaluation by market prices. As a whole, von Mises' critique can be summarised as the narrow theoretical view that rational economic computation cannot exist apart from evaluation in the market, competitive capital investment also included in such evaluation.

Weber

M. Weber (1864–1920), in Chapter II 'Sociological Categories of Economic Action', Part One, of his *Economy and Society* (1921), similarly stated that rational economic accounting cannot be achieved in a socialist economy planned in kind. According to Weber, in an economy planned in kind, economic calculation of costs through the comparison of different kinds of means of production and qualitatively different final products, is more than difficult to solve.

> Monetary accounting attains the highest level of rationality, as an instrument of calculatory orientation of economic action, when it is applied in the form of capital accounting. The substantive precondition here is a thorough market freedom'.[5] At the same time, in a planned economy, economic actions tend to be heteronomous, short of autonomy, motivation, and thus the economy must 'weaken the incentive to labour'.[6]

Halm

G. Halm followed Pierson's and von Mises' arguments in his paper 'Further Considerations on the Possibility of Adequate Calculation in a Socialist Community' (1935), and stressed that the role of interest and ground rent is indispensable to secure rational utilisation of relatively scarce capital, or capital goods, and land. 'The socialist economy no more provides such a pricing process of capital-goods than it provides a process of interest-determination' (*H*, p. 164). By the same token, rational determination of rent would not be possible either.

Barone

Before these arguments, E. Barone in his article 'The Ministry of Production in the Collectivist State' (1908), applied Walras' and Pareto's mathematical approach of general equilibrium theory, and sought the rational way for the Ministry of Production to maximise collective welfare by selecting combinations of factors of production which were publicly owned. In so far as the purpose of the Ministry of Production in the collectivist state is to obtain the collective maximum benefit, the Ministry has to determine 'ratios of equivalence between the various services and between the various products and between products and services' (*H*, p. 267). Even if the Ministry begins without money and prices,

> all the economic categories of the old regime must reappear, though may be with other names: prices, salaries, interest, rent, profit, sav-

ing, etc. Not only that; ... the same two fundamental conditions which characterise free competition reappear, and the maximum is more nearly attained the more perfectly they are realized. We refer, of course, to the conditions of minimum cost of production and the equalisation of price to cost of production (*H*, p. 289).

Barone also noted that 'it would be a tremendous – a gigantic – work' to solve on paper 'so great number of simultaneous equations' even by assuming given technical coefficients, and that 'the determination of the coefficients economically most advantageous can only be done in an experimental way', not *a priori* on paper (*H*, pp. 287–8). In short, his application of the general equilibrium theory showed that a socialist economy is practically incapable of constructing a production plan maximising collective welfare, and that the plan, if it were ever achieved, would substantially result in the re-emergence of the economic order of a free competitive market economy.

Hayek

Hayek collected these articles in *Collectivist Economic Planning*, and added his own arguments by reviewing the debate in the following way. Socialism faces the economic problem of distributing a limited amount of resources among a practically infinite number of purposes. Although there are many kinds of socialism, the way in which Marxism has been interpreted by the social democratic parties on the Continent of Europe envisages collective ownership and unified direction of the use of all material resources of production, combined with freedom of choice in consumption and freedom in the choice of occupation (*H*, pp. 17–18). When, however, it is possible to combine labour, land and material resources in many different ways in order to produce a good, the absence of a standard of value makes it impossible to decide which method is the most rational. A similar 'economic problem arises as soon as different purposes compete for the available resources' (*H*, p. 6). In a market economy, these problems are solved by the functioning of the price system based upon individual decision-making. As an alleged standard of value, 'the labour theory of value was the product of a search after some illusory substance of value' (*H*, p. 24). However, H.D. Dickinson had shown, following Barone's analysis, that on the assumption of complete knowledge of all relevant data, the values and quantities of goods to be produced might be determined by the application of the general equilibrium theory of prices.[7]

Hayek admits that 'this is not an impossibility in the sense that it is logically contradictory' (*H*, p. 207), but believes that it is impractical for the following two reasons.

First, the initiative of the manager of an individual enterprise is based upon minutely detailed knowledge of the technological processes, the possibilities for economising on raw materials, the changes in technologies, and the shifts in consumers' tastes. The central planning authority would not be able to collect all this detailed and changing information so as to incorporate it into the plan.

Secondly, even if the difficulty of collecting relevant data was somehow overcome, the number of different products entering into the system of simultaneous equations would be too large for practicable solution.

> At present we can hardly say what their number is, but it is hardly an exaggeration to assume that in a fairly advanced society, the order of magnitude would be at least in the hundreds of thousands. This means that, at each successive moment, every one of the decisions would have to be based on the solution of an equal number of simultaneous differential equations, a task which, with any means known at present, could not be carried out in a lifetime (*H*, p. 212).

Particularly in making the first point, Hayek emphasised the importance of decentralised, partial, but precise, knowledge and information, which tends to change in an advanced economy. He saw in the pricing system a social mechanism for organising and adjusting individual decisions based on such partial information. Technological innovations are facilitated and promoted at innumerable points by utilising such contextual knowledge in a market economy. The central planning authority cannot gather all this information and so substitute itself for a market economy. Lack of initiative for technological innovation in the Soviet bureaucratically centralised planned economy must be closely related to this problem. Hayek's critique of socialism on this aspect originates in his economic philosophy of neo-liberalism, concerned with how to conceive of the human ability to cope on an individual basis with perennially limited local knowledge and information. The point was repeated in his later writings[8] by emphasising the positive function of the spontaneous and innovative dynamic order of a market economy in the face of the socio–technological argument for economic activity from above.

Based on this belief Hayek wrote that 'Practically all observers seem to agree that even compared with pre-War Russia the position of the great masses has deteriorated' (*H*, p. 205). This remark, like von Mises' assessment of Soviet economic difficulties in the 1920s, was neither objective nor correct. In economic terms the industrialisation of the Soviet Union in the 1930s, based on the five year plan, was successfully achieved, even if under the oppressive political rule of Stalin. The disaster of mass unemployment which plagued capitalist countries at that time, was absent in the Soviet Union. The improvement of the economic conditions of the Soviet people during the period after the Second World War and until the middle of the 1970s, is even more evident. Actually, the various theoretical critiques of socialism summarised by Hayek from the standpoint of neo-liberalism, used to be regarded as a somewhat irrelevant and forgettable theoretical episode of the pre-war period. However, with the deepening crisis of the Soviet Union and the Eastern European countries, eventually resulting in the collapse of those economies, those critiques have enjoyed a powerful resurgence, and now act as guide to economic reforms aiming at total marketisation. Therefore, it is imperative for the future of socialism to challenge Hayek's recapitulation of the theoretical critique of the socialist economy.

THEORETICAL DEFENCES OF THE RATIONALITY OF A SOCIALIST ECONOMY

Will a socialist economy inevitably be an irrational economic system because it lacks a rational basis for economic computation, particularly for means of production publicly owned?

Dickinson

Dealing with the above issue, raised by von Mises, Dickinson showed in his 1933 *Economic Journal* paper that rational price formation for the means of production is theoretically possible in a socialist economy, even if the latter had the social characteristics assumed by von Mises. In Dickinson's formulation, a demand curve for each type of consumption good can be derived by observing reactions in the consumer market in which the selling agencies raise prices when stocks fall short and lower prices when stocks accumulate. Then, 'on the basis of the orders sent back by selling agencies the manufacturing organisations will be able to draw up a demand curve for their products'.[9] Similarly, a demand curve for the ultimate factors of production (such as parcels of land, mineral resources, certain numbers of workers registered as willing to do certain jobs) can also be obtained. Since the quantities of these ultimate factors of production are known, the Supreme Economic Council (SEC) can fix their prices according to demand curves, and so as to ensure their full employment.

> Then the productive organisations will slow down or stop the production of these goods where demand price is below the cost price and will expand the production of those goods whose demand price is above cost.[10]

They will also try to substitute one factor for another, and thus modify their demand for the factors. By this process of successive approximation, 'a true economic price for each factor', together with its allocation to different uses, will be established imputed from the demand for the marginal product.

Once the system has started functioning, the SEC would be able to solve the problem mathematically on the basis of full statistical information concerning, (1) a demand function for each consumption good, (2) a function connecting a unit of each consumption good to the quantities of factors used in its production, (3) a function for each product expressing the condition that selling price must equal the sum of the prices of the factors of production, (4) a supply function for each factor of production relating available quantity to price. 'The whole thing could be resolved into a set of simultaneous equations'.[11] As we have seen, Hayek criticised this part of Dickinson's view as practically impossible. It is worth noting that Dickinson also suggested an early non-mathematical successive approximation approach, shared by F.M. Taylor and O. Lange.

Dickinson further stated that in his view of socialism, the return to natural resources, interest on capital and surcharges for risk, would be determined or calculated as mere accounting sums to be paid into the Social Fund. The return to labour, or the value imputed to human effort, would be determined according to the value of consumption goods, and it would be contributed into a common pool by enterprises as part of their costs, or paid out of their sales proceeds. Social distribution of earnings could be decided independently on some principle, 'say equal income for everybody, or a system of payments according to need'.[12] The simplest solution to the problem of scarcity or redundance of certain types of labour, which would appear under such a distribution system given free choice of employment, would be to pay each labourer the value of his or her labour reflecting the balance between demand and supply. The resultant inequality in personal earnings would be reduced as education and vocational training became free and available to all. A large number of other social services (medical, cultural and recreational) provided free of charge, would further diminish inequalities in real income. A steeply progressive surtax could also be levied.

It is instructive to read Dickinson's argument regarding the role of interest in a socialist community. In deciding whether a tunnel should be built through a hill for a railway line, or the hill should be bypassed, the authorities have to decide how long it would take for the economy in operation to offset the extra cost of building the tunnel. If the extra construction cost is only five times the excess annual operation if no tunnel existed, 'it is almost certainly worth while to build the tunnel. If it is a hundred times more, the tunnel is almost certainly not worth while'.[13] In choosing between such investment plans, the rate of interest must play the role of a benchmark. The lower the rate of interest, the more comprehensive and easier the investment plans would become. The SEC may either fix the rate of interest for the year and then earmark the necessary quantity of capital from the total social income, or it could fix the amount of capital to be raised and then let the rate of interest for the year be freely determined. If the tempo of technical innovation rises, or if public tastes become more volatile, the amount of capital to be raised would increase.

Thus, Dickinson attempted to show that the pricing and allocation of means of production publicly owned can be undertaken in a socialist economy at least as rationally as in a market economy. He also replied to Halm as regards the possibility of incorporating the rational functions of interest in a socialist planned economy. As we have seen in Chapter 3 (pp. 75–7), the role of the rate of interest can be broader than that of a mere benchmark for choosing between investment plans. The rate of interest can become part of a mechanism mobilising for investment idle funds held by enterprises and citizens. Together with the potential for flexible expansion of the supply of s-money and credit, this can serve as a strategic policy instrument for the macroeconomic management of a socialist economy. Its role would naturally be greater when the economic decision-making for investment and saving will have been decentralised. At the same time, in any type of socialist economy the social decision to invest can be made more or less flexibly by taking into consideration socially determined priorities, or conditions other than the rate of interest as a benchmark.

Taylor

In 'The Guidance of Production in a Socialist State' (1929) F.M. Taylor argued that a socialist economic system was rationally possible and, before Dickinson, developed a trial and error approach to determining the effective role of a community's primary factors of production. In Taylor's model of socialism the State possesses the entire apparatus of production and guides all production operations. As sole producer the State buys productive services from citizens, and allows the latter freely to purchase consumption goods. By means of such purchases, citizens call on the State to produce what they want. In fixing the selling price of any commodity, 'the economic authorities would set that price at a point which fully covered the cost of producing said commodity',[14] or they would have to meet the drain on the primary factors of the community. The authorities would also construct tentative factor-valuation tables and continue their productive operations by using those tables, as well as make all necessary corrections of the tables. The valuation of a factor would be increased if the factor stock became short, and decreased if the stock became excessive. By this trial and error method the authorities would reach correct valuations of the primary factors, and achieve the right use of the economic resources.

Lange

The method of trial and error, which was also partly contained in Dickinson's paper, had presented a roundabout solution to the problem raised by Hayek concerning the practical impossibility of solving on paper a gigantic set of simultaneous equations. O. Lange adopted the idea and, in a way, provided a conclusion for the whole debate in his paper 'On the Economic Theory of Socialism' (1936–7).

In this paper, Lange assumes a socialist society with public ownership of the means of production, but also freedom of choice in consumption and employment, or a genuine market for consumers' goods and for the services of labour. He also assumes that 'the preference of consumers, as expressed by their demand prices, are guiding criteria in production and in the allocation of resources'.[15] The income of consumers is composed of the receipts for the labour services performed, together with the individual's share in the income derived from the capital and natural resources owned by society. The latter portion of the social dividend should not have any influence on the choice of occupation, and can therefore be distributed in many different ways, for instance, equally per head of population, or according to age, or size of family. The Central Planning Board (CPB) can determine the rate of accumulation arbitrarily or strategically, before distributing the social dividend to the individuals.

The CPB imposes two rules on the managers of production; first, the choice of combination of factors must minimise the average cost of production, so that the marginal productivity of factors is equalised; second, the scale of output should be determined at the level at which marginal cost becomes equal to the price of the product. When managers of firms or industries operate according to these rules, prices of services of labour and consumers' goods are determined in the market. Prices of means of production are initially put forth by the CPB as accounting prices, or parametric indicators by which alternatives are quantitatively compared. Given such prices, the quantities of means of production demanded and supplied would also be determined. If the prices put forth by the CPB failed to make demand and supply meet, the error would appear objectively as a surplus or a deficit of the goods or resources in question. The price of a commodity has to be raised if demand exceeds supply and lowered if the reverse is the case.

Thus, so long as the parametric function of prices is maintained, a set of equilibrium accounting prices can be determined through a process of trial and error, much like in a competitive market. The CPB does not need to possess 'complete lists' of demand and supply functions. 'Neither the Central Planning Board have to solve hundreds of thousands (as Professor Hayek expects) or millions (as Professor Robbins thinks) of equations'.[16] What is necessary is simply to observe the result of selections and decisions by the consumers and managers of production plants, made on the basis of their limited concerns and limited knowledge of prices. The trial and error procedure would work much better and more swiftly to reach the correct equilibrium prices in a socialist economy rather than in a competitive market, for the CPB has a much wider knowledge of what is going in the entire economic system. The argument by von Mises, Hayek and others that in a socialist economy the accounting prices of capital goods and of productive resources in public ownership cannot rationally be determined must thus be rejected.

Lange further shows that the trial and error procedure is also applicable to a socialist economy with neither freedom of choice in consumption nor freedom of choice of occupation. In that case, the CPB would decide which commodities are to be produced, and in what quantities. It would distribute consumers' goods by rationing, and assign workers to occupations. Still, rational accounting prices can be determined by reflecting 'the preference of bureaucrats in the CPB, instead of those of consumers'.[17] In Lange's view, however, the system cannot be recommended because of its undemocratic character.

Lange demonstrated that economic calculation with reference to the means of production publicly held can be rationally undertaken through a trial and error procedure, in spite of Hayek's critique of the practical feasibility of determining the prices of means of production by solving a huge set of simultaneous equations. This was indeed a powerful answer to the central problem raised by von Mises and Hayek, among others, concerning the capacity of socialism to utilise the factors of production rationally.

Hayek's Response

Hayek replied to Taylor and Lange in his paper 'Competitive "Solution"' (1940). In his reply, Hayek, first casts doubt on whether Taylor's and Lange's solution shows any advantage of socialist planning over a competitive market economy. Secondly, he argues that Taylor and Lange were trapped by static equilibrium theory and neglected the incessant changes of the relevant factors involved in reaching equilibrium prices; they did not make it clear in their solution how long prices would be fixed. Thirdly, the trial and error procedure is not applicable to many machines, buildings and ships which cannot be standardised, and which are made to individual special order. Further, without the possibility of free entry into an industry, or real price competition, there will not be sufficient motivation for an entrepreneur to discover the cheapest method of production. Thus, Hayek shifted his emphasis away from the original issue of the rational calculability of the prices of means of production publicly owned toward the ability of a real market economy to organise the changeable factors of production using localised specific knowledge and information. This shift is rather a move away from the problem of rational economic calculability in a socialist economy, posed earlier by von Mises and Hayek.

As Hayek emphasises, the motive for innovation is certainly important. However, this motive can be secured for socialised enterprises in market socialism, or even under a fixed price system, by allowing such enterprises to obtain a certain extra s-profit if they manage to reduce the cost of production, or to produce a new type of product. The prices of new products must be determined promptly, and for a certain time they must afford an extra return to encourage innovation.

Unlike in Soviet central planning, the existence of many rival enterprises within each industry is a desirable factor, promoting the motive to innovate. Differences in remuneration according as enterprises succeed or fail, should be allowed within limits. The competitive motive to succeed through innovation could be strengthened if the management of enterprises was made relatively independent and could reap extra rewards within limits. This result could be achieved even if the means of production were publicly owned, as is evidenced by the fact that managers and workers in Japanese firms are motivated to innovate and work hard despite not possessing large amounts of shares of their corporations.

The period during which prices will remain fixed within an officially fixed price system need not be five years, but could be reduced to one or two years depending on the planning and calculation capacity of the CPB. Nowadays, the period can be shortened by utilising improved microelectronics information technologies, and its length does not seem a fundamental problem.

Hayek's critique of socialism subsequently shifted further away from his earlier position regarding rational economic calculability, and in his later writings, such as *The Road to Serfdom* (1944),[18] Hayek stressed his view of the incompatibility between human liberty and socialism.

Dobb

In the course of the debate on socialist economic calculation, the Austrian marginal utility theory which imputes the values of capital goods to prices of consumer goods determined in the market, was more or less taken for granted not only by the anti-socialist Pierson, von Mises, Halm, and Hayek, but also by the pro-socialist Dickinson, Taylor and Lange. Taylor and Lange's trial and error procedure employed their opponents' theoretical framework, and showed that a rational price system, and the rational allocation of resources, are plausible in a socialist economy, similarly to (or better than) a capitalist market economy. M. Dobb (1900–76) and P.M. Sweezy (1910–) criticised the theoretical framework of the debate itself, and attempted to demonstrate the superiority of socialist economic planning from the point of view of Marxist political economy.

For instance, in his paper 'Economic Theory and the Problems of a Socialist Economy' (1933),[19] Dobb argued that the theoretical framework of the debate depended on the narrowly limited view of marginalist price theory based on individual consumer preference. In Chapter 8 of

Political Economy and Capitalism (1937), titled 'The Question of Economic Law in a Socialist Economy', Dobb enlarged on this point and put across the following argument. In the entire debate it has been implied that

> in essentials the same economic laws must rule in a socialist economy as rule in a capitalist economy, so that the economic problem must have the same general shape and be handled by similar mechanisms in the two systems.[20]

However, in a socialist economy, where the major decisions of investment are integrated into a coherent whole, mistakes, discontinuities, and economic difficulties caused by short-sighted investment in a capitalist economy will be avoided. Socialist investment decisions would be arrived at with a more egalitarian attitude regarding the present and the future. The pattern of development would thus be determined flexibly, and without being constrained by the rate of interest in the market.[21]

It is true that even in a socialist economy, in order to compare economic quantities, diverse goods must be reducible to quantitative terms according to a scale of priorities. The scale of priorities need not, however, be determined by arbitrary market prices, but

> might be constructed in an authoritative manner, as a doctor prescribes a diet for a patient, or on the basis of sampling opinion by means of questionnaires, or on the basis of information supplied by co-operative societies, or by a combination of these methods.[22]

A free consumers' market can also be incorporated into the socialist economy. Large-scale allocations alone need to be made by the central authorities, and their detailed assignment can be decentralised to subordinate authorities possessing more detailed information. There would be no need for the planning authorities to have 'millions of equations' 'of which Professors Hayek and Robbins speak with so much scorn'.[23] In practice, and always starting from a pre-existing situation, prices of products can be operationally altered.

Thus Dobb had in mind a trial and error procedure for determination of prices in a socialist economy similar to Taylor and Lange. However, he opposed the application of marginal utility theory of prices to socialism since the theory always started from the passive individual consumers' selection of goods. 'The laws which will rule a socialist economy will be different in essential respects from those which rule a capitalist economy'.[24] For instance, customers can take positive initiatives for new types of goods and services, co-operative social consumption can be much expanded, and more rational social determination of investment plans can be made possible in a socialist economy. Dobb assumed that as the importance of such social decisions increased, the role of the theory of value 'would be small or non-existent, and at any rate a rapidly diminishing one'.[25] This view matched the 'orthodox' Marxist position that the role of political economy, or economics, would end with the realisation of a socialist society, and the science would be replaced by technology. However, the inclusion of a free consumers' market, and the economic calculation of costs of products and investment, as we have seen, will require some theoretical analysis of the values, or s-prices, of goods and services in a socialist economy. Therefore, there will still be a role of value theory in socialism, even if the role of social decision-making will certainly increase.

In fact Dobb provided a perspective of his own regarding the increasing relevance of the Marxist theory of value by stating that

> an economic plan which distributes capital resources in the most productive manner will necessarily, ... produce a system of prices analogous to Marx's 'prices of production'. But this will not be a position of equilibrium. In the degree that capital accumulation proceeds, and the productive equipment of society extended, this dispersion of prices away from their labour-values will tend to disappear.[26]

The reason for the last argument is that the proportion of living labour (the source of profit) relative to accumulated past labour tends to decline, a trend which Marx also assumed in his law of the tendency of the rate of profit to fall. However, it is not likely that the dispersion of prices away from labour-values will disappear due to a decrease in the proportion of living labour relative to accumulated past labour. The reason is that the amount of past labour embodied in the means of production is repeatedly devalued as the productivity of labour increases. A simpler procedure for making prices equal to labour s-values, as we have seen on pp. 67–8, would be to calculate the costs of production by a full s-wage model in which all the social net income is distributed to individual workers who are subsequently levied by society.

Sweezy

In Part III of his book *Socialism* (1949), Sweezy also reviewed and commented on the socialist economic calculation debate. According to him, and as a reply to the anti-socialist case of von Mises, Hayek and others, 'Lange's paper may be regarded as having finally removed any doubts about the capacity of socialism to utilize resources rationally'.[27] Real-life socialism, however, would not necessarily conform to Lange's model. The 'most striking feature of Lange's model is that the function of the Central Planning Board is virtually confined to providing a substitute for the market as coordinator of the activities of the various plants and industries'.[28] The CPB appears simply as a price-fixing agency. Production decisions are left to a myriad of independent units, just like in capitalism. Although such a system is conceivable, it does not take advantage of the constructive possibilities of economic planning.

In an actual socialist society, the CPB can lay down 'concrete directives which will be binding on the managers of socialised industries and plants'.[29] In such a case, comprehensive planning is compatible with money calculation, as shown by the experience of the Soviet Union, and this money calculation can be performed formally in accordance with Lange's procedure. The Sections of the CPB can even be instructed to follow exactly the same rules as those in Lange's trial and error procedure determining prices and the allocation of resources. If conditions, such as consumers' tastes, techniques of production, and availability of natural resources, are static, the two systems would arrive at the same end result. However, if there are changes in the conditions, the path of development in the planned system must be quite different from that in the unplanned market system.

The logical possibility of rational accounting and resource allocation does not always ensure the attainment of these goals in practice.

> There will be areas of indeterminacy, miscalculations, errors of execution. But this is true of all systems, including competitive capitalism, monopolistic capitalism, unplanned collectivism, and planned socialism; and in this respect it seems safe to say that planned socialism need not fear comparison with its hypothetical and actual rivals.[30]

Sweezy thus attempted theoretically to demonstrate the rational feasibility of the Soviet type of comprehensively planned economy, not only in opposition to the anti-socialist case, but also in contrast to Lange's model of an unplanned collectivist economy. His arguments in the same book concerning the possibility of providing incentives to work, improved efficiency, and increasing freedom in socialism are also instructive and interesting. However, we have to note that a comprehensively planned economy is apt to be accompanied by a hypertrophy of oppressive State power, such as was experienced in the Soviet type of society. As we shall see in the next chapter, Sweezy himself has become very critical of this type of society. So long as a socialist economy cannot exist without planning, it is clearly essential to devise democratic rules and practices in constructing the central economic plans. In order to promote positive participation and initiative by working people, relegation of certain parts of decision-making to local authorities, industries and enterprises is also worth democratic consideration. Furthermore, co-ordination among decentralised economic units may require certain roles for the market, or s-market, beyond what Sweezy has assumed here.

On the other hand, however, Sweezy accepted that Lange's model, based on marginal utility theory, can be applied to a socialist economy even under comprehensive planning. He did not particularly investigate how the Marxist labour theory of value could provide the theoretical grounds for rational accounting and allocation of resources in socialism. Since Dobb's reference to the labour theory of value was not so positive in this respect, both Dobb and Sweezy seem to have accepted Austrian neo-classical price theory as a common theoretical framework for the socialist economic calculation debate. Their opposition to neo-classical price theory and their support for the labour theory of value in their other works, is somehow not logically related to their comments on the debate.

Lange on Computers

Three decades later Lange returned to the debate in 'The Computer and the Market' (1967). He wrote:

Were I to rewrite my essay today my task would be much simpler. My answer to Hayek and Robbins would be: so what's the trouble? Let us put the simultaneous equations on an electronic computer and we shall obtain the solution in less than a second. The market process with its cumbersome tatonnements appears old-fashioned.[31]

In his view, the market mechanism may be regarded as a computing device for solving a system of simultaneous equations on the feedback principle. The market serves as one of the oldest historical devices for solving simultaneous equations via a social rather than a physical process. If the capacity of electronic computers remains still limited, the market is to be used. The market has in a sense a broader capacity.

An important limitation of the market, however, is

> that it treats the accounting problem only in static terms, i.e. as an equilibrium problem. It does not provide a sufficient foundation for the solution of growth and development problems. In particular, it does not provide an adequate basis for long-term economic planning.[32]

Indeed, electronic computers can fulfil a function which the market was never able to perform namely, the calculation of future shadow prices in long-term development plans based on an objective function (for instance, maximising the increase of national income over a certain period) and given certain constraints.

Lange may have over-estimated the growth of the capacity of computer technology. Alternatively he may have under-estimated the practical difficulty of gathering and ordering the huge volume of economic information to be contained within simultaneous equations, as well as how rapidly consumers' tastes can change before computation starts. It has to be admitted, however, that the recent development of ME (micro-electronics) information technologies has much improved the capacity of gathering and handling a variety of information. Typical examples of such advances are the POS (point of sales) system, which can instantly channel sales information from shops back to the distributing mechanism and the production lines, and demand information gathered by credit card users as well as by a computerised ordering system. These would make Lange's expectation of socialist economic calculation by means of computers more realistic than ever before. If strategically important items to be computed are separated from other items to be left to the market, and if the former are systematically segmented by the decentralisation of decision-making, the areas which can be dealt with by computer information technologies have been decisively expanded in recent years.

It is particularly interesting to note that Lange considered the market mechanism and computers as similar devices which can be substituted for each other. The two devices may then also be used as complements for each other, or some part of the functions of one may easily be replaced by the functions of the other. The technological grounds for such combinations in a socialist economy actually seem to have expanded in the wake of the recent information revolution in the advanced capitalist economies.

ARGUMENTS FOR MARKET SOCIALISM

Socialist economists, such as Lange, Dobb, and Sweezy, asserted the feasibility of a rational socialist economy against the arguments of von Mises, Hayek and others. They also believed in and looked forward to the continuous growth of the Soviet planned economy. In fact, the Soviet economy repeatedly exceeded the targets of the five year plans, its growth compared favourably to the capitalist countries engulfed in the Great Depression of the 1930s, it successfully confronted the severe trials of the Second World War, and seemed to demonstrate the viability of the new economic system.

The actual operation of the Soviet economy was, however, different from the functioning of the Lange model. Soviet prices were officially fixed, based on cost calculations, and not subject to the changing balance between demand and supply (except for the free market prices of kolkhoz products which amounted to just 3 percent of total retail prices). Prices were determined by the central planning authority, together with the allocation of means of production and investment. The characteristics of the Soviet economic system were more faithfully reflected in Dobb's and Sweezy's theoretical model.

The basic characteristics of the Soviet economic system were not altered by the so-called profit controversy, initiated by a *Pravda* article by E. G. Liberman in September 1962.[33] Neither were these characteristics significantly affected by the reform of the price system in 1966–7 which followed the controversy. In this reform, the accounting basis for net earnings, or s-profit to be added to the cost of products, changed from the running costs to the total amount of the production fund (total s-capital, including fixed equipment). This took place in order to promote the more appropriate use of fixed funds. A charge (or s-interest) for the use of production funds was introduced for the same purpose. The forming of economic incentive funds was allowed out of funds reserved from the s-profit of enterprises. However, the kernel of Liberman's proposal namely, to bring about elastic price formation in the direction of market socialism, was not implemented.

In Eastern Europe, the economic reform of 1965 decisively moved Yugoslavia toward a model of decentralised market socialism. The latter was based on the country's characteristic practice of workers' self-management which was adopted in the 1950s independently of Soviet political control. In Czechoslovakia, the economic reforms of 1965–8 surpassed those in the Soviet Union, including elastic price formation, and started to be combined with demands for political democratisation. At the summit of the Czech reform movement during the Spring of Prague in 1968, however, Soviet military interference froze and reversed the reform movement. Hungarian economic reform implementing the new economic mechanism from the beginning of 1968 was allowed to remain as an exception within the Soviet bloc, so long as it did not develop into political reform.

Theoretical arguments for market socialism were repeatedly forged in the heat of the East European reform movements, together with critiques of the Soviet model of centrally planned economy. Such arguments gained power as the 'abrasion' and crisis of the Soviet and Eastern European economies deepened. They theoretically prepared for the Eastern European revolutions of 1989, and the dissolution of the Soviet Union in 1991. Let us review some of the representative arguments.

Brus

W. Brus (1921–), who co-operated with O. Lange in planning the Polish economic reform of 1956–7 and then moved to the UK, presented a functional model of a socialist economy in 'The Functional Model of Socialism'.[34] He proposed to classify economic decisions into the following three areas. (1) Basic macroeconomic decisions, such as those concerning the economic growth rate, the rate of accumulation, the division between communal and private consumption, and the regional industrial structure. These must be taken by the central planning authority in a socialist economy. The central authority would also regulate, directly or indirectly, wages, prices and the rate of interest. (2) The choice of private consumption goods within a given income, and the choice of occupation. These should be undertaken in a free market. (3) Operational economic decisions concerning the size and the composition of input and output, the methods of production, the selection of suppliers and purchasers, as well as the detailed determination of emoluments, which should be taken by individual enterprises or industrial sectors.

In comparison with the Lange model, in which the central authority appeared as a passive auctioneer, the Brus model was more concrete and practicable in its theoretical structure, and accorded a more positive role to the central authority in determining macroeconomic strategies. Together with the assumption of social ownership of the basic means of production, this aspect of the Brus model is worth noting as indicating the socialist character of his construction at that time. The assumption of a consumption goods market and a jobs market in the Brus model was held in common with Lange and others in the socialist calculation debate, but was a more market-oriented feature than those to be found in the actual Soviet type of economy. A clear characteristic of the Brus model was to locate individual enterprises or industries as operational organs able to make decisions by themselves. In this aspect, the model is clearly a type of decentralised market socialism, which can serve to weaken central bureaucratic power and to broaden the opportunities for democratic participation and workers' control.[35] The Brus model presenting possible economic reforms combining the market with central planning, exercised a strong influence on Soviet and Eastern European reform movements, as well as on Chinese economic reform.

Brus himself seems to have been subsequently much influenced by the process of the reform movements themselves, and wrote *From Marx to Market* (1988) together with K. Laski. Brus' view in this book is that the combination of planning and market cannot but be inconsistent in one way or another as an economic system. Therefore, the initial introduction of the market will have to proceed to more comprehensive marketisation. The limits of the transition from the integrated ownership of property, which is a characteristic of socialist economy, to decentralised ownership, which is more suitable to a market economy, cannot be precisely determined. As Brus put it, the transition may be open-ended. With comprehensive marketisation, the economy would become unstable, it would generate the economic problems of depression and unemployment, and so macroeconomic Keynesian or Kaleckian policies would, once again, become necessary.

Was Brus' first model theoretically incorrect and so abandoned, or was it altered into the second model simply to suit and to lead the more recent East European reform movements? Here is a methodological problem to bear in mind in the course of our exposition.

Kornai

In Hungary, J. Kornai (1928–) characterised the Soviet type of centrally planned economy as a shortage economy. In a series of works,[36] Kornai described the following three types of shortage phenomena.

The first type is horizontal shortage which occurs between the seller and the buyer. Faced with shortage, the buyer, typically a consumer, generally has to endure long queueing, and often has to accept the forced substitution of the original good, the tiring search for goods on foot, the postponement of purchase or, even, the abandonment of purchase. The second type is vertical shortage which typically appears when firms in a bureaucratic hierarchy are allotted various resources and products. In the case of products and services distributed by the authorities to consumers, such as state-owned housing tenancies, vertical shortage is combined with horizontal shortage. The third type of shortage is inter-firm shortage, or bottlenecks, of certain raw materials or skilled workers.

One type of shortage often gives rise to another and so shortage phenomena tend to exacerbate each other. As certain raw materials remain unutilised, due to shortage of other raw materials or components, the surplus or slack of unutilised raw materials, or resources, also tends to increase in tandem with the shortage economy. Shortage phenomena and the uncertainty of obtaining supplies induce the building up of large stocks of both factory inputs and household consumer goods whenever such goods are available. This stockpiling, in turn, strengthens the shortage phenomena. Because of the existence of a shortage economy, (1) consumers' welfare is decreased, and (2) the efficiency of production is much reduced. Furthermore, (3) the central authority and the bureaucrats can behave dictatorially in the one-sided sellers' market, and people have to live permanently asking for favours, looking for useful personal connections and offering bribes. At the same time, (4) the seller or producer is in such a strong position against buyers that the incentive to improve product quality, or to innovate, is lost.

The system-specific causes for these phenomena 'are linked with the effect, the shortage syndrome'.

> One such is, for instance, the interest of the firms' managers in gaining the recognition of their superiors. Others include the soft budget constraint and investment hunger. These three phenomena, ... form a major, direct cause of shortage, but they are also effects; they derived integrally from the system's deeper traits: the typical structure of power, ideology, ownership, and coordination.[37]

The budget constraint of firms is soft and elastic because there exists adjustability of prices of products according to costs, the state gives subsidies to firms in difficulties, there is a soft tax system with many possible exemptions, and there also exists a soft credit system negotiable *a posteriori*. Thus, unlike capitalist firms with hard budget constraints, firms in a semi-monetised socialist economy tend to pile up stocks of raw materials, and to 'run away' with expansion and investment regardless of the real demand for their products and profitability.

Kornai proposed a transition from a semi-monetised economy with soft budget constraints for firms to a truly monetised economy with hard budget constraints as a solution for the shortage syndrome in 'classical socialism'. Although bureaucratic control is necessary in socialism in order to guarantee the fair distribution of income, to promote economic activities with socially favourable external effects, to curb economic activities with unfavourable external effects, and to supervise or nationalise monopolistic firms, a market mechanism for firms has to be developed in many areas outside bureaucratic co-ordination. Thus, Kornai substantially pointed to the path of market socialism with a dominant role of the market economy. In the actual process of the Eastern European social revolutions of 1989, he further proposed as a necessary reform the transition from socialism to a fully capitalist market economy.[38]

As a diagnosis of the state of the Soviet type of economy, particularly in the 1970s and 1980s, Kornai's description of the shortage syndrome is sharp and comprehensive. His insight into the economic influence of the institutional and social relations within the Soviet type of bureaucratic hierarchy was a significant contribution to economics. In his analysis of the causes of the shortage economy, however, he tended to treat the specific features of the Soviet type of socioeconomic order much too generally as characteristics of 'classic socialism', or of the centrally planned socialist economy. As a result his analysis of the causes of shortage is neither completely persuasive nor satisfactory. In fact it is circular, as he himself admitted.

In so far as Kornai stresses the system-specific factors in the behaviour of firms under the Soviet type of bureaucracy, he does not successfully explain the shortage phenomena on the consumer side. Kornai makes much of a presumed general tendency toward excess demand for free services. However, in many capitalist countries the provision of free education, free public libraries, and free or cheap medical services (especially in the UK), works relatively well and without shortage phenomena. A precondition for this success, though, is sufficient supply capacity together with fairly inelastic demand. It might have been political mismanagement of the Soviet type of societies to have provided certain consumer goods and services for free, or exceedingly cheaply, without being able to supply these goods in sufficient volume to meet social need. Maintaining a low share of consumer goods relative to producer and military goods in the total output may also have been a similar political mistake. Such mismanagement should not be identified as an unavoidable defect of a socialist economy in general.

As Kornai correctly points out, bureaucratically controlled Soviet-type societies faced a serious problem of insufficiency of effort by firms to supply goods and services in accordance with social need, as well as a problem of unbalanced shortages of various production inputs. Although Kornai calls these societies 'classic socialism,' they actually presented a very disfigured image of classic co-operative socialism, and certainly not an image of democratic socialism with effective control over the power and functions of bureaucrats. By identifying the experience of Soviet-type economies with classic socialism in general, Kornai overlooked the possibility of democratic control over the bureaucrats and their planning. Even under soft budget constraints, the shortage syndrome may not appear, or may be greatly reduced, if individual firms can themselves more precisely assess and improve their activities by employing certain indices, including terms of s-prices. We have to admit, however, that there remains the serious problem of how to achieve both efficient and democratic control of bureaucrats, and also of how to establish non-selfish social consciousness among working people in a normally operating socialist society after the initial phase of revolutions and wars. The role of education and culture is important here, and so is the role of a more effectively democratic political system which would utilise advanced information technologies.

At the same time, Kornai fails to explain, or even to formulate, the problem of how the Soviet economy could enjoy relatively high economic growth until the middle of the 1970s, and why this growth turned into unprecedented economic stagnation and subsequent crisis. The problem cannot be solved by referring to the general characteristics of 'classic socialism'. The damaging effect of the heavy burden of military spending, which was also left out of Kornai's considerations, can be neither totally reduced to the logic of the bureaucratic system nor to the essence of socialism.

On the whole, Kornai's assessment of socialism and his identification of it with the experience of the Soviet type of societies is too negative. Kornai tends to idealise the market economy, or the capitalist market economy, as a way out of the shortage economy, but he disregards the fundamental defects of a capitalist market system, especially for working people. Democratic socialism should strive to overcome the shortage syndrome of the Soviet model, as well as the unstable, unequal, and oppressive economic order of capitalism which frequently generates over-production and mass unemployment. Probably because of over-generalisation, Kornai's diagnosis of the shortage economy was not strongly linked to a socialist prescription, and was in fact used in order to recommend not simply market socialism but the full transition to a capitalist economy.

Selucky

In Czechoslovakia R. Selucky worked for the reform movement until the Spring of Prague in 1968, then he moved to Ottawa University, and published *Marxism, Socialism, Freedom* (1979). His major concern was to reconstruct socialism and expand freedom and democracy.
According to Selucky,

> While Marx's economic concept of socialism consists of a single social-wide factory based on vertical (hierarchical) relations of superiority and subordination, his political concept of socialism consists of a free association of self-managed work and social communities based on horizontal relations of equality. Whoever accepts in full Marx's first concept has to give up the latter, and vice versa: they are mutually exclusive.[39]

At the same time, Marx's and Engels' dream that in a communist society it would be possible 'to hunt in the morning, fish in the afternoon, rear cattle in the evening, criticize after dinner'[40] is not realistic for the professional work of today, and therefore the social division of labour cannot be abolished. Marx was also not right when he argued that

> Only the products of mutually independent acts of labour, performed in isolation, can confront each other as commodities (I, p. 132).

Just as the exchange of commodities sprang out of relations between communities, 'the causal connection of an autonomy of producers with private property is both methodological and theoretical error'.[41]
On the basis of these reflections, Selucky proposes the following 'general model of democratic socialism'. Labour to be the sole source of income; the means of production to be owned socially and managed by those who make use them; enterprises to be autonomous from the State, independent of each other, and to operate within the framework

of the market, the latter being regulated by a central indicative plan; incomes to be distributed according to one's contribution to work output; health and education services, and social benefits for the disabled to be distributed according to one's needs.[42]

Selucky's proposal of market socialism was thus based on workers' self-management of enterprises, and was composed through a textual re-examination of Marx's works, especial emphasis being laid on securing political and social freedom. Selucky's method, however, is still rather inflexible since he presents his model as the sole general alternative to the Soviet type of society. Both the viability of a centrally planned economy under certain conditions, and the actual economic achievements of the Soviet model are totally neglected. The essential tendency of the market system toward instability and inequality is also neglected.

Selucky's re-examination of Marx's works, furthermore, seems incomplete. His refutation of Marx's concept of socialism as a single social-wide factory, for instance, may derive from a misreading of Marx's text concerning the one nation, one factory argument, which we examined in Chapter 3 (pp. 61–2). Selucky should have explored further the many and useful implications of Marx's theory of value for socialism, or even for market socialism.

Nove

More recently the British economist A. Nove (1913–94) wrote *The Economics of Feasible Socialism* (1983). His notion of feasible socialism was clearly defined, being the socialism which can conceivably be achieved within the time span of one generation or the next fifty years. Nove, thus, intended to avoid the pitfalls of over-generalisation.

Nove subjects the legacy of Marx to a severe re-examination and questions the validity of 'the romantic – utopian – religious elements of the Marxian tradition'.[43] His opinion is that Marxist value theory has contributed little to economic calculation, the measurement of opportunity costs, or the choice between alternatives under socialism.

> Marx has himself caused much confusion in viewing use-values as incommensurable, and, above all, by an artificial and unjustified separation between value and use-values.[44]

Nove further charges that under Marx's influence Soviet prices were based simply on cost and disregarded use-values. While any society

should try to increase the difference between cost and result, one cannot measure and compare the socially useful effect, or the use-value, of shoes, ships, sealing wax and cabbages, except in terms of money.
In the USSR there were 12 million identifiably different products, close to 50,000 industrial establishments, and 48,000 plan 'positions'.[45]

The more choice there is, the less the predictability, for obvious reasons. It is therefore tempting for planners to limit or even eliminate choice.[46]

Although Marx clearly stated that rewards should be in accordance with work in the first stage of a socialist society, how should rewards differ with respect to skill or physical intensity of work? Because of this ambiguity, Marx's principle of pay 'according to work' was 'interpreted in the USSR as justifying wide pay differentials, based on a mixture of criteria: skill, rank, heavy work, location (e.g. in the Arctic), and so on'.[47]

Marx's view that production relations and plans would be 'simple' and 'transparent' in a socialist society 'was seriously mistaken'. 'The elimination of commodity production, ... implies a degree of centralisation which has a multilevel, hierarchically organized plan-bureaucracy as its functionally inescapable accompaniment'. This in turn conflicts with the aim of meaningful workers participation' and 'must cause alienation'.[48] From this point of view, Nove examines the historical experience in the Soviet Union, Eastern Europe, and China, and presents the following sketch of feasible socialism.

The political system is assumed to be a multiparty democracy with periodic parliamentary elections; there can be many types of production unit, so as to encourage citizens' private and group initiatives, for instance, state enterprises, socialised enterprises with workers' self-management, co-operative enterprises, small-scale enterprises with definite limits of operation, and individual agents such as freelance journalists, plumbers, artists; there would not be large-scale private ownership of the means of production; very large state enterprises with a monopoly position would face tripartite supervision from the State, the users and the workers, just as Selucky had recommended; the many competitive (socialised or co-operative) firms in an industry would 'base their activities on negotiations with their customers';[49] according to Hungarian experience, technologically innovative information would circulate more freely if it could command a price.[50]

In this model, the functions of central planning would include the following; determination of major investment; monitoring decentralised investment in order to avoid duplication; administering 'naturally' important productive activities, such as electricity, oil, railways; setting the ground-rules for the free sectors with reserve powers of intervention; some regulation of foreign trade. 'In those sectors where externalities are significant, intervention is essential'. There will also be the basic task of

> determining the share of total GDP to devote to investment, as distinct from current consumption, and this in turn would affect the rules that are made to ensure adequate savings (either by way of taxation or through the use of retained profits of enterprises, or both).[51]

Democratic voting would determine the boundary between the commercial or market sectors, and those sectors in which listed goods and services would be provided for free. However, the voters might not wish to make the list of free goods and services too long, as they 'would appreciate that free goods and services need to be paid for, and that the longer the list the smaller the personal disposable income'.[52]

Contained within the difference between cost and result, and as part of prices, there would be profit, differential rent, and interest. However, interest and rent would be payments made to the State, and profit would be taxed. The reward for labour would be seen to relate closely to labour's average productivity, and the degree of income differentiation would be related to such factors as 'supply and demand for different kinds of labour, social policy, the need for incentives, compensation for heavy or disagreeable work'.[53] Attempts will be made to broaden the opportunities for job change and specialisation changes for those who wish to do so. The right to form free trade unions would be indispensable, but unions and management will have to adjust the total number of jobs through work-sharing, if technical progress is of a massively labour-saving kind, 'The duty to provide work would override considerations of micro profitability'.[54]

Nove thus presented the argument for market socialism in the line of the socialist economic calculation debate. Since his book can be seen as a representative recent work in favour of market socialism, let us consider it somewhat more fully. There is, first of all, an important confusion in Nove's understanding of value theory. According to Nove, one cause of the failure of the Soviet centrally planned economy can be found in the unjustified separation between value and use-value or, more broadly, in Marx's view of use-values as not commensurable magnitudes. Nove is on weak theoretical grounds when he assumes the comparative measurability of the use-value of different goods in terms of prices. Except for very early Austrian theorists, utilities are generally thought of as not measurable even by the neo-classical marginal theorists. The latter assume that at the point of contact between the budget constraint surface and an indifferent curve, quantities demanded of commodities and relative prices are determined so as to maximise consumers' satisfaction. What is necessary is to be able to compare the relative degree of utility in the psychological selection of goods in the mind of individual consumer, and not to be able to measure the absolute amount of utility.

A rise (fall) in the market price of a commodity would generally signify that the demand for the commodity is excessive (short) relative to the supply, but not that its use-value or utility has necessarily increased (decreased). So far as the commodity is a reproducible good, a rise (fall) in its market price in a competitive market economy would induce an increase (decrease) in its production. As a result, the gravitational center of the various fluctuating market prices would generally coincide with the equilibrium prices in the Sraffian system, or Marx's prices of production, both of the latter being objectively determined on the basis of social and technological relations of reproduction. Excepting certain commodities, such as curios whose prices depend solely on scarcity, the exchange values of the decisively important reproducible commodities in our economic life are generally determined by production costs. However great its use-value, the exchange-value of a commodity with a low unit cost of production would be small. The value of a commodity which retains exactly the same use-value would decline, if its production cost were reduced due to technological development.

Further, Nove criticises the Marxist idea of determining prices based directly on the labour-time embodied in commodities, and sees this concept as a source of difficulties in the Soviet model of economy. However, the exact relationship between the publicly fixed prices of goods and the labour-time embodied in them, was neither assessed nor considered in Soviet planning. A planned economy organised on the basis of labour-time is a social system which has not yet been realised.

As Nove points out, it is certainly worth consideration how properly to adjust supply to consumers' needs and choices in a socialist economy. However, the necessary adjustment of supply is plausible even with fixed prices, if certain indicators are used, such as stocks of products, length of order lists, and the rate of capacity utilisation, as we see in the practice of monopolistic firms. There are cases of successful adjustment of supply and demand regarding socially common consumption both in capitalist and in 'socialist' societies. We can conceive of various theoretical models for solving this problem. Market socialism can undoubtedly be one such model, although which goods and services are to be assigned to the market has to be democratically determined and regularly re-examined. Nove has proposed the use of democratic voting in this respect.

Nove also stresses the essential role of free market prices in measuring economic efficiency by comparing costs and output. However, market prices are apt to fluctuate unstably, and often they are not a suitable standard for making investment decisions. If it was accepted that a part of the extra s-profit obtained through technological innovation is to be distributed among members of enterprises as revenue to increase the incentive to work, the same effect would be secured more easily with stable prices objectively grounded on the technological structure of reproduction. Furthermore, so long as market prices are the sole rational measurement of goods and services, the social cost of using free goods and services would be impossible rationally to measure. Prices of goods and services of 'the very large state enterprises', or 'naturally' important productive activities, even according to Nove, would not be subject to competitive market pricing. Thus, prices which are based on costs of reproduction (or on embodied labour-time, if the latter could be determined) must be theoretically more consistent as the economic measurement of those categories of goods and services. This type of calculation of costs (or labour-time) must also be desirable for the monitoring of the social functions of free market prices. If the negotiations of consumers with competitive firms in Nove's model is to be effective, information regarding such calculation of costs in comparison with actual market prices would be really necessary.

Nove also points out that the issue of how to reduce skilled or complex labour into simple labour in measuring economic efficiency or determining distribution according to labour, is a fundamental difficulty of Marx's theory. His solution, namely, to rely on the market assessing the achievement of labour, or determining wages, is somewhat inconsistent with his prescription of undertaking policies guaranteeing a certain degree of equalisation of incomes. The grounds on which Nove supports the principle of income equalisation are not at all clear. As I have already argued in Chapter 3 (pp. 53–7), such a principle is easily supported by the concept that the contribution of labour-time is basically equal for all workers regardless of educational or training costs. In a socialist society an additional remuneration for the necessities of life, or incentive payments for certain hard occupations and so on, could be socially determined but not on the grounds of a presumed unequal ability to labour. At the same time, the costs of education and training should be, as far as possible, expended socially in order to guarantee equal opportunities for all members of society.

One cannot but agree with Nove when he stresses the egalitarian principle and workers' participation in a socialist society. In the same spirit, one could also concur with many aspects of his plan for feasible socialism, if the latter was presented as one of many possible models. However, his arguments regarding the necessity of the comprehensive introduction of the market, though typical among market socialists, are not theoretically persuasive enough. Nove's model of socialism is constructed in a very narrow theoretical manner. It suffers by its denial of Marx's value theory, and by connecting the direct and simple measurement of consumers' needs and of economic efficiency with the need for a subjective theory of value. Nove's theoretical oversight of the passive position of consumers in a capitalist market economy, despite his emphasis on the role of consumers in a socialist economy, is also related to this fundamental theoretical view. The negative, but powerful, influence of the Austrian critique of socialism, which we saw in the calculation debate, can thus be traced even in the current arguments in favour of market socialism.

THE RECENT DEBATES ON THE MARKET AND SOCIALISM

Against the background of Perestroika and Eastern Europe's move toward reform, Nove's argument of feasible socialism initiated a contemporary debate on the market and socialism. The socialist economic calculation debate, broadly speaking, was revived after several decades, and its theme was widened in an interesting contemporary fashion. Let us consider some representative arguments of this recent debate.

Mandel

E. Mandel was first to criticise Nove and to assume an opposite point of view in his article 'In Defence of Socialist Planning' (1986). According to Mandel, an effective answer to Nove's objections to socialist planning with no commodity production can be provided if one follows Marx's method and starts from the basic historical trend of capitalist development. As capitalism developed, the planned organisation of work expanded with the growing size of factories, and reached beyond the factory to the level of the firm in monopoly capitalism. Planned organisation has even become international at the level of transnational corporations. Consequently, the market allocation of labour has been radically reduced. Market and planning, furthermore, are fundamentally different ways of allocating resources and labour, but they can both be found under various political forms: there can be 'despotic' planning as well as 'democratic' planning. The malfunctioning of the Soviet Union, Eastern Europe and China arose out of the immature historical conditions for socialism. These societies are not in any meaningful sense socialist but, rather, transitional economies. In fact, the material, technical and human resources needed for planning exist in the most advanced capitalist countries.

Nove argued that there are about 12 million different goods in the USSR, and that only the market could ever perform the function of allocating these rationally. Against this argument, Mandel writes:

> Already today, in the most advanced capitalist countries, the bulk of both consumer and producer goods are not produced in any way in response to 'market signals' shifting violently from year to year, let alone month to month. The bulk of current production corresponds to established consumption patterns and predetermined production techniques that are largely if not completely independent of the market.[55]

The role of made-to-order consumer goods is also increasing. With the increase in social wealth, the number of goods and services characterised by inelasticity of demand could progressively increase. At least 80 percent of the consumption of the average consumer is now insesitive to price fluctuations. Already in the richest industrialised countries the overall consumption of food, clothing and footwear, measured in terms of calorie-intake, square metres of cloth and pairs of shoes, has become satiated and has started to decline.

Therefore, the production and allocation of certain goods and services which satisfy fundamental needs, such as basic food and drink, shelter and associated goods and services (heating, electricity, running water, furniture), education and health provision, transport to the workplace, a minimum of recreation and leisure, can be treated as objective conditions at a given period in any country. These goods and services can easily become subject to planning. Even if money and prices were used, money relations could easily be quasi-market or pseudo-market relations: 'The absence of market competition in no way necessitates a lack of product innovation.'[56] Most discoveries and innovations have been made wholly outside any commercial nexus, and will continue to be made given the natural propensity of ordinary producers to save their own labour, and the existence of unforced intellectual–scientific curiosity.

On these grounds, an annual congress of workers' and people's councils would determine in a democratic way the length of the working week; the needs to be satisfied as priority (free distribution); the volume of resources devoted to growth; the volume of resources left for non-essential goods and services to be distributed through the money mechanism; the minimum and maximum money incomes; the pricing policy for marketable goods and services. A coherent general plan would then be drawn up based on these choices, utilising input–output tables. Self-managing bodies in each industry would further divide the workload among the existing producer units, and project the creation of new such units, if necessary.

Such a system would not yet be pure socialism, but it would still be a transition towards socialism. It is not true that the only choice for humanity is between the despotic direction of labour and the market economy. The third alternative way is in democratically articulated and centralised self-management, the planned self-rule of the associated producers.

These arguments by Mandel rely on the traditional Marxist conception of socialism. Market and planning are seen as mutual opposites, more sharply so than in the view of Dobb and Sweezy. Mandel thus asserts that the promotion of a planned economy based on the democratically articulated and centralised association of producers is both fully possible and desirable.

Nove replied in 'Market and Socialism' (1987).[57] His argument was that Mandel does not understand the overwhelming complexity of marketless planning, comprising several million types and varieties of goods and services, produced and provided by hundreds of thousands of enterprises. In Nove's opinion, it does not make much sense here to assert some vague democratic solution, a world of abundance with the capacity to meet all reasonable input requirements, and a static equilibrium without changes in the existing patterns of production and consumption. Mandel's *tertium datur* cannot be a solution.

Mandel came back with *The Myth of Market Socialism* (1988).[58] In Mandel's view, the shortcomings of the Soviet economy, which were so strongly emphasised by Nove, did not result from the 'principles of central planning', but have to be seen within the framework of relative backwardness, isolation and bureaucratic mismanagement of the Soviet Union. From the very nature and the historical experience of market economies in capitalist countries, it is definitely an illusion to want to maintain a sizable market economy whilst avoiding mass unemployment and numerous disastrous firm bankruptcies. Nove put forth a list of goods to be provided independently of the desire to make money, such as health, education, public housing, post and telecommunications, urban public transportation, environmental protection, water supply, street lighting and cleaning, and parks. If to this list one adds cultural and information services and basic food and clothing, one would cover 70–80 percent of civilian expenditure in most industrialised countries, leaving a minor sector of the economy at the disposal of market relations. Would it not be preferable from the macro–social point of view to abolish personal cars and to devote the thoroughfares of all cities to small buses passing, say, every three minutes? Nove also ignores the point that market relations could wither away for goods whose elasticity of demand approaches zero, or has even become negative. Nuclear annihilation, destruction of eco-systems and the biosphere, hunger in the third world, and massive impoverishment in the northern hemisphere would not be solved by the market economy. The crux of the debate concerns, in Mandel's opinion, not the greatest possible efficiency (which in any case is not precisely defined), but the greatest possible human freedom, or emancipation from externally imposed constraints on individuals, whether these are economic or political or socio–cultural. It is a debate about the self-determination of human existence.

Chris Harman in *The Myth of Market Socialism* (1989)[59] presents a similar critique of Nove, denouncing the irrational shortcomings of the market economy in a capitalist society, and arguing in favour of an advance away from the market mechanism toward conscious control without a market.

Auerbach, Desai and Shamsavari

P. Auerbach, M. Desai and A. Shamsavari, in 'The Transition from Actually Existing Capitalism' (1988), intervened in the debate between Nove and Mandel, and advanced the following comments. The setbacks suffered by socialist parties in Western Europe have, paradoxically, revived the question of the feasibility of socialism in advanced capitalist countries. Together with the radical rethinking taking place in contemporary socialist countries, this has made market socialism once again the object of analysis after nearly fifty years. Mandel, following a long Marxist tradition, based his critique of Nove on a perceived tendency of the market allocation of labour to decline as large capitalist factories and enterprises continue to grow. The internal organisation of the large capitalist enterprises has certainly been expanded, and has become more sophisticated and developed. 'But no evidence exists to indicate that these developments have taken place at the expense of market-based activities.'[60] A measure of the extent to which firms tend to be 'planned' in an economy would be the ratio of value added to sales. While this ratio in the US economy displayed an increase in the period from 1880 to 1920, it did not show a tendency to rise in the half-century after 1920.

In the real world, there has been not a mutually exclusive relation but, rather, a dialectical and symbiotic connection between planning and the market. For instance, administrative planning to impose uniformity of standards and specifications on machine tools, as well as electrical parts and equipment, made possible the development of markets and the commodification of these products. In the steel industry, the traditional strategy of vertical integration has been thwarted by the emergence of world-wide markets in coal and iron ore in recent decades. This was, at least partly, a result of the planned decisions of the Japanese steel industry. Many giant corporations have used a multi-divisional structure, in order to stimulate the discipline of the market within the corporation structure. Even the most recent triumphs of capitalist planning and co-ordination within and between enterprises, such as the famous Japanese kanban system for the control of inventories, have emerged as a result of market pressure.[61]

According to Auerbach, Desai and Shamsavari, these comments and observations do not by themselves support market socialism: they are also applicable to a rationally organised economy without a market. If we assume that a rich array of markets is necessary in order to offer signals for rational decision-making, society's internal organisational structures must be arranged so as to generate these markets. This is also true of the present Russian economic reforms. However, planning has an intrinsic and inevitable role to play, especially in a socialist economy, not just in response to problems of 'market failure', as suggested by market socialists. Planning of investment and research by enterprises, as well as helping to co-ordinate these enterprise activities in the future, remain significant activities in socialism. The most innovative forms of economic planning would involve the re-fashioning of work to suit the needs and desires of the population – what is now called 'manpower planning'. 'The realisation of human potential is, of course, the greatest and most valuable weapon in the socialist arsenal.'[62]

Auerbach, Desai and Shamsavari thus sharply criticised Mandel's traditional view that the market and planning are mutually exclusive. They also persuasively showed that it is incorrect to treat the growth of capitalist firms as an indication of the increasing relative weight of planning, or of a corresponding decrease in the importance of the market, both of these tendencies traditionally regarded as preconditions for socialist planning. Most of their comments were, however, not favourable to socialism, as they themselves admitted. Though their concluding remark on the necessity of 'manpower planning' suggests an interesting possibility for the future, they did not fully examine the argument in favour of market socialism in its substantial content.

Elson

D. Elson attempted more positively to tackle this issue in her article 'Market Socialism or Socialisation of the Market?' (1988). She shares Mandel's view that there is an alternative between the market and bureaucratic planning. On the other hand, she also agrees with Nove that the price mechanism is an indispensable instrument of co-ordination for a socialist economy, but argues that it must be socialised. Her starting point is the reproduction of labour power. This includes the unpaid labour process in the household and the community, which has been an argument much elaborated by feminists. From this point of view, she stresses the politics of use-values, and of popular participation in planning through direct co-operation between the organisations of producers and the households which use their products. Nove places little value on self-organisation at the grass roots, and is suspicious of the role of trade unions.

Further according to Elson, the neo-classical school does not see the need to distinguish labour from other factors of production. However, 'Labour power is not fully commodified because it is not produced as a commodity'.[63] While considering this specificity of labour, Elson asks how social arrangements can be created which enable working people to take initiatives in economic decision-making. Nove presents a 'bargaining model' of a market economy, where individual buyers can refuse to buy, can go elsewhere, and can bargain. In the great majority of cases, however, choice by households can only be exercised within a pre-specified set of goods at pre-specified prices. Nove's 'feasible socialism', which aims at raising the position of consumers as buyers by adopting a bargaining model of the market, is more utopian than at first sight appears.

Most of the economic theory literature on plan versus the market, in Elson's view, fails to consider markets as social institutions. Instead, they confine their image of the market to one of the following three options: a bargaining type of market; an auction type of market; a broker-organised type of market. These images are insubstantial because they ignore the fact that markets require informational functions which have related costs and demand resources. Hayek for example assumed that the market provides information costlessly.

> Too often the claim for the superiority of market allocation has been based on a comparison between a market system with exogenously or costlessly given prices and a planned system with a multitude of visible administrative costs.[64]

At the same time, a market does not directly reveal information about the intentions, desires and values of its participants, but transmits information solely about the outcome of decisions taken in the dark. This blindness is one of the important characteristics of an anarchical market economy. Hence the relevance of trade associations or business lunches, where information is swapped. Still, however, information flows are very fragmented, and information gathering activities are both duplicated and wasteful.

Apart from the plan/market dichotomy, there is a third kind of co-ordination nexus to be found in informal relationships, such as implicit contracts, moral commitments, interrelationships based on trust and reciprocity, which have been called the 'invisible handshake' by A. Okun.[65] Much of the literature on the economic success of Japan, South Korea, and Taiwan makes a similar point. Although the 'invisible handshake' in capitalism tends to be the 'invisible arm twist', socialists must make sure that co-operation is genuinely a product of trust and goodwill so as truly to create a third way.

In Elson's view of socialism, the process of the reproduction of labour power must be the independent variable to which the accumulation process conforms. The foundation for household choice and freedom would be two-fold: the provision, free of charge of basic services (with particular characteristics of interdependencies and externalities), such as health, education, water and sanitation; and the provision to all citizens, in their own right, of a minimum money income to cover the purchase of sufficient food, clothing, shelter and household goods providing a basic living standard.

To the first category of free services, Elson adds access to information networks: print, telephones, photocopiers, fax machines, computers, etc. because a necessary condition for socialising the market is equal and easy access to information. A Wage Commission would provide information about job vacancies and job seekers, and the Commission would also democratically produce basic norms regarding both the basic wages paid to different occupations and across-the-board increases in those basic wages. A Price Commission would similarly form price norms based on average unit costs, and the mark-up determined by the investment needs of the economy. This type of pricing procedure was earlier adopted by Kalecki, and differs from Lange's trial and error procedure. The annual review would then decide the extent to which cost and demand changes (as revealed in inventory changes) have necessitated changes in prices. A firm with lower than average costs would make a larger than average surplus, and would possess funds to pay higher bonuses to its workers.

As for staple consumer goods and services which account for a large proportion of household expenditure, detailed information on price formation is to be openly provided. Elson proposes that a Consumer Union should be formed to act as a network co-ordinator between households and enterprises. In such an economic order, open access to information would be the key to conscious control of the socialist economy. It is desirable to develop networks which prefigure those in a socialist order, and to weave a whole host of issues, ranging from market regulation, environmental issues and consumer protection, to industrial democracy and national industrial strategies, into a coherent campaign around open access to information.

The content of Elson's view of socialism is thus different from Mandel's third way, and offers support for the notion of market socialism. However, in opposition to Nove's argument, Elson restructures the concept of market socialism by advocating the socialisation of the market from a Marxist and feminist point of view. Price norms are to be based on average unit costs and mark-ups and, unlike Nove's argument based on neo-classical theory, they would not be subject to the balance between demand and supply in the market. The peculiarity of the reproduction of labour power is also much stressed. The ways of controlling firms, particularly those supplying means of consumption, have to be reconstructed in the direction of letting workers positively act as a social subjective agent. Joan Robinson's argument that it is up to socialist economies to find some way of making consumers' sovereignty a reality[66] must be fulfilled. Also noteworthy is Elson's assertion that a market should be considered not simply as an abstract level place of exchange, but as a concrete social institution. Especially in a capitalist market, economic information is concentrated in firms, and therefore there is much overlap, fragmentation and concealment. One of Elson's key strategies for the socialist conscious control of the economy is to make economic information socially open and freely accessible.

It is notable that the demand to increase the availability of information to the public has become an important issue for democratic socialism, both in the form of glasnost in the course of Perestroika and in the Western argument of the socialisation of the market. It is clear though, that mere free access to economic information would not suffice. Socialist organisations such as consumers' unions, workers unions, and social institutions which democratically operate firms, set prices and determine State and local budgets, have to be created in order to make the accessibility of information actually useful for socialist purposes.

At the same time, it should be admitted that there are certain kinds of information which are known and transmitted inside firms and workplaces alone. This would typically include some skills or the management of personal relations learned at work. This information is, thus, unsuitable for free access. Besides, even information which can be socially transmitted is so voluminous in each industry, firm and workplace that its entire amount could not be handled by a single central planning board. Therefore economic information is dispersed and difficult to gather by a single planning board in a double sense. This dispersed specific nature of knowledge is stressed by Hayek as one reason for the irrationality of a centrally planned economy. However, as R.Blackburn argues, following Elson, 'the dispersed nature of knowledge could also be deployed against a narrow capitalistic entrepreneurialism by advocates of social and worker self-management'.[67] A socialised market can be a social institution which will encourage the meeting of free individual minds upon the basis of easy access to necessary information, provided that this can be publicly transmitted.

On the other hand, so long as the socialised market works on the basis of price norms determined by a Price Commission on the principle of average cost plus mark-up, and as the mark-up may be subject to strategic differentiation, the functions of the market would indeed be socialised and quite different from the ordinary conception of market socialism. The price system in Elson's socialised market would not be far away from the *s*-price system in a planned socialist economy. The difference may be limited to the freedom of purchase or sale by each individual economic agent. The conception of market socialism can, thus, become diversified not only as regards the extent of the non-market sectors of the economy, but also as regards the very functions of the market itself. The market can be free and competitive, the balance between demand and supply determining prices; it can be organised, monopolistic firms dominating the determination of prices; it can be democratically socialised, average costs being marked-up according to social priorities.

Bardhan and Roemer

More recent representative contributions for and against market socialism are collected in P.K. Bardhan and J.E. Roemer (eds), *Market Socialism: The Current Debate* (1993). In the Introduction, the editors identify five stages in the history of the idea of market socialism following Hayek. The first stage was marked by the realisation by socialists that prices, and not a 'natural unit' such as energy or labour, must be used for economic calculation under socialism. In the second stage Dickinson, among others, asserted the calculability of the correct prices in a socialist economy by using Walrasian general equilibrium theory and solving a complicated system of simultaneous equations. The third stage was marked by the realisation, by Lange and others, that markets of some kind would be required to find the socialist equilibrium. The fourth stage was the period of market reforms in the East European countries and in Soviet Perestroika, in which Kornai's theory of soft budget constraint was presented. The fifth stage is the present debate.

The typical arguments in the fifth stage are represented by the contributions of Bardhan, Roemer, Weisskopf, Drèze and Fleubery in the collected papers. They share the common assumption that firms operate

> independently of the state control, with a board of directors representing either workers or various institutions (banks, mutual funds, pension funds) that hold stock in the firms or are responsible for their financing.[68]

Their models of market socialism differ from capitalism under social democracy by excluding private ownership and allowing for various forms of public ownership of firms. The mechanism for equalising income out of profit is thus maintained. Roemer explicitly rejects social democracy as a species of socialism 'because the mechanism for equalizing income is not stable, being based upon redistributive taxation and not a change in property rights'.[69] In contrast to the Soviet type of 'Communist model', however, their models of market socialism preclude both political dictatorship and the allocation of many goods by central administration.

According to Bardhan and Roemer,

> how to monitor the managers of public firms to maximize profits, to get them involved in competitive races for innovation, to discipline laxity, and how to separate political from economic criteria in decision making – these are central economic issues any model of market socialism must address.[70]

These issues are also related to issues of incentive compatibility and agency problems. They regard free markets and the connected institutional settings as indispensable for solving these issues. Their arguments are reminiscent of the communications I have had with B. Rowthorn and A. Glyn in the process of preparing this book, as mentioned in the Preface.

One would agree with many of their arguments regarding the fifth stage of the concept of market socialism if these are presented as a possible and promising way for socialism 'with some chance of existing today',[71] either in Eastern Europe or in the West. One could also agree with the view that the Japanese model of management is frequently thought to provide evidence for the possible separation of the motive to innovate from the managers' property in their firms. Neverthless, I suspect that Bardhan and Roemer over-estimate the monitoring function of banks and keiretsu (group) firms in fostering innovation under the Japanese type of management, by neglecting the other institutional characteristics of Japanese firms, such as the lifetime employment system for regular employees, and the promotion system incorporating a method of employee assessment. From the standpoint of the Japanese experience, flexible innovative change cannot really be achieved simply by managers, but must also be founded on the loyal co-operation and the initiative of workers at the shopfloor.

Conscious co-operation and initiatives by workers for the improvement of the methods of production, or for changes in products are, in my view, indispensable for successful innovative changes in capitalism, in market socialism, and in socialism with a more restricted market. The mere existence of a market does not suffice in this respect. Denial of political dictatorship should not deprive socialism of its advantage in mobilising workers' own conscious co-operative initiative. Bardhan and Roemer's fifth generation model of market socialism seems to over-react to the failure of the Soviet type of socialism in so far as it demands the strict separation of political from economic motivation. Likewise, it sets too much store by the functions of the free market in solving all the difficult problems of successful innovation. Should we then remain pessimistic with respect to innovative changes in a public sector which has politically regulated prices for its products? Bardhan and Roemer also seem to over-stress the role of managers of firms rather than that of workers, engineers and R & D professional scientists in providing economic dynamism.

Possible solutions for allocative efficiency, as well as for the motive to innovate, by firms in a socialist economy must not be limited to Bardhan and Roemer's fifth generation model of market socialism with a completely free competitive market, if one takes a longer-run view or considers a wider range of socio–historical circumstances.

MULTIPLICITY OF THE MODELS OF A SOCIALIST ECONOMY

As we have seen in this chapter, there has been a long debate concerning the theoretical feasibility of socialism. This debate has also dealt with a further question, namely, what type of socialist economy is conceivable and desirable. The entire historical process of the formation, growth, crisis, and fall of the Soviet type of socialism has been the background of this debate, and substantially influenced its content. This debate is not, and can not be, complete since the socioeconomic problems of the capitalist economy continually generate hopes of, and demand for, socialism. The fall of the USSR did not reduce but actually increased the intellectual interest in the future of socialism around the world. We will now briefly note some important points to be borne in mind in order to further the discussion.

Relevance of the Marxist Theory of Value

Firstly, though mostly implicitly, value theory has been on trial as the basic frame of reference for theoretical models of socialism. In the first round of the socialist economic calculation debate, von Mises,

Hayek and others, who asserted the impossibility of rational economic calculation in a centrally planned economy, denounced Marx's labour theory of value. To support their position on how to collect information, and calculate the rational equilibrium prices, they relied on the marginal utility theory of value, the theory of imputation for the values of the means of production, as well as on general equilibrium theory. Dickinson, Taylor, and Lange, who argued in favour of the rational economic calculability in a centrally planned economy against the Austrian critics of socialism, also used a similar neo-classical general equilibrium theory of prices as a basic frame of reference. Nor did Dobb and Sweezy, who at the time positively suported the Soviet type of centrally planned socialism, actually present the Marxist labour theory of value as a foundation for their arguments.

In the recent Western debate on feasible socialism, arguments for straightforward market socialism, such as those of Nove, tend to see in Marxist value theory one of the causes of irrational confusion in a socialist economy. In Nove's opinion, Marxist value theory unduly neglects the role of demand, or users' estimation, in determining prices. Participants in the debate, such as Mandel, Desai, Elson, Bardhan and Roemer who argued from a socialist point of view, did not particularly refer to the issues concerning value theory. Since most of these theorists have also been prominent participants in the value controversies of recent years and advocates of the Marxist value theory (as Dobb and Sweezy defended Marxist value theory in the initial phase of the transformation controversy), this is evidently a rather mysterious lacuna of the entire debate.

While reconsidering Marx's economic theories for socialism in Chapter 3, we attempted to examine ways for filling this lacuna. Marx's value theory, which clarifies the distinction between the forms and substance of value as well as the significance of the labour process as eternal economic norms common to all social formations, is potentially applicable to various models of socialist economy. This is in contrast to the naturalistic labour theory of value of the classical school. The application of Marx's value theory need not be confined simply to theoretical support for a model of strict equal exchange of labour among labour products, or to theoretical support for the Soviet model of inelastic prices based on costs and determined by a central body. Marx's labour theory of value is also a value theory of labour, as paraphrased by Elson.[72] The theory claims to ascertain how the social relations of labour-time are socially obtained and distributed through the forms of value.

130   *Theories*

Even in a model of market socialism in which a considerable part of the total produce is traded in a competitive market, it must be both desirable and necessary to confirm as far as possible how much labour-time is embodied in each product, and how much is distributed to each industry, firm or worker. This confirmation would act as a foundation for the co-operative, conscious control of the economy based on the subjective activity of workers. To effect this purpose we can expect effectively to utilise information technologies and to use some type of input–output analysis. Theoretical and statistical estimation and inference must also play a certain role in examining the social relations of labour-time.

In any form of socialism, how to define the cost of labour in terms of price (or s-wages) will always be an important question. As the communal part of consumption expands in a socialist economy, the money s-wage rate can be correspondingly reduced. Therefore, if money expenditure is taken as the cost of production, the cost of living labour will be systematically undervalued. This may affect the choice of technological path. One way of avoiding this distortion is to distribute the whole of the social income to workers in the form of s-wages, without normally leaving any surplus. Then, the reproducible price system has to contain prices exactly proportional to the labour-time embodied in each product, as we have already argued. The price system can be made to arrive at such a condition without any calculation, but simply through a trial and error procedure in the market. In this model both the social surplus labour-time and the necessary labour-time to be communally consumed, must be levied from s-wages. The co-operative firms may collect such funds for society. The money payment for workers must thus be confined simply to a portion of s-wages while total s-wages will serve as a nominal cost for the price of the product. In case prices of products are subject to market fluctuations, the industries enjoying increased prices in the market would gain a return above the costs of production, and would be encouraged to expand production by employing this surplus. The industries facing reduced prices and thus unable to recoup their costs fully would make losses, and they would be forced to reduce production. How severely this contraction would be undertaken would depend on how rigidly social levies would be paid. In order to make the reduction of employment gradual, the social levies must be less rigidly imposed for some period of time.

In a certain type of socialist economy without market prices there is a danger of a vicious circle comprising the relative shortage of demand for a product, its reduced production, and an increase in its average costs of production. In such an economy, social arrangements to collect information on the movement of stocks of products, and to adjust the size of production in accordance with social need, must be effectively incorporated. The socialist form of industrial reserve army, as we have already argued, may also facilitate such arrangements to some extent.

In a socialist economy in which necessary labour-time is distributed in the form of s-wages and the price norms are determined on the basis of average costs plus mark-up, the rate of mark-up need not necessarily be equalised, and can be strategically differentiated according to social priority, as Elson has suggested. The differentiated rate of mark-up should be related in this case not to the bonus payment of workers, but only to the rate of investment.

Under any price system, extra s-profit would be obtained by firms with superior conditions of operation, or by firms which successfully introduced new type of products. In the case in which such superior conditions resulted from the fertility or the location of land that can be monopolised, then the extra s-profit must be levied by society as differential s-rent. By contrast, a part of the extra s-profit due to either technological or product innovation may be retained by the firm to be distributed to the workers and managers as a bonus in order to promote incentives for further technological progress. In order to avoid the difficulties which centrally planned bureaucratic economies have in promoting innovative changes, it is desirable to allow autonomous decentralised operations by many rival firms in every industry to a certain extent. Social reserves of resources and labour-power (in the socialist form of a reserve army) must also be present and must be utilised flexibly by firms. Incentives and motivation for innovation would then be compatible with various systems of pricing, and it would not be restricted to the pricing system of a free market. Such incentives would also be compatible also with a variety of forms of public property in firms.

In a socialist economy in which market prices are employed, a democratic consensus should be arrived at as regards the kinds of goods and services to be subject to market prices, the range of fluctuation of prices in comparison with the planned standard of prices, and the rule of how to cope with surpluses or losses of firms due to fluctuations of market prices.

It has been repeatedly pointed out in the long debate on socialism that a fundamental difficulty in examining the social relation between prices and labour-time is the reduction of skilled or complex labour-time to simple labour. However, since skilled or complex labour is also a form of expenditure of the universal human ability to labour, there is fundamentally no need for us to evaluate skilled or complex labour-time differently from simple labour, as we have already argued in Chapter 3 (pp. 53–7). This point is quite separate from the social need to cover the costs of education and training of skilled or complex labour-power. In any form of socialism, it would be desirable socially and sufficiently to secure the costs of education, and of the acquisition of skills or professional knowledge, as an element of a free education and training service. If the entire costs of education and training are socialised, there is no reason why skilled workers should obtain more income than unskilled workers from the view of reproduction of skilled labour-power.

All socialists, including market socialists, recognise that an important task of socialism is to equalise incomes. The importance of this task is agreed upon even by some critics of socialism. Our reinterpretation of skilled or complex labour-time is consonant with the egalitarian principle for socialism which sees the basis for economic activity in the universal human ability to labour. Upon this recognition, a certain range of differentiated s-wages can be introduced as an expedient incentive for the spontaneous move of workers to harder jobs or inconvenient geographical areas.

Through these considerations, we see that the Marxist labour theory of value can be used flexibly as a frame of reference for various types of socialism. We can conceive of a type of socialism containing a free competitive market for a certain range of goods and services, or another type in which prices are officially set by a central board by simulating the market. A centrally planned socialist economy would also be a feasible option, either at an early stage of industrialisation, or in a highly developed rich society containing many democratic organisations. The combination of these socialist forms in separate economic areas is also conceivable. In any form of socialism, the social relations of labour-time existing behind the price (or s-price) system must also be examined so as to clarify the social functions of plan and price (or s-price) for workers.

Arguments for or against socialism which are based on neo-classical theories cannot generally comprehend the broad applicability of Marx's theory of value, and tend hastily to conclude that a major reason for the failure of the Soviet type of planned economy was the various theoretical defects of the Marxist theory. The same kind of argument believes that economic rationality cannot be achieved except through a competitive market, and therefore perceives of a narrowly limited market socialism as the only possible model of socialism. Such a model of socialism necessarily becomes theoretically inconsistent when one tries to incorporate into the model the socialist demands for an egalitarian distribution of income, increases in socialised consumption, and the protection of ecological environments. Marx's labour theory of value, if its depth is understood and applied properly, would enable us to overcome such narrow limitations or inconsistencies in the arguments for socialism based on neo-classical theory.

The Possibility of Multiple Models

Secondly, participants from both camps have tended to assert the existence of an ideal economic system as an exclusive and unique solution, starting with the total negation of the rationality of socialist economic planning. This may have, directly or indirectly, reflected the attitude of Soviet 'orthodox' Marxism, which insisted that the Soviet type of centrally planned economy was the only correct way to socialism. After the fall of Soviet Marxism, however, the range of conceptions of and options for feasible models of socialism has been much extended. Among socialists, the possibility of democratic selection from among various social models, or changes of choice according to the concrete historical conditions of each society, has become more and more evident for the foreseeable future.

Marx's conception of socialism or communism as 'an association of free men'(I. p.171) without a market, generally thought of as a reversal of the comprehensive market economy under capitalism, may still serve as a basic frame of reference or as a distant goal. However, feasible models of socialism must belong to a different level of consideration. Just as we need a stages theory of capitalist development on a research level separate and different from the level of the basic principles of the capitalist economy (in order to make the actual analysis of an individual capitalist economy more flexible and richer at a third level of research), we should carefully distinguish among different levels of consideration for socialism. The possibility, at a similar level of stages theory, of multiple models of socialism for the foreseeable future would not directly negate Marx's basic conception of communism.

From the point of view of recognising the possibility of multiple models of socialism at the level of stages theory, it is improper to neglect the historical conditions which enabled the Soviet type of planned economy to grow actively, if accompanied by socio–political oppression. Arguments for market socialism which assume an absolute form are apt to neglect the historical fact of, and the conditions for, the relatively rapid economic growth of the USSR for over a half century. It is likewise improper to see economic models of market socialism as being in opposition to Marxism.

An economic model of market socialism containing a free competitive market for certain goods and services is indeed one among many possible options open. However, it is evidently an over-generalisation influenced by the narrow neo-classical view, to regard such a model as the only feasible type of socialism with rational economic calculation and incentives for innovation. Similarly it cannot be true that the price form has rational significance only within a free competitive market.

As most market socialists would agree, one strength of a socialist society evidently lies in its ability to expand the socially communal type of consumption, and to provide a safety net for all members of society outside the narrow 'rationality' of a market order. What level of education, health care, pensions for the aged and so forth, shall then be provided as socially free services? Shall the funds necessary for communal consumption and accumulation be levied on s-wages as well as on the surplus of firms? How broad shall the range of differentiation of incomes be in order to secure incentives and the reallocation of workers upon the basis of the egalitarian principle? On these issues, among others, a socialist society can clearly set up a wide range of options subject to democratic decision, even accompanied by a free competitive market of considerable size, as well as by a decentralised social order encouraging the activities of self-managing local communities and co-operative firms.

Diversity of public forms of property in the means of production or firms must correspondingly be incorporated. For instance, in one type of socialist economy land must be basically owned by the whole people or the State, whereas some firms may be owned by the State, some by local communities, some by co-operative workers. Although private ownership of firms must be basically excluded, the possible combination of public forms of property in firms can be diverse. Besides, even the State-owned firms can be run by contracted managers (as in China recently), or by co-operating workers. In any form of socialist economic order, the existence of many rival firms with a certain autonomy is desirable in order to promote innovative changes. At the same time, the strategies for the fullest possible disclosure of economic information to the public, and the 'socialisation of the market', in Elson's phrase, are indeed important and practicable steps in intensifying economic democracy and in facilitating innovative dynamism. How widely and properly such options for democratic social decision-making are understood is, in a sense, a test for the various arguments and theories on feasible economic models of socialism. An advantage of the Marxist school compared to the neo-classical one is, in my view, its command of a wider perspective on this issue, since its originality lies in the theoretical study of the socio–historical nature of economic life not confined to the market order.

The theoretical recognition of a wide range of feasible economic models of socialism does not mean that any model can be chosen independently of the given historical conditions of a society. The range of actually feasible models of socialism must certainly be adapted to the given historical and social conditions of a society, including the ideologies prevalent among its people. One task of the theory of socialism must be to show the breadth of optional models even within a given historical context, and to criticise the prejudice or one-sidedness of certain judgements or ideologies. On the other hand, recognising the existence of a wide range of models of feasible socialism does not exclude the possibility that the various models of socialist economy would in the very long run universally increase the conscious control of economic life independent of the anarchical market order, and would converge toward a model of an associational economy without a market, such as Marx had suggested.

Practical Relevance

In the deepening crisis of the Soviet type of centralised socialism, the concept of market socialism was presented as a radical critique of the existing order, and actually inspired the reform movements in Eastern Europe. It is, thus, rather amazing to see how the concept could not survive the fall of the Soviet type of socialism, and was rapidly replaced by neo-liberal policy demanding immediate and comprehensive marketisation. This may suggest that market socialism would, in practice, require complicated social arrangements, or compromises among people, which are difficult to realise by a weakened political leadership. The free market theorists Hayek and M. Friedman seem to have won the day, beating not just Marx and Lenin, but also Lange, Brus, and Nove. Conversely, all socialist thought and theories seem to have lost their role and relevance as a guide to the understanding and the making of existing socialist policies.

If theoretical models of the socialist economy were significant only as a practical guide for foreseeing and determining the policy stance of actually existing socialist countries, then not just the model of the centrally planned economy, but also the models of market socialism seem to have lost all actual meaning. This would at least partly explain why Brus in his joint work with K. Laski *From Marx to Market* (1988), changed his previous position favouring market socialism, as we have already seen. Even after this change and his move toward a type of Keynesianism, Brus could not regain much prestige as the tide of policy change in Poland, his country of origin, and other Eastern European countries moved so rapidly toward neo-liberalism. However, this actual policy shift does not even remotely eliminate the theoretical and practical relevance of Brus' earlier model of market socialism, nor that of whole variety of other models of socialist economy. This is just as the dominance of neo-liberalism in the major capitalist countries could not eliminate the theoretical and practical relevance of Keynesianism.

Indeed, as the economic crisis deepens in Russia and other CIS countries, as well as in Eastern European countries, neo-liberalism is fast giving rise to disillusionment. There are signs of a revival of the popular need and hope for socialist movements, theories and thought in these countries. Disillusionment with neo-liberalism is widespread also in capitalist countries, now in the process of deepening depression after the collapse of financial bubbles. Since the feeling of chaotic loss of social orientation is dominant in the capitalist world, it is significant for the future of humanity to maintain and clarify the characteristics of various feasible models of socialism as a foundation for socialist thought and movements which will continue to reappear in one form or another. In such co-operative attempts the deep crisis of socialism may be turned into an opportunity for overcoming the unfortunate history of repeated splits and antagonisms within the socialist movement due to different models and strategies. One of the practically relevant aspects of the theoretical study of the feasibility of various models of socialism can thus be the renewal of the ideological basis for easy co-operation among the people who would support a socialist future.

Critiques of the Capitalist Market Economy

It is interesting to note that the long debate on the socialist economy has generated a reconsideration not only of models of socialism, but also of the functioning of the market economy. Starting with the abstract theoretical image of the auction-type market in general equilibrium theory, the theoretical conception of the market, even that of critics of socialism such as Hayek, was enriched to form an image of dispersed knowledge and information in a dynamic and spontaneous market order. Socialists also became aware of the fact that different social relations, such as policies, institutions, customs, organisations, and the methods of dealing with information, plans and decisions, are combined in a market mechanism, and considerably affect the workings of a market economy. More or less related to this recognition, arguments for market socialism, or the socialisation of the market, have also been recently presented. The difficulty of introducing a market order into the former socialist countries provided fresh evidence for the importance of the social relations which make the market system workable.

In examining feasible models of socialism, with or without a free market, it is therefore essential to study the workings of the market in conjunction with other social relations. Since the fully developed workings of the market economy are seen in advanced capitalist countries, we have to study and to consider what is actually happening in the capitalist world, if only for the sake of examining the feasibility of the future of socialism. It is notable in this context that the recent debate on socialism has more and more frequently referred to the Japanese economic system. Japanese capitalism has become a model of the most efficient and advanced capitalism in the very process of the great world depression starting in 1973, and has tended to be idealised as a harmonious economic order even by Western socialists. As Marx intended to provide foundations for socialism by studying critically the most advanced capitalism of his day in England, we should study carefully the actual workings of the market economy in the advanced capitalist countries, including Japan in our own age.

As I have argued elsewhere,[73] the main source of the relative strength of international competitiveness, and of the relative stability of the Japanese economy has been the Japanese style of firm management. Especially in big corporations, the Japanese style of management has effectively secured the workers' loyalty to their company by promoting the consciousness of a solid member of the firm through life-time employment for regular workers, trade union organisations based on the company, and a seniority wage/promotion system. The Japanese style of management has generally organised a team system at the workplace, promoted multi-skills through learning-by-doing in a rotation system, and formed a broad intra-firm labour market. A promotion system leading all the way to the top director positions is formally open to all regular workers. Together with small group activities, such as the QC (quality control) circle or the ZD (zero defect) movements, the Japanese style of management has served to enhance the incentive to work, and the sense of participation among workers, thus facilitating the introduction of technological innovations. On the positive side, the system contains certain elements of co-operation, development plans for the human capacity to work, and a subjective sense of participation among working people, which would be a useful example not only to capitalist managers and workers in other countries, but also to socialist self-managed firms for the future.

Furthermore, the general tendency of managers to take a longer view for their investment strategies, and the 'invisible handshake' co-operative relations among firms, as well as among politicians, bureaucrats and business circles in Japan, are also social relations which cannot be reduced to the simple image of the competitive free market. There seems to be room to consider if such social relations can be reformed into a co-ordination mechanism in a socialist economy, freed from the currently dominant influence of capitalist chrematistic motivation and still containing innovative dynamism.

Other means for handling economic information and promoting flexible co-ordination within various models of socialist economy, increasingly employed in the capitalist world, are the flexible and swift adjustment of production and supply in accord with the motion of social demand through the POS (point of sales) information system, the tendency to move toward production to order by an automated mass production system with flexible multi-model products, and the easy acquisition of information regarding the motion of social consumption by means of digital electronic card purchasing systems. The much increased organisational power of co-operative movements based on sophisticated information technologies actually reveals the renewed possibility for economic co-ordination among people outside chrematistic capitalist motivation. The technical and social feasibility of Lange's suggestion to substitute the computer for the market, and of Elson's demand for the socialisation of the market through the disclosure of economic information, seem to have increased, though not necessarily in the form of Lange's idea of centralised computing.

Despite all these positive possibilities for the future of socialism, we should not neglect the fact that in capitalist countries co-ordination and co-operation among people outside the market are realised and work in still narrowly limited areas, mostly under the overwhelming influence of the motion of capital. In the case of Japan, for instance, her strength as one of the most advanced economic powers in the world has been concentrated in improving the international competitive power and the financial positions of capitalist firms. By contrast, the notoriously long working hours, coupled with exhausting long-distance commuting to work, the syndrome of chronic fatigue, and the rising number of karoshi (deaths from overwork) among working people, have been persistent and difficult problems to solve. Among advanced capitalist countries, the sharpest discrepancy between rising labour productivity and stagnant real wages has been found in Japanese manufacturing industries.[74] Workers who engage in dissident activities and are critical of their company's policies, either as individuals or through minority unions, are severely oppressed and discriminated against.

Meanwhile, the Japanese economy, and especially the working people, have been exposed to the damage of repeated depressions. In the shock following the collapse of the recent financial bubble, the Japanese style of labour management has itself been badly shaken. Even regular workers in big corporations are now often thrown out of life-long employment and made unemployed. The threat of unemployment and the real difficulties faced by middle-aged unemployed workers are indeed disastrous, as their labour market is narrower than the market for the cheaper young labour force. The 'invisible handshake' co-operative relationship between politicians, bureaucrats, and business circles has become a hotbed for endless corruption scandals, such as Lockheed, Recruit, Kyowa, Sagawa Express, Giant Construction Companies, etc. involving almost all the leading politicians of the former ruling Liberal Democratic Party (LDP).

Thus we have to recognise that even in Japan, seemingly the most harmonious and stable advanced capitalist country, which is also one of countries with the most egalitarian distribution of family income, the capitalist market economy is not at all really secure, agreeable, and fair for most of the working people. The necessity of critical analysis of contemporary capitalist market economy based on Marxist political economy is, thus, still very significant. The relevance of the arguments for the future of democratic socialism would also be illuminated by such critiques of the capitalist market economy in our own age.

Part III

Realities

5 The Nature of the Soviet Type of Society

ANOMALIES IN THE SOVIET ORDER

Three Major Anomalies

According to the ideas and theories set forth by Marx and Engels, after a proletarian revolution society will, and must, elevate the working class to the position of ruling class, promote thorough democracy, decompose the bourgeois relations of production, and nationalise, or make public, the ownership of land and the means of production. Then, in the course of the development of history, class distinctions will disappear, public power will lose its political character, the State will wither away, and an associational society will blossom, in which 'the free development of each is the condition for the free development of all' (*MECW*, 6, p. 506). The entire process should also incorporate the principle of proletarian internationalism. The Soviet and other postrevolutionary 'socialist' countries, which contained about 35 percent of the population of the world, all started with such ideas and theories.

The reality of actual development in these countries, however, did not easily accord with the classical theory of socialism of Marx and Engels. There were three major and mutually related anomalies: an undemocratic and oppressive social order; international and domestic friction among nations and peoples; economic stagnation and crisis, which became severe in the 1970s and 1980s.

Following the classic Marxist ideas and theories, land and the major means of production were certainly nationalised, or turned into public property. However, the state did not wither away, contrary to original Marxist theories. The power of the state, which was in the hands of privileged persons such as Communist Party executives at various levels, bureaucrats of higher ranks, and military officers, was rather strengthened and actually hypertrophied.

M.S. Voslensky's *Nomenklatura* (1980),[1] contained an analysis of the process of formation, the life style, the scope of privileges, the substantial content of exploitation, and the internal composition of a 'ruling class' in the USSR. According to Voslensky's estimates, about

3 million persons, a little less than 1.2 percent of the total population of the USSR, (or 750,000 persons, roughly 4 percent of the total Communist Party membership plus their families), formed the commanding 'red aristocracy' called Nomenklatura.

Under the domination of the Nomenklatura working people in Soviet-type societies did not have the democratic rights of free speech, opposition, and participation in the process of social decision-making at various levels. Although their jobs were secure, working people were actually not fully emancipated and true masters of society. Workers and farmers were still alienated, socially oppressed, and might be regarded as having been in the position of a ruled class. The Chinese Cultural Revolution, which hoped to revolutionise this social order, did not succeed, caused disastrous socioeconomic confusion for about 10 years, and ended in failure with the death of Mao Zedong in 1976.

The economic development of Soviet-type societies became 'abraded', or stagnated. These societies fell into a serious crisis in the 1980s, in spite of expecting to be able continuously to increase their productive power and to improve the economic conditions for working people, since they were presumably liberated form the fetters of capitalist relations of production. The symptoms of this economic crisis were shown in the stagnation of labour productivity, and the difficulties in improving the quality of products and the efficiency of production. The average annual growth rate of GNP in the USSR, for example, fell from 9.2 percent in the sixth five year plan lasting until 1960, to 7.8 percent in the eighth five year plan lasting until 1970, to 3.5 percent in the tenth five year plan lasting until 1980. The eleventh five year plan could not achieve the lowered target of 3.4-3.7 percent, and was ending with almost zero real growth when Gorbachev began Perestroika (meaning restructuring in Russian). Eastern European 'socialist' countries were experiencing a similar, or more severe, economic stagnation and crisis at the time.

In international relations, friendship in the spirit of proletarian internationalism gradually became a mirage. Especially after the de-Stalinisation of 1956, international conflicts and strife, often of a bloody military nature, regularly broke out among 'socialist countries'. We saw for example the Hungarian invasion of 1956, the Soviet–Chinese split after 1959, the Czechoslovak invasion of 1968, military strife between Vietnam, Cambodia, and China in 1979, and the Soviet invasion of Afghanistan in the same year. Those conflicts and strife were probably related, in one way or another, to the hypertrophy of state power, as well as to the difficulty of resolving friction among nations.

The Polish Solidarity movement, which started in the summer of

1980, sprang from the anomalous political and economic crisis of the Soviet type of societies, and served as a flash of lightening enabling us to see these problems more clearly. Under the threat of Soviet military intervention, Polish social unrest was suppressed at that time by the formation of Jaruzelski's military government, though the ruling Polish United Workers' Party (PUWP) lost its government position, the first time ever for such a party in the 'communist' world. It was apparent that this arrangement could not be a final solution. The suppression of the Solidarity movement created latent social tension, and as Gorbachev's Perestroika changed the international environment the resurrection of the Solidarity democratisation movement was provoked in 1989, igniting a series of Eastern European revolutions.

The Reversed Role of 'Orthodox' Marxism

When the Solidarity movement began in 1980 it was reported that one of the demands of the Polish students was to drop theories of Marxism as an obligatory subject of university courses. A similar demand, and an antagonistic feeling toward 'orthodox' Marxism, were popular among democratisation movements in 'socialist countries' towards the end of 1980s. At that time, the Soviet government condemned such demands and tendencies as evidence that rightward revisionism played an important role in the movements. The accusation was not totally wide of the mark, but neither was it a persuasive defence of the role of 'orthodox' Marxism. The antagonistic feeling toward Marxist theories expressed the popular sentiment against the conservative role of the Soviet type of 'orthodox' Marxism. Such Marxism ideologically concealed the real problems of the Soviet type of societies and defended the existing social order.

This is reminiscent of the memoirs of Z. Mlynar, *Nachfrost* (1978), who was the secretary of the central committee of the Czechoslovak Communist Party under A. Dubček. The book powerfully argues that the Czech reform movement of the Prague Spring, despite popular support for its ideal of humanistic reform of communism, was violently suppressed from the outside by the Soviet ruling stratum in the very name of proletarian internationalism. Just as in a capitalist society the social mechanism of the exploitation of working people is substantially maintained under the legal form and concept of human rights to liberty and equality, in the Soviet type of society 'orthodox' Marxist–Leninist theories were used, both internationally and domestically, for the opposite of what they intended, namely, to sustain the social order repressing working people.

In the 'orthodox' Soviet Marxist view, Soviet society had already completed the transition from capitalism to socialism during the 20 years after the October Revolution. It then started a harmonious transition to communism characterised by friendly co-operation among the working class, the farmer class, and the intelligentsia, based on growing social productive powers. This conception was formulated in Stalin's Constitutional Law (1936), and was inherited by Khrushchev and Brezhnev. It was grounded on 'orthodox' Marxist economic theories in ways which we shall consider below.

For 'orthodox' Marxist economic theories, the fundamental contradiction of capitalism lies in the contradiction between the social character of productive power and the private character of appropriation. Crises of over-production were themselves thought to derive from this contradiction. The generalised private character of appropriation, which contradicts the tendency of productive powers to develop without limit, had its roots in private ownership in capitalist society, especially in the means of production. Therefore, the principal aim of socialism, thought to be the solution to the fundamental contradictions of capitalism, was to remove the private, capitalistic ownership of the means of production. According to the formula of historical materialism, capitalistic bourgeois society must be the last class society in human history. Once the capitalist social order was abolished a socialist society would be inevitably realised, without any oppressive class relations. Working people would become masters of society. The harmonious further development of the socialist order of distribution according to labour into a higher communist order of distribution according to need was guaranteed simply by the elevation of society's productive power in the due course of time.

Given this theoretical view, it was naturally envisaged that Soviet society, in which nationalisation, or the public ownership of means of production, was generally completed, already was a harmonious socialist society without antagonistic social classes. To acknowledge that oppressive social conditions were imposed on working people, and that the latter were anything but masters of Soviet society, was treated as impossible and absurd by the officials. Thus, in an ironical twist of history, 'orthodox' Marxist theories, originally intended as weapons for the emancipation of working people, served as an oppressive ideology defending the existing social order in the Soviet type of societies. Hence, resentment against Marxism and socialism in general could easily spread and became popular among anti-establishment movements in these societies.

Although one can understand it, this resentment still seems an over-reaction to the distorted features of Marxism in the Soviet type of societies, and, as the British say, it may be a case of throwing out the baby with the bath water. It should be noted in this regard that critiques of the anomalous nature of the Soviet type of societies had been presented in many ways among Marxists long before the actual fall.

MARXIST CRITIQUES: THE REAL NATURE OF THE SOVIET TYPE OF SOCIETIES

The Marxist critiques of the anomalous nature of the Soviet type of societies belong to two major currents. One defines such societies as basically a kind of workers' state, or a sort of socialist society, although it also attempts to criticise their disfigured character. The other treats such societies as non-socialist class societies. The former current further contains the following three different points of view.

Disfigured Socialist Societies

(1) The first view, which could be regarded as closest to 'orthodox' Soviet theory, saw the various anomalous phenomena of the Soviet type of societies as originating in the fact that socialism was still in its very early age. For example, I. Fujita, *The Theory of Socialist Societies* (1980, in Japanese),[2] argued this position. We cannot deny that, as far as the long run of world history is concerned, the Soviet type of societies contained certain international and domestic distortions due to the fact that socialism was still in its transitional period. One would have expected, however, that the weight of transitional problems would have tended to decrease with the development of the socialist countries. Instead, the oppressive and hierarchical mechanisms of Soviet society were not mitigated, but rather hardened, in the very process of that society's economic development into the second largest industrial country in the world. The first view, therefore, is not satisfactory.

(2) The second view emphasised Stalinisation. R.A. Medvedev, in *Let History Judge* (1989),[3] for example, argued that the Soviet history of oppression of the working people systematically arose out of the personal characteristics of Stalin, his personality defects, and his inclination to foster the personality cult. J. Elleinstein, in *The Stalin Phenomenon* (1976),[4] also emphasised the role of Stalin's personal character in shaping the Soviet type of distorted socialist societies, though the

author located Stalin's personal role within a wider historical, economic and political environment. This type of view can explain more convincingly than the first the reasons why the socio–political distortions lasted, and in fact intensified, throughout the long process of Soviet industrialisation.

Moreover, this type of view seems to be supported by the historical fact that political brutality, the repeated use of terror, and political purges, declined after de-Stalinisation. However, the privileged social position of upper-class bureaucrats and the oppressed social conditions of working people were not much mitigated in the quarter of a century after Stalin died in 1953. The Brezhnev regime of 1964–82, especially, was called neo-Stalinism, and restrengthened Soviet undemocratic social features. This strongly suggests that the distorted character of the Soviet type of societies can neither be completely attributed to Stalin's personality nor to his personal political errors.

(3) The third type of view attempted to examine the socioeconomic grounds for the distortions of socialism under Stalinism. For example, L. Trotsky (1879-1940), who had been the greatest political rival of Stalin after Lenin's death, developed a view of this kind instead of simply ascribing the faults of the Soviet social order to Stalin's personality defects. According to Trotsky in *The Revolution Betrayed* (1937),[5] as well as in other writings, technocratic professionals formed a consolidated social stratum of privileged bureaucrats, as a result of having been placed in the position of managing agents or attorneys of the working people. This ultimately arose because working people lacked the professional knowledge and ability to run society, a fact reflecting the general backwardness of Soviet society. A second social revolution was then proposed by Trotsky as a necessary step in order to expel the privileged bureaucrats. E. Mandel took up this assertion, and defined the Soviet Union as 'a bureaucratically degenerated workers' state'.[6]

As P. Sweezy commented, however, it became difficult properly to understand the nature of Soviet society on the grounds of backwardness as the country grew into the second industrial power in the world.[7] The spread of basic as well as higher education in the Soviet Union significantly raised the cultural and intellectual level of working people, and solved the problem of shortage of technocratic professionals, which was conceived of as one reason for the bureaucrats' privileged position.

A. Hegedüs, who served as the prime minister of Hungary in 1955–6, argued that a professional ruling group forming bureaucratic relations, and having the exclusive right of decision-making, would be necessary even in a socialist society so long as economic growth and efficiency were sought. Based on this hard-headed recognition, Hegedüs asserted the significance of permiting and promoting popular movements in order effectively to control the bureaucrats.[8]

These three types of view face the common problem of explaining why working people had remained subjugated and oppressed for so long by the State and Party bureaucrats, despite their alleged social position as ruling class and masters of the socialist society. It is indeed hard to see why effective control over the bureaucrats was so difficult to bring about in a 'socialist' society. What was the meaning of the regime's hostility toward, and the suppression of, the workers' and citizens' movements demanding reform of the social system in Eastern Europe? Did the Soviet type of post-revolutionary societies deteriorate into some kind of restructured class society, totally opposite to the original goal of Marxist revolution to abolish all oppressive ruling classes?

Or Class Societies?

There are actually two more types of view, which treat Soviet societies more critically as class societies. In constructing these views the nature of class relations is certainly important. The first type defined Soviet societies as State capitalism, the second defined them as a new kind of class society.

(1) C. Bettelheim, *Les Luttes de classes en USSR* (4 vols, 1974)[9] examined the history of the Soviet Union and maintained that a sort of capitalism had revived, and that a State bourgeoisie comprised the ruling class of the USSR. This extended historical study coincided with the Chinese critique of the Soviet Union in the period of the Chinese Cultural Revolution. If this type of argument is correct, then State capitalism must have also existed in East European countries, as well as in China excepting the period of the Cultural Revolution.

Characterising the oppressive nature of the Soviet type of societies as State capitalism tends to be based on the following two points; (1) capitalism must be the final form of class society according to the formula of historical materialism, and (2) the (s-)wage form as well as the (s-)price form of products did exist in those societies, and workers and farmers could be seen as having been exploited.

However, a series of problems easily arises out of such a characterisation of Soviet society. The (s-)wage form and the (s-)price form were officially planned and fixed, and their motion was quite different from free market movement of wages and prices necessary for capitalism to develop. It is, further, not persuasive to identify the State and Party bureaucrats, who did not have private ownership of the means of production or shares in firms, with capitalists as a class. Actually, the pattern of behaviour of those bureaucrats in managing either individual firms or the whole economy, was quite different from that of capitalists. Unlike capitalism, workers were generally immune from the threat of unemployment. There was no immanent drive to increase productivity in individual firms. Moreover, if there was State capitalism in the Soviet type of societies, why has the transition to a capitalist market economy, which started in 1989 in Eastern Europe and in 1991 in CIS, been so difficult and destructive?

(2) P. Sweezy in a series of papers collected in *Post-Revolutionary Society* (1980),[10] while commenting favourably on Bettelheim's work on the history of the USSR, eventually formed a different type of view. Sweezy asserts that, in the post-revolutionary Soviet type of society, a new model of class society, neither socialism nor capitalism, emerged through a historical reversal of the position of leadership, whereby the higher stratum of bureaucrats came to dominate the Party and the State. This was a powerful attempt to overcome the problems of the other types of view on the anomalies in the Soviet type of society, and to present a proper Marxist theoretical frame of reference for contemporary world history by revising a part of the formula of historical materialism. Sweezy laid considerable emphasis on the fact that the higher stratum of bureaucrats in the Soviet type of society could maintain and reproduce their privileged positions from generation to generation through the education system and the promotion mechanism. He identified that as a strong reason why the bureaucrats could be characterised as an established ruling class.

The role of education, as well as of the centralisation of both knowledge and information, in helping to form a ruling class which holds political power and controls the economic base, was also stressed by R. Bahro, in *The Alternative in Eastern Europe* (1978).[11] In this work, this aspect of the Soviet type of society was investigated by comparing these societies to the Asiatic mode of production. In the latter, the foundations of the social power of the ruling class lay indeed in monopolised knowledge of social life, customs, and the timing of agricultural work, often taking the form of religious secrets.

S. Amin called the ruling class of the Soviet type of society a State class.[12] Voslensky called it a Nomenklatura class while revealing the reality of privileges in its daily life.[13] D. Singer, *The Road to Gdansk*

Nature of the Soviet Type of Society

(1981),[14] also examined the realities of a privileged class in the Soviet Union and Poland, and suggested the possibility of an actual upsurge of class struggle alongside the deepening economic crisis in those countries.

It has to be said that many non-socialist phenomena in the Soviet type of society, such as the hypertrophy of the State, the depoliticisation of working people, the suppression of liberty, the banning of anti-government critiques and of reform movements, the marginalisation of minorities, the maintenance of excessively powerful military forces, and international military interventions, would become much easier to understand if we thought of these phenomena as aiming at strengthening and consolidating the position of a ruling class feeding off the State. If the Soviet type of society had changed into such a new class society, then the ideal of socialism would emerge unharmed from the failure of the social order in those societies. Thus this type of view is indeed theoretically attractive. However, there are several reasons why one cannot be fully satisfied with this type of view either.

Class-like Disfigured Socialism

For one thing, there is a problem in reconciling this view with the traditional Marxist theory of class society. In Marxist theory, the foundation of class rule was commonly seen to lie in some form of exclusive (or monopolistic) appropriation (or ownership) of the major part of the means of production. This can be clearly seen in ancient slave societies, medieval feudal societies, and modern capitalist societies, although not so clearly in the case of the Asiatic mode of production in which village communities maintained autonomous control of farmland, despite paying tribute to the State. By contrast, the concept of a new class society in the Soviet Union, Eastern Europe, China and elsewhere, as developed by Sweezy and others, relies on the sociologist's or the political scientist's approach since it emphasises the role of education and the promotion system in consolidating the social basis for the privileged class. Although this is an interesting point worth further consideration, especially in comparing such societies with various Asiatic modes of production as Bahro suggested, the economic grounds for the State class in Soviet type societies was not persuasively established, except in the somewhat circular way of relating it to the functions of the privileged bureaucrats in the State or Party organs.

It is also not clear that the powerful ruling-class-like position of

State and Party bureaucrats was entirely anti-working class. The legitimacy of their rule rather lay in working for the workers in the name of socialism. This was not merely a propaganda slogan. Education, medical services, child care, general welfare, and real personal income, were obviously improved, with some degree of egalitarianism. It was possible for workers to believe in a better future life in the workers' own socialist countries as long as economic growth continued. In exchange for such gradual improvement of social and personal economic life, and for job security, the ruling-class-like bureaucrats could claim the support of the majority of working people. Put differently, in exchange for improvements in economic life the majority of working people accepted the de-politicised and regimented social order, still being to a certain extent the subject and not merely the object of society. It would have been impossible to arrive at and to sustain the ruling-class-like position of State and Party bureaucrats without some subjective, even if half-hearted, co-operation by the workers. This basic condition for the working of the Soviet type of society was made increasingly clear in the process of the deepening economic crisis, as well as during the events of the 1989 East European revolutions.

The concept of a new class society cannot account for the depth and dynamism of the role of the working people in support of the powerful bureaucrats. The position of the privileged bureaucrats should rather be specified as a class-like distortion within a degenerated socialist society. In particular, Soviet-type societies had their foundations provided by Marxist thought and theories, and declared themselves to be socialist. Working people, the ruling politicians and bureaucrats, as well as the rest of the world believed this to be true. Such a general belief must have had certain social functions and cannot be rejected as unreal. Marxists should, therefore, assume the responsibility of clarifying the process which caused the distortions and failure of Soviet-type societies. They should place this process within the historical development of socialism, instead of disregarding it as unrelated to socialism.

The belief commonly found in those societies, however, that their social order was the only correct and inevitable way to socialism, was fallacious. Their failure was not at all the failure of socialism in general. If the theory of new class society assumed that socialism would never reach a deteriorated form similar to Soviet type societies, this would also be too narrow a view to be realistic. Though the ideals, or final goals of socialism are definitely sound, actual socialist economies can assume a wide variety of forms in different historical periods and social backgrounds. This is similar to the historical fact that capitalism could develop in various concrete ways in different periods and societies. In any case, the future of socialism must be strengthened by learning the lessons of the tragic distortions and failures of Soviet type of societies.

ARGUMENTS FOR REFORMS AND THE FUTURE OF SOCIALISM

Decentralisation and Self-management

It is a notable fact that Marxists repeatedly strove to overcome the anomalies of the oppressive Soviet type societies. Since a focal point of such anomalies was the hypertrophy of power of the State and Party bureaucrats, the arguments for reform emphasised the plausibility of a more decentralised and democratic economic order, as opposed to the Soviet type of centralised economic planning. Theoretically, it is conceivable that central planning can be run by democratic social decision-making without ruling-class-like privileged bureaucrats. However, the strong reaction against the oppressive top-down nature of the Soviet social order, and its association with central planning, led the arguments of the reform movements of socialism in the direction of decentralisation. This tendency was also partly shown in the ideas of the Chinese Cultural Revolution.

As economic growth in the Soviet Union and Eastern Europe became increasingly difficult, political economists, especially those supporting the reform movements in Eastern Europe, tended to emphasise the significance of democratic decentralisation as an effective means to stop the 'abrasion' of the socialist economy and to regain the economy's functional efficiency. Thus, they demanded democratisation based on the decentralisation of decision-making in favouring the autonomy of regional and industrial units, as well as workers' self-management of individual firms. Correspondingly, it was argued that the range of strategically important products and services remaining within the centralised planning of supply and distribution, should be reduced and limited. Since there was no powerful alternative model of an adjustment mechanism allowing relatively autonomous firms to supply and distribute various goods and services in accordance with social needs, it was recommended that a market economy be incorporated into the socialist economy in combination with central planning.

For instance, O. Sik, who led the reform movement in Czechoslovakia as the vice prime minister of the Prague Spring (1968), presented this perspective for reformed socialism in his *Argumente für den Dritten Weg* (1973).[15] J. Kosta, who co-operated with Sik, followed up and demonstrated in a more theoretical way a similar position in his *Sozialistische Planwirtshaft* (1974).[16] A series of other arguments in favour of market socialism, such as these by W. Brus and others, which we saw in Chapter 4, also generally emphasised the importance of decentralisation. The mutually close relationship between economic and political decision-making was typically expounded by Brus in *The Economics and Politics of Socialism* (1973).[17] F. Fejto[18] pointed to the influence which Soviet foreign policy, including the Soviet-Chinese conflict, had on these movements.

In Yugoslavia, the reform movement brought about the 1974 Constitutional Law in the spirit of worker's self-management. Enterprises were renamed 'work organisation of associated labour', and were to be divided into smaller sized units in order to minimise the danger of bureaucratisation.[19] On the basis of this unique historical achievement, the ideals and actual institutional framework of the reform were put forth by E. Kardelj, in *Self-Management and Democracy* (1981).[20] The experiment of workers' self-management in Yugoslavia naturally attracted a great deal of international interest among Marxists, as a promising way out of the disfigured Soviet type of socialism. It was a pity that the experiment was impossible to maintain in the process of economic deterioration, more or less common in the Soviet block in the 1980s, which increased conflict among regions and peoples, eventually destroying the country.

Soviet leaders after Brezhnev constantly criticised these Eastern European reform movements as the road to revisionism, and frequently intervened to suppress them in one way or another. However, the Marxist reaction to such oppressive international Soviet interventions, starting with the Hungarian invasion of 1956, served as an important moment to re-strengthen not only the East European reform movements, but also non-Soviet neo-Marxism, such as Euro-communism or Eurosocialism, in Western Europe and other parts of the world. In Japan, Uno theorists, such as T. Ouchi in *A Study of a New Vision of Socialism* (1979), in Japanese,[21] stressed that the basic task of socialism is to emancipate workers from the commodity form of labour-power, a task which could not be achieved by mere central planning based on the nationalisation of the means of production. Arguments for decentralisation, regional autonomy, and democratic workers' self-management thus became a keynote for many contemporary lines of Marxist thought and political movements in the world, not limited to the Eastern European countries. The failure of socialism in the Soviet Union and Eastern Europe does not detract from the significance of such arguments for the future of socialism.

How to Increase Economic Efficiency

The arguments for sounder socialism were much concerned with the problem of economic stagnation and inefficiency of Soviet-type societies, often in combination with the problem of the undemocratic and oppressive social order. There are at least three points to be considered on this score: (1) the role of bureaucracy, (2) the introduction of the market economy, and (3) the nature of technologies and ecological issues.

The Role of Bureaucracy

As Hegedüs pointed out, when economic efficiency is pursued the formation of some kind of bureaucracy may be inevitable both in a centralised system and in decentralised economic planning. This relates to the difficulty of pursuing both efficiency and the dissolution of the division of labour on a social scale as well as at the workplace for the foreseeable future. The pursuit of efficiency contains the danger that jobs will be stratified, and this will lead to oppression of workers in the lower ranks. However, the experimental attempt during the Chinese Cultural Revolution hastily to abolish the professional bureaucracy with a privileged position in the division of labour by assigning the bureaucrats to agricultural rural employment, could not but lead to a decline in economic efficiency. The attempt had to end and turned into the modernisation line after 1978.

It would be a more practical view for quite some time, as Hegedüs argued, to see the formation of a group of professional bureaucrats as unavoidable in a socialist economy, and thus set the socialist task of democratically controlling the bureaucrats. We need not think thereby that bureaucrats would continuously hold fixed privileged positions with authoritarian powers to make decisions. Socialism should not neglect the final goal of dissolving State power and the privileged interests of bureaucrats through an increase in the participation of liberated working people in social life.

In a conscious move in this direction, the privileged power of bureaucrats should certainly be limited and reduced. Attempts should be repeatedly made to put the social functions of bureaucrats under the more democratic control of working people by such means as elections, referenda, and fixed terms of service. Such attempts would be made easier if the means of production were to be socialised in the form of decentralised workers' self-management with an increased role for local communities. The socialisation of the means of production in this direction is not conceptually identical with their nationalisation under a strong State power, and it should be pursued uninterruptedly so as to reduce the power and the number of bureaucrats. Maintaining economic efficiency in this type of economic development remains a most challenging problem for the future of socialism.

The Introduction of the Market Economy

One solution for the problem of achieving economic efficiency in a decentralised socialist society seemed to be the introduction of the market economy. In fact the Eastern European reform movements mostly proposed that the road to market socialism be taken. As we have seen in Chapter 4 (pp. 105–17), the advocates of market socialism expected that inefficiencies in the Soviet type of centrally planned economy, such as misallocation of resources and lack of motivation to innovate and work efficiently, would be overcome by introducing the market economy.

Theoretically it is indeed conceivable to combine plan and market in various models as, for instance, in Brus' functional model of socialist economy. There can be certain ways of measuring and improving the efficiency of the planned part of the economy by using s-prices, as we have argued. However, a series of practical socioeconomic difficulties exist in the path of market socialism.

Although the introduction of the market economy was frequently proposed as a corrective for the power and the excessive functions of the bureaucrats, the actual process of marketisation requires the presence of a strong political power to break the existing vested interests of the bureaucrats. At the same time, powerful social control, often exercised by bureaucrats, is also necessary in order to keep an eye on and regulate the unevenness of private income and asset possession. This could be achieved, for instance, by means of socialist levies, taxes (s-taxes), or by setting official bands for market prices. Without such egalitarian policies, the introduction of the market economy in a socialist society would increase social discontent due to the resultant irregularity among the mass of the people. Social unity or conformity would then come under threat, and socialism might be abandoned in the direction of a thoroughly capitalist free market economy. As the scope of the free market expands in a socialist economy, the intrinsic instability of the market economy will reappear in the form of macroeconomic fluctuations. This will cause a lot of inefficiency, evidence of which we see in the phase of depression in a capitalist economy. One strong point of a socialist economy relative to a capitalist one would be macroeconomic stabilisation through the combined effect of control of the market economy and planning. In these regards, the introduction of the market order into a socialist economy requires rather strong social control, often linked with the economic functions of bureaucracy.

As we shall see in Chapter 7, actually the introduction of the market economy has been much more successful under the strong leadership of the Communist Party in China after 1978, and in Vietnam after 1990 (at least for the time being), rather than in Eastern Europe and the CIS, where Communist Party rule was dissolved. Yugoslav experimental reform also found it difficult to construct a proper adjustment mechanism in addition to the market, among work organisations of associated labour, or among rural regions. As a result, rural and urban disparities increasingly established the background for the tragic ethnic conflicts currently taking place there.

Thus, even though the vested interest of bureaucrats should not be defended, reformulating the necessary social control over the market economy in the direction of socialism remains a major consideration. Introduction of the market economy cannot be a complete answer to the issues concerning economic efficiency.

The Nature of Technologies and Ecological Issues

It has been generally believed that the development of natural science and of industrial technologies, and the road toward the elevation of the material standard of living, must be neutral as regards the nature of the social relations of production. Thus, economic development and increases in economic efficiency were pursued in the Soviet Union and its allied countries through the introduction of both industrial technologies and consumption patterns which were already in existence in the leading capitalist countries. If the development of both industrial technologies and consumption patterns was indeed neutrally linear and independent of the nature of social systems, it would not be at all problematic, rather it would be recommended, for a socialist economy to imitate the technologies and consumption patterns of the advanced capitalist countries.

However, the general belief in the desirability of the capitalistic development of science and technologies, as well as of the consumption patterns based on them, has been seriously shaken with the emergence of several important global problems. These include: limited natural resources, especially energy; deteriorating ecological environments, for instance caused by the accumulation of carbon dioxide in the atmosphere; the threat of nuclear disasters; the deterioration of the quality of foodstufffs giving rise to organic farming. Arguments in favour of alternative technologies convincingly maintain that the development of industrial technologies, at least after a certain stage, and the resultant consumption patterns, such as we see in the modern automobile society excessively reliant on the personal car, are not the one and only possible path of economic growth.

Nevertheless, the Soviet policy of constructing large-scale heavy industrial complexes and factories was uncritical of the disfigured nature of the expansion of productive powers in capitalist development, and extensively reproduced this expansion in a statist fashion. There were some, but not many, policy attempts in Soviet-type societies to develop new productive technologies and new attractive consumption patterns, in accordance with the principles of socialist economic formation rather than capitalism. As a result the American-style automobile society remained a longed-for dream for the mass of people in the Soviet Union and Eastern European countries.

If efficiency of scale was accepted as absolutely true in all fields of economic activity, it could easily be used to legitimate centralised bureaucratic control of nationalised industries. Reforming socialism in the direction of decentralised workers' self-management would then be very difficult, if not impossible. Thus, prudent social discretion is necessary, and choices must be altered from time to time regarding which industrial areas are suited to efficiency of scale and which are not. In researching and developing technologies, a socialist society must carefully choose the alternative paths more suited to workers' democratic self-management, and not necessarily large-scale technologies which easily feed statism. Such considerations seem quite necessary and desirable to facilitate the dissolution of bureaucratic control from above, to promote socialisation (separate from mere nationalisation) of the means of production, and to foster the democratic emancipation of working people.

Generally speaking, the increase in economic efficiency in order to minimise costs for given results is an economic norm common for any form of society and, as such, it must be pursued as far as possible.

Socialism can aspire to achieve this general economic norm in a more humane manner, away from the capitalistic constraints of cost accounting. For instance, the acceptable technologies could possibly be broadened if actual labour-time, rather than the capitalistic calculation of wage cost, is to be economised. This sort of consideration for technological development must be quite important for a socialist economy, particularly since nominal wages may become lower in a certain type of socialism which promotes increased social consumption, as we have argued in chapter 3 (p. 53). However, in socialism the increase in labour productivity itself should also not be taken for an absolute aim, unlike the increase in the productivity of capital in a capitalist economy. The pace and direction of growth of labour productivity must be suitably adjusted from the point of view of ecological harmony with nature, or of broader considerations for easier associational life and work.

Consequently, it is essential for socialism to organise democratic politics of use-values. This requires the popular participation of households, in co-operation with producers, in deciding what type of goods and services are to be provided. The pattern of consumption in capitalism, which is totally individualistic and selfish, as symbolised by the automobile society, has to be criticised and practically overcome through such a social process. The actual possibility of the latter is already discernible, if still weak, in the many attempts to form consumers' co-operatives, workers' co-operative movements, and citizens' regional mutual aid activities in advanced capitalist countries.

Nevertheless, in the actual development of past socialist economies, industrial technologies, as well as the style of consumption, generated in the capitalist economies tended to be introduced uncritically, and were often naively admired as advanced civilisation. The advantage of socialism in being able to restructure industrial technologies and the content of popular consumption in capitalism through the socially conscious politics of use-values, was not really and fully demonstrated. This must be one reason for the unexpected fragility of past socialist economies, and would explain, at least partly, why reforming them was so prone to full-scale marketisation of the economy leading to capitalism. In this regard, the future of socialism requires that the causes and significance of the failure of past centralised socialist economies be examined still further, coupled with the critical reconsideration of the logic and actual reality of the capitalist economies.

6 Achievements and Crisis

THE SOVIET TYPE OF PLANNED ECONOMY

Characteristic Features

The Soviet economy from the time of the first five year plan of 1928, the post-Second World War Eastern European economies, and the Chinese socialist economy of the 1950s and 1960s, were all generally characterised as centrally planned economies. In order to make clear the causes and the significance of the failure of the centrally planned socialist economies we have to review their economic system and their basic conditions of functioning.

The fundamental aim of those economies was to overcome the anarchical nature of capitalism, as well as the latter's intrinsic tendency toward overproduction and economic crises. Thus, they aimed at solving the problems of mass unemployment, exploitation, and poverty of working people under capitalism, and intended to construct a classless society by making working people the real subject of society. This ideal was based on a certain understanding of Marxism which sees the root of the socioeconomic problems of capitalism in the anarchical and exploitative nature of capitalist appropriation. In particular, the concentration of private ownership of means of production into units of capital was seen as a fundamental issue, because it enables capital to use the commodity labour-power of workers in an anarchical, exploitative, and thus crisis-ridden economic order. Based on this, it was generally believed that a socialist economy should nationalise the land and the means of production as property of the whole of the people, and it should also bring about a centrally planned economy so as to uproot the economic difficulties and contradictions of capitalism.

In the Soviet Union, which led other socialist economies as a typical advanced model of socialism, the State actually owned the land, the main means and other ancillaries of production. The national economic plans were centrally built by Gosplan (the national planning board). These plans assigned precise tasks, or work quotas, called norms, to the bureaucrats managing industries and State firms. Gossnab (the State committee for supplying raw materials and machines) also assigned and distributed equipment and raw materials necessary to achieve the norms. The whole of such planning and distribution was under the control of the bureaucrats and the political leaders of the State and the Communist Party.

The annual economic plan set both physical quantities and input–output prices for industries. The actual product of each industry or firm as compared to the norm given from above was usually assessed simply in terms of quantity of output, without much caring about quality. The huge labour of constructing complicated economic plans and setting norms for a large number of industries and firms used to be performed mostly on the basis of aiming for output levels a certain percentage higher than the output of the preceding year(s). The prices of resources and products were officially fixed, and were insensitive to changes in the balance between demand and supply, to qualitative differences between products, and to changes in productivity. The distribution of income to workers in the form of s-money (s-wages) according to a classification of job categories and ranks, was also officially planned and fixed by the State on relatively egalitarian grounds.

In such a centrally planned economy, a large proportion of the net surplus (s-profit) of each firm was absorbed by the State, and redistributed according to the economic plan. Conversely, firms which made net deficits could easily procure subsidies, or loans, from the State as part of the redistribution of the socialised surplus. Indeed, the deficit of a firm or an industry might well have been the result of unfavourable price relations which were beyond the responsibility of the firm or industry. Firms were, thus, under what Kornai called a 'soft-budget constraint', and could continue operations even with successive deficits and excessive numbers of workers on their books without serious threat of closure or failure. Workers in such firms had a strong and secure right to their jobs, and were generally immune from the danger of unemployment, although they were also oppressed and controlled from above in the vertical bureaucratic system of central planning.

Achievements

It is worth noting as an objective fact that the Soviet model of a centrally planned socialist economy was not always stagnant as an economic and social system, but rather showed an ability to grow faster than most of the capitalist countries for many years until the 1960s. Von Mises' arguments, which saw mere irrationality, destruction and annihilation in the Soviet centrally planned economy, were clearly incorrect for this period. Though these achievements were accompanied by socio–political problems of oppression for workers, they remain a historical fact which contradicts the anti-socialist critiques of the workability of a centrally planned economy put forth during the socialist economic calculation debate.

The Soviet five year plans were introduced in 1928 and in subsequent years achieved rapid industrial growth, while the capitalist world suffered the inter-war Great Depression and mass unemployment. The official Soviet index of industrial production grew at an average annual rate of 16.8 percent from 1928 to 1940. Even Western estimates for the same period range from 8.4 percent to 13.6 percent per annum.[1] Although agricultural production fell by 20 percent from 1928 to 1932, and had not recovered by the late 1930s, the rapidity of industrial growth rate is evident for any of these estimates. In contrast to the capitalist world, the Soviet economy was crisis-free, exempt from unemployment, and seemed to present a hopeful alternative to deeply diseased capitalism.

During the Second World War the Soviet economy managed to bear the huge costs of defending the country against fascism. Throughout the subsequent cold war period it has been estimated that the Soviet economy had to spend annually about 15 percent of GDP (twice as big a proportion as that of the USA) on wasteful military expenditure. Despite this heavy burden, the Soviet economy continued to grow faster than most of the advanced capitalist countries, if not as fast as Japan during the latter's High Growth Period, 1953–73 (see Table 6.1).

Table 6.1 Estimation of the growth rate of Soviet real national income (percentage of annual average for each period)

Periods	Soviet official data	Selunin and Hanin	CIA
1951–60	10.3	7.2	5.1
1961–65	6.5	4.4	4.8
1966–70	7.8	4.1	5.0
1971–75	5.7	3.2	3.1
1976–80	4.3	1.0	2.2
1981–85	3.6	0.6	1.8

Source: S. Shimamura, *The Soviet Economy and Statistics*, 1989, in Japanese.

Even though the Soviet official statistics of Table 6.1 may over-estimate Soviet economic growth, the revised estimates by Selunin and Hanin, published in a Soviet journal,[2] and the CIA estimates, still show a growth rate above that of the USA and many other capitalist countries until the middle of the 1970s. Through continuous economic growth and industrialisation the Soviet economy overcame the backwardness of Russian society prior to the Revolution, and became the second industrial power of the world. The Soviet Union could boast two thirds of the industrial output of the USA and nearly equal military power. By the middle of the 1970s, for instance, the country produced nearly 50 percent more crude steel than either the USA or Japan. National income *per capita* in the Soviet Union and in the Eastern European socialist countries was generally estimated at about one half of that in the USA and 80 percent of that in the EEC.[3]

Certainly it should not be ignored that the high economic growth in the Soviet Union was achieved through a high investment rate, and on the basis of restricted level of consumption, as well as by utilising import technology on a massive scale from the West. If we compare Soviet economic growth with Asian countries at a similar initial level of development, it appears less impressive. Having said this, we should still recognise that the Soviet type of centrally planned economy showed viability and fairly rapid economic growth for decades. We should also not dismiss lightly the fact that the Soviet Union, as well as the Eastern European socialist economies, achieved successes such as full employment, a strongly guaranteed right to work for workers, the participation of women in a broad range of increasingly complex occupations, relatively egalitarian economic life for people, including a safe pension system for the aged, free or cheap schooling, public facilities for babies and children, higher education, medical services, transport, basic means of consumption and dwellings. In general, these economies did to a certain degree exhibit the features of economic life in a workers' state.

These achievements of the Soviet model of economy had a strong impact on the capitalist world, and served as an effective lateral pressure promoting the development of the welfare state and of social democracy based on the trade union movement in the advanced capitalist countries. The continuous growth of the 'actually existing' socialist economies also served to assist liberation movements in third world countries morally, financially and sometimes militarily. As a result, these liberation movements often established socialist pro-Soviet political regimes soon after a social revolution. Thus, following China, socialist regimes were successfully established in countries such as North Vietnam, Indonesia, Cuba, Ethiopia, South Yemen, and Nicaragua.

The Basic Conditions for Growth

Certain basic conditions existed which allowed the Soviet centrally planned economy to grow for many years, and to develop into a leading industrial country. These conditions became increasingly clear and significant in the very process of deepening crisis and failure of the Soviet economy in the 1980s.

First of all, the Soviet Union had a favourable geographical condition enabling it to construct a leading one-state socialism. The country had not merely the largest national territory in the world, but was rich in various natural resources, such as coal, oil, and metal ore, which could be domestically utilised for industrialisation. It was possible for central economic plans to find domestic extra supplies of energy and raw materials necessary for industrial growth. As a result, the Soviet economy was relatively free of disturbances caused by foreign trade and participation in the fluctuating world market. It is interesting to note that both superpowers of the cold war era, the USA and the USSR, were rich in natural resources suitable for domestically-oriented economic growth. This probably contributed to their tendency toward self-centred international politics unconcerned with the historical and social circumstances of other countries.

Second, in so far as Soviet economic growth depended mostly on industrialisation and urbanisation, the abundant working population which could be mobilised from the rural agricultural areas was quite important for the continuation of growth. Throughout the period of the five year plans, the agricultural sector tended to miss the planned output targets and remained stagnant. The difficulty of improving economic life in the rural agricultural sector, however, facilitated the mobilisation of the necessary working population for industrialisation. The introduction of combine harvesters, tractors, and other machines, as well as chemical fertilisers and agricultural chemicals in kolkhozes and sovkhozes (social and national collective farms), also economised on the working population on the land and made the latter even more available for industrialisation. Especially as industrialisation was based on the extensive mode of accumulation which extended reproduction without much intensive innovation in technology, it was of the essence to have access to additional industrial workers almost in proportion to the growth rate of industrial output.

Third, the extensive mode of industrial accumulation, continuing the construction of similar large-scale factories and adding equipment and raw materials to already existing factories without much altering technology, indeed facilitated bureaucratic management through the central economic plans. The latter could be annually drawn up by simply adding a certain percentage to the norms achieved in the preceding years. The managers of each industry and firm could also easily expect to accomplish the given norms by following the practice of the preceding years. Thus, given bureaucratic practices at various levels, industrial innovation was hard to initiate and to achieve. However, the bureaucratic centrally planned economic system worked and effected a relatively high economic growth so long as the technology of the main industries remained basically the same, or changed slowly, as in the period from the 1930s to the 1960s. The industrial technologies of this period also tended to favour economies of scale in heavy industries, they were suitable for large-scale factories and firms, such as steel plants, and so they were easily subject to bureaucratic central planning. Moreover, the cardinal role which military industry played, further facilitated the bureaucratic control of central planning in the Soviet type of economy by its political nature and not only on technological grounds.

Last, but not least, the co-operation of working people was indispensable to the functioning of the Soviet type of planned economy. Unlike a capitalist economy in which selfish economic actions can be co-ordinated through the market mechanism in the absence of a unified social will, socialist economic planning needs more direct social co-operation among working people. Without the moral support of the majority of working people, the centrally planned economy cannot achieve the various norms, and will become an economy of shortage. Despite the Austrian school's critique of centrally planned economies, and despite the critique of the Soviet economy by the advocates of a full market economy, the Soviet economy was able to function so long as it managed to secure the co-operation of workers for a considerable length of time.

There is no doubt that a strong negative element of threats, official inquiries, informing, arrests and terror, was employed in securing the co-operation of workers. This element was very evident during the Stalin years, but was maintained, if in a milder bureaucratic form, even in the period after Stalin. However, a positive element also existed in the workers' will to co-operate in constructing a new workers' society according to socialist ideals, in fighting against the brutal fascist military invasion in the 1940s and against the perceived US military menace, in supporting liberation movements in other countries, and finally in improving their own economic conditions. While the cold war imposed a heavy burden of military expenditure onto the Soviet economy, it also served to maintain the consciousness of social co-operation in the face of international politico–military tension. (The cold war was also useful to US political leadership in securing support both domestically and internationally.) It was thus imperative for the centrally planned economy to secure positive co-operation of working people for the socioeconomic order. As long as the improvement of economic life was uninterrupted, positive co-operation by workers could be grounded on the hope of a better life in the future and was actively provided both in the Soviet Union and in the Soviet bloc, especially among the dedicated people of the generations which fought for the socialist revolution and against fascism.

STAGNATION AND CRISIS

Economic Difficulties

As we can see in Table 6.1, the growth rate of the Soviet economy began to decline in the 1970s, and became stagnant after the latter half of the decade. The country's actual growth rate was generally estimated at almost zero after the beginning of the 1980s. Selunin and Hanin's critical estimate in Table 6.1 for this period is thought of as realistic by many Soviet and foreign economists.

In the first half of the 1970s, the Soviet economy still seemed to be doing relatively well in comparison with the capitalist countries which generally suffered from an acute inflationary crisis in 1973–5. However, in the second half of the 1970s, when the advanced capitalist countries experienced a measure of economic recovery, the Soviet economy began to worsen and deteriorated throughout the 1980s. Never in the history of the Soviet Union had such severe stagnation and crisis been encountered, with the exception of the initial years of confusion due to civil war and armed intervention from abroad. Given that the socialist planned economy was believed to be crisis-free because it had resolved the inner contradictions of the capitalist economy, the Soviet Union's stagnation and crisis was a real shock to political leaders and to working people.

The difficulties of the Soviet economy were not limited to a quantitative fall of the rate of growth. Qualitative stagnation and lack of innovation in industrial activities were also present. In the 1970s and 1980s the advanced capitalist countries raised the sophistication of consumer durables by introducing ME information technologies in the mass production of multiple car models, audio-visual equipment and so forth, in an attempt to restructure their economies. By contrast, the Soviet Union and the Eastern European economies failed to innovate and to expand the production of consumer goods. Thus the quantitative and qualitative gap in consumption between the advanced capitalist countries and the Soviet bloc further widened in this period.

M. Gorbachev openly admitted these difficulties in 1987 in the course of his arguments about the necessity of Perestroika. He stated that,

> At this stage – this became particularly clear in the latter half of the seventies – something happened that was at first sight inexplicable. The country began to lose momentum. Economic failures became more frequent. Difficulties began to accumulate and deteriorate, and unresolved problems to multiply. Elements of what we call stagnation and other phenomena alien to socialism began to appear in the life of society... In the last fifteen years, the national income growth rate had declined by more than a half and by the beginning of the eighties had fallen to a level close to economic stagnation... Moreover, the gap in the efficiency of production, quality of products, scientific and technological development, the production of advanced technology and the use of advanced techniques began to widen, and not to our advantage.[4]

Constraints of Labouring Population and Primary Products

Why did the Soviet economy unexpectedly deteriorate and fall into such stagnation and difficulties? The causes must be found in the changes in the factors which had sustained the continuous growth of the Soviet economy. In so far as Soviet economic growth had depended mainly on urban industrialisation, and especially on the extensive mode of accumulation in heavy industries, the ready availability of an elastic supply of natural resources and labour-power was indispensable.

When the advanced capitalist economies fell into an acute inflationary crisis in 1973 and the subsequent great depression, the Soviet and Eastern European economies still seemed completely free of this deadlock. The crisis of the advanced capitalist countries was due to the over-accumulation of capital relative to the elasticity of supply of the labouring population and of primary products. As a result of that process, there occurred a sharp rise in wages and the prices of primary products in the world market, as well as a profit squeeze. As the Bretton Woods monetary system broke down, the swollen supply of money and credit added a strongly inflationary aspect to the over-accumulation crisis of this period.[5] Since a disturbing rise in wages, prices of primary products and the general price level were absent in the Soviet Union and the Eastern European economies, it tended to be assumed that these countries were free from the economic crisis of our age in a manner similar to the Soviet economy in the 1930s. In retrospect, however, very similar fundamental constraints on economic growth were crystallising and began to emerge in the Soviet bloc, a little later and more slowly, but also more persistently than in the capitalist countries.

By absorbing surplus labouring population from agricultural rural areas, and by mobilising the female labour force, as well as by taking advantage of the relatively rapid natural increase of the labouring population, the Soviet economy could increase the number of wage- (or salary-) workers at the annual average rate of 9.5 percent during the first two five year plans. In the course of industrialisation of the extensive type the ranks of the reserve army of labour in the rural areas and among women became thinner, and as the rate of the natural increase of the population had by 1980 fallen to below half the level of 1960, the annual average rate of increase in the number of wage (or salary) workers declined to 3.8 percent in the 1960s, 2.2 percent in the 1970s, and 0.9 percent in 1980–5.[6] The decline in the rate after the 1970s partly reflected overall economic stagnation but, more fundamentally, it represented an insuperable constraint on the continuation of rapid economic growth in the same extensive mode. If Soviet economic growth was to continue at a fast pace a more intensive mode of accumulation with increasing labour productivity was necessary.

At the same time, natural resources, which were initially relatively abundant within the Soviet Union, were used in an increasingly extensive mode, starting with the most easily accessible mines, forests and so on, so that resources gradually became relatively scarce and costly. While mining production could still increase by 28 percent in 1970–5, it could only register 8 percent growth in 1980–5. Furthermore, the mode of utilisation of natural resources, energy, and raw materials was often wasteful because of bureaucratic management simply promoting extensive quantitative accumulation. As a result, Soviet industry, while producing twice as much steel and consuming 10 percent more of electricity, produced a far smaller total output than US industry. Similarly, despite producing 80 percent more of chemical fertilisers and three times as many tractors, the Soviet economy produced a much smaller agricultural output than the USA.[7] The supply constraint of natural resources and primary products was thus intensified by the wasteful and extensive way of using these goods.

Thus, some years after the over-accumulation crisis in the advanced capitalist countries, the Soviet economy unexpectedly encountered a basically similar difficulty of exhaustion of the elastic supply of labour, raw materials and primary products. In the Soviet officially fixed price system, however, the appearance of this difficulty was quite different from the inflationary crisis in the capitalist world.

The Economy of Shortage with Co-ordination Failure

The characteristics of what Kornai called a shortage economy[8] were clearly reinforced by the relative shortage of labour, raw materials and primary products and resulted in a vicious circle of economic stagnation. The relative shortage of primary products and raw materials strengthened the position of bureaucrats and organisations as suppliers or distributors of these goods. The managers of firms were under pressure to fulfil their norms in time and, therefore, in need of these products as inputs. Thus, they were forced to curry favour and to look for personal connections by offering bribes. Unlike in a capitalist economy, they could not purchase what they needed by offering a higher price. The uncertainty of obtaining supplies induced the building up of large stocks of various inputs whenever these were available. The resultant excessive stockpiling of inputs generally intensified their shortage, often in an uneven way, and further exacerbated the shortages of finished products.

As military industry was given political priority and could command preferential treatment, the large proportion of the Gross National Product which it absorbed, amounting to at least 15 percent of the total, became a heavier burden than ever. Under the circumstances, the further economic burden imposed by the Star Wars arms competition initiated by president Reagan's military strategy in the 1980s, accelerated the phenomena of shortage. Shortage phenomena certainly also spread to consumer goods. In addition to the high proportion of important inputs absorbed by the military sector, the traditional Soviet policy of giving priority to the production of the means of production, (probably as a result of misinterpetating Marx's schema of expanded reproduction), resulted in neglecting the supply of more and better consumer goods, the improvement of the distribution system, and the quality of the service industry. The supply of consumer durables such as audio equipment and personal cars which were regarded as luxury goods, was restricted through planning. The prices of these luxury goods were officially set at very high levels. Consequently, dissatisfaction among working people increased as they began to be aware of the growing difference with high mass consumption in the advanced capitalist countries, as well as in the rapidly growing Asian NIEs. Given the quantitatively and qualitatively stagnant consumption in the shortage economy, the privileged consumption of the Nomenklatura, with easy access to consumer durables and imported goods at special shops, was naturally felt more sharply by people as undemocratic and corrupt.

Workers, while suffering from a shortage of consumer goods, could take advantage of their position as suppliers of labour in a shortage economy. Unlike in a capitalist economy, labour shortages could not easily induce a rise in the wage rate under the officially fixed price system. However, as well as possessing the traditional workers' right to their jobs, Soviet workers became completely immune to the fear of dismissal, or to a forced move to an unpopular job, regardless of their diligence at work. Changing jobs had been made legal in 1956 and gradually became much easier for workers so that administrative action to restrict it was required in the 1980s.[9]

As in the advanced capitalist countries during the labour shortage phase at the very beginning of the 1970s, labour discipline in the Soviet economy deteriorated through absenteeism, sabotage, and a lazy pace at work. Unlike in the capitalist countries, however, labour discipline could not easily be restored through the threat of dismissal in the process of recession. With guaranteed jobs and wages, especially under the condition of relative shortage of labouring population, workers could be lazy and even get drunk at work without facing penalties. Workers tended to conserve their energy for 'moonlighting', i.e. unofficial work after the official working hours, paid by private customers. Workers even used the shopfloor and the raw materials at their workplaces in the course of such 'moonlighting' in the second or underground economy. The conditions of labour adversely influenced the first or official economy, reduced its productivity and growth, and intensified the economy of shortage.

Thus, the co-operation of workers which was indispensable for the smooth working of the planned economy was eroded in the process of economic stagnation, and as the generations dedicated to socialism started to pass away, so as to make the achievement of norms more and more difficult at various levels. Private self-interest began to escape the control of the official conomy, to absorb more and more of resources and human energy, and to assume the form of an underground, grey economy not possessing the proper order of a market economy. The size of this underground economy, compared to the official one, was variously estimated at 10–50 percent.[10]

The so-called co-ordination failure in the Soviet planned economy, which caused a serious imbalance between the severe shortage of some goods and the excessive supply of others, was a natural result of the vicious circle of economic difficulties in an economy of shortage.

Difficulties of Restructuring

In a capitalist economy, economic crises and depressions force restructuring and 'rationalisation' in order to revitalise the economic activities of capitalist firms. These difficult phases of economic activity are not only destructive but may also be creative in many respects. In the case of the great depression after 1973, innovation through the introduction of more and more sophisticated ME technologies was broadly promoted in the process of restructuring. Such innovation served to economise significantly on both labour-power and the consumption of energy by industry. Combined with the pressure of mass unemployment, it resolved the difficulty of labour shortage for capitalist firms. Simultaneously, labour discipline could be tightened again under the threat of dismissal. The relative shortage of primary products, including oil, was also mitigated and reversed through industrial restructuring, as well as through increased global capacity to supply oil and other primary products via the market mechanism.

By contrast, the Soviet type of bureaucratic centrally planned economy could not foster renewal and restructuring. So long as achieving the annual physical quantity of norms was regarded as the most important aim for bureaucrats in order to maintain their positions, or to be promoted to higher ones, there were systematic efforts at various levels to secure safe plan targets, not much above the output of the preceding year(s). Risky industrial technological changes as well as product innovations which would radically change norms, tended to be avoided. Excess productive capacity, excessive raw material stocks, and a redundant labour-force, were apt to be held within firms so as to facilitate the fulfilment of norms. Thus the shortage economy was further reinforced.

Consequently, the Soviet type of bureaucratic central planning, which had been able to function and to maintain economic growth in the process of extensive accumulation without much technological change, turned out to be unsuitable for industrial renovation. If, as Hegedüs argued, the emergence of a professional bureaucratic group would be unavoidable in a socialist planned economy, is it possible for democratic popular movements to tackle the problem of the bureaucrats' inelastic attachment to the status quo, as the latter was seen in the Soviet experience? On some occasions, democratic movements can be slow in terms of time, and may even be counter-productive in bringing about effective change. The entire structure of a socialist society, therefore, must be carefully arranged in two respects as far as this issue is concerned. On the one hand, it is important always to be on the alert to prevent the consolidation of the bureaucrats' own conservative interest in maintaining the status quo. This could be done, for instance, by limiting the bureaucrats' period of service and by adopting a system of personnel rotation. On the other hand, various ways of decentralising decision-making with respect to industrial investments, through facilitating workers' socialist self-management, would surely reduce the danger of bureaucratic rigidity toward industrial change. At the same time, it must be made certain that the conscious goals of the bureaucrats are primarily in the social interest, and not in maintaining their own established positions.

In the case of Japan, for instance, the bureaucrats are beyond the democratic control of the popular movement, and they are generally in secure employment lasting to retirement in their late fifties. Although they are certainly conservative as far as defending their own administrative offices and positions are concerned, they have worked not to obstruct, but, on the whole, rather to facilitate industrial renovation. Their secure position, and the Japanese custom of appointing bureaucrats to responsible positions in private companies after their retirement from the public service, has enabled the bureaucrats to adopt a longer-term and broad perspective favouring industrial growth. A similar incentive on the part of the bureaucrats to work for industrial renovation aiming at growth has to be integrated into a socialist economic order, upon the basis of democratic workers' self-management of firms. To some extent, democratic interchange of personnel between administrative offices and industrial firms would also help, just as the rotation of personnel across departments within Japanese large companies has worked to maintain flexibility toward industrial change and renovation.

Since it was so difficult to restructure the Soviet type of economy because of its established bureaucratic system, the Soviet type of society could not overcome economic stagnation once the latter began. It must be noted, however, that the crisis of the Soviet type of economy, unlike a certain type of capitalist crisis, did not result in a destructive spiral of collapse but, rather, maintained a certain stagnant stability. Economic stagnation, however, was very persistent, difficult to overcome within the existing social order, and began to assume the form of a socio–political crisis of legitimacy for the existing system of government and administration.

The Case of Socioeconomic Crisis in China

The socioeconomic crisis of China was different. Chinese socialism initially followed the Soviet model of centrally planned industrialisation, as in the first five year plan of 1953–7. During the Great Leap Forward (1958–61) China attempted to build a more self-reliant socialist economy, including the construction of the people's communes in rural villages. However, the attempt failed, resulting in a disastrous shortage of consumption goods, particularly food, due to the over-hasty policy of priority for the heavy industries, the loss of motivation on the part of farmers, natural calamities, and reduced economic aid from the Soviet Union. It is estimated that between 16 and 27 million people died in the economic turmoil and starvation of the period of the Great Leap Forward.[11]

In 1961 Adjustment Policies were undertaken so as to restore the level of production in agriculture and light industry by reducing the priority of heavy industry. Subsequently, in 1962 Mao Zedong began to stress that the attempts of the bourgeoisie to revive could be expected to continue throughout the entire period of socialism, and so the class struggle of the proletariat against the bourgeoisie was always necessary. This very left-wing view reflected not only the complex domestic rivalries among different political groups on the direction of socialist economic construction, but also international tension and dangers. Mao and his supporters in the top positions of the Chinese Communist Party felt that it was urgent to prepare militarily and ideologically for a possible confrontation with the Soviet Union, as well as against the menace of American imperialism. The US military intervention in Vietnam was a serious threat to China.

Thus, from an international standpoint, it was not accidental that the Cultural Revolution was initiated by Mao in 1966, soon after the US bombing of North Vietnam which began openly in 1965. The Cultural Revolution promoted a mass movement which aimed at organising a commune-type social order from below, through the various levels of administration, schools, universities, firms, and local rural communities. The Cultural Revolution emphasised the significance of proletarian class struggle against the existing privileged politicians, bureaucrats, intellectuals, and the remaining bourgeoisie, or people who were supposed to belong to the bourgeoisie. The movement contained certain ideals of true socialism by the people for the people, while intending radically to alter the top-down bureaucratic Soviet type of social order. It was actually argued that the Soviet type of society was state capitalism and not socialism.

In retrospect, the social upheaval during the Cultural Revolution, sometimes approaching the level of civil war, affected economic activity not as much as the turmoil of the Great Leap Forward. After a period of stagnation during 1966–9 agricultural production grew at 3.0–4.2 percent annually (except in 1972). Total social production also grew in the 1970s. However, the Chinese economy was out of balance because of assigning too high a priority to military industries. The economy was also stagnant in a qualitative sense, and even deteriorated, as technical experts and professionals were sent to rural communes, while higher education was in confusion. Thus, the Chinese economy became fragile toward the end of the period of Cultural Revolution. Moreover, intense political unrest followed the death of Mao and, in 1976, an earthquake devastated the coastal area of Pohai. Thus in 1976–7, the Chinese economy was in turmoil, and agricultural production even fell in absolute terms.

The bureaucratic central planning system, similar to that of the Soviet Union, was maintained for Chinese heavy industries often related to military production. Nevertheless, Chinese management of large firms partakes substantially of the nature of a commune, looking after workers for their entire life, often including cheap or free accommodation for their families and the payment of pensions. At the same time, Chinese socialism is forced to rely, both politically and economically, predominantly on farmers who in the 1970s still made up three quarters of the working population. Mao's tendency to emphasise the importance of the commune type of social formation for socialism, reflected, to a certain extent, the social weight of farmers and rural communities.

The attempt to construct Chinese-style socialism thus still contained an aspect of bureaucratic central planning in the principal sectors of the nationalised industries with all the problems to be found in the Soviet Union. At the same time, Chinese-style socialism stressed the importance of forming rural communes from below, particularly during the Great Leap Forward and the Cultural Revolution. How to coordinate relatively independent communes, rural areas, urban industries, and firms, remained a significant problem, and added to the economic imbalance and sense of crisis. A further difficulty was to maintain the motivation to work in the egalitarian peoples communes in the rural areas as well as in the large firms. Finally, technological stagnation also became a serious concern.

The introduction of a market economy together with the dissolution of people's communes was regarded as a promising way out of these difficulties and problems when Deng Xiaoping initiated the four modernisation policies concerning agriculture, manufacturing, defence, and science and technology. This type of reform coincided with and led the reforms in the Soviet Union and Eastern Europe in the 1980s, although its preconditions were not actually the same.

7 The Reforms and Systemic Change

At first sight, the reforms in the centrally planned economies of the Soviet Union, Eastern Europe, and China seem on the same track leading to a market economy. However, things are not always what they seem and the reforms actually differ considerably in their features and content. The initiative for reform in Eastern Europe sprang from a broad workers' and citizens' movement, whilst in China and the Soviet Union the initiative was taken by the top leaders of the ruling Communist Party. The weight of reform in the Soviet Union and in Eastern Europe was concentrated on the political issues of democratisation, freedom of speech and of the press, and independence for all nations and peoples. The aim of the reforms was to transform the existing Communist Party regime and to alter the international order in the Soviet bloc. In China, the reforms were concentrated on the economic aspects of society, rather than on the political system, and they were effected in more gradual steps. Below we will review the outlines and the development of reforms in some detail, while comparing the effects of the different type of reform adopted in each of the above cases.

PERESTROIKA AND THE RUSSIAN TRAGEDY

Perestroika

Perestroika was launched by M. Gorbachev soon after his rise to the position of secretary general of the Soviet Communist Party in 1985. It was a campaign aimed at the general renewal of the Soviet socio-economic system. Because it promoted Glasnost (disclosure of information), freedom of expression, and democratisation, Perestroika gathered popular support especially among professionals and intellectuals. In contrast to the 1989 Eastern European revolutions, Perestroika was driven from above, aimed at maintaining Communist Party rule, and was based mainly on the enthusiasm of the revitalised intelligentsia. Gorbachev clearly stated that 'we will proceed toward better socialism rather than away from it'.[1] While Perestroika shared these features with reforms

The Reforms and Systemic Change

in China, its focus was obviously socio–political, as shown by the demands for Glasnost and freedom of opinion, as well as the critique of privilege and corruption. These characteristics reflected the considerable growth in the numbers and power of the professional and intellectual backers of Perestroika as a result of the historical development of Soviet society.

As economic stagnation deepened, the legitimacy of Communist Party leadership had somehow to be re-strengthened. In the beginning, reforming the undemocratic controls on expression and delivering Glasnost seemed to serve this purpose. Especially among professionals and the intelligentsia, who had become increasingly acquainted with the Western social order of freedom of political opinion and criticism, the unpopularity of the Soviet type of undemocratic social order had grown. Given that diminished co-operative discipline among working people had increased the difficulties of the Soviet economy, Gorbachev, and his followers in the government and the upper echelons of the administration, might have hoped that Perestroika and democratisation would restore workers' support, co-operation and discipline within the planned economy. In retrospect, Gorbachev's group actually failed to prepare an accurate analysis of the causes of stagnation and crisis in the Soviet economy, and consequently they did not put forward systematic policy steps aiming at overcoming the economic problems. As far as reforming the economy is concerned, Perestroika went through three different phases without ever possessing a well prepared economic strategy.

First, during 1985–6 the policy of Perestroika aimed at restoring worker discipline through a general tightening of morals. In 1985, in order to cure alcoholism and to prevent drinking at work, a campaign against alcohol was launched. Many villages and communities stopped the sale of alcohol, and official alcohol sales indeed fell by a half in two years. In 1986, State quality control was intensified. A struggle against unearned income was also launched in order to limit and to reduce the second, unofficial economy. These campaigns, however, were felt by the majority of workers as a severe tightening of their condition without real economic compensation, and at odds with liberalisation and the democratisation of social life. Since Perestroika was not initiated by a popular movement from below, the campaigns to restore worker discipline were naturally understood as intensification of labour, austerity, and re-strengthened control from above. These campaigns could not successfully revive the incentive to work and to co-operate, nor to limit the second economy, and thus failed to reactivate the Soviet economy.

Secondly, after the end of 1986, when small size private enterprises were made legal, the autonomy of enterprises began to be tolerated and expanded. A new law of State enterprises, effective from the beginning of 1987, abolished obligatory norms and adopted a self-supporting accounting system, letting individual firms purchase raw materials and pay wages through their own sales or finance. The proposed transformation of the distribution system, run by Gosnab, into a wholesale trading system, however, did not proceed smoothly because of the resistance of the existing administration. As a result, State orders for products, which were meant to be gradually limited to the strategically important industries alone, actually continued to take up 100 percent of the total without interruption. Although a self-supporting accounting system with more autonomous activity for State enterprises was allowed, neither the revision of the planned price system nor the co-ordinating function of the market mechanism worked as intended. While the functioning of the control system of the planned economy was considerably disturbed, the operation of a market economy was still far from being realised. Various imbalances and confusion inevitably spread to production and distribution, worsening the phenomena of shortage in the official economy. The rate of inflation was estimated at above 10 percent by 1989, and the absolute standard of living of the Soviet people began to decline.

Thirdly, in order to cope with the deepening economic crisis, it was decided by the Supreme Council of the Soviet Union in October 1990 that a full-scale transition to a market economy should take place within a period 18 months–2 years. This was declared not to contradict the Soviet people's choice of socialism, so long as it was combined with macroeconomic policies which would not allow inflation, unemployment, excessive disparities in income or in regional development, and as it was accompanied by effective social welfare policies.

The first step was an emergency programme to cut the budget deficit so as to curb the vicious inflation, stop the fall in production, and promote a transition of State enterprises to non-State ownership (i.e. to collective, co-operative, or joint-stock forms of ownership). The second step would be to make prices and financial controls more flexible, though more than one third of commodity prices would still be officially fixed. The third step would be to bring housing and the wages system within the ambit of the market. In the fourth step, the complete competitive environment of a self-adjusting market economy would be created by eliminating State control and by freeing the exchange of the rouble with foreign currencies.

These policies of complete and rapid marketisation of the entire Soviet economy were assumed necessary not only to solve the economic crisis of the planned economy, but also in order to be able to appeal to the IMF and other Western institutions, as well as the London summit of May 1991, and ask for economic aid and rescue loans. Bearing in mind such considerations, these policies clearly showed the strong influence of neo-liberal Western economic advisers, such as J. Sachs. The consistency of these policies with socialism was dubious from the outset, and the policies were misguided in proposing that such a tremendous transformation of the economy could take place within 2 years at most. As it turned out, even the first step of the emergency programme was unsuccessful. The cumulative deficit of the State budget, State debt, and the total amount of currency continued to swell. As a result, the already vicious inflation became further aggravated, threw productive activity into turmoil, and reduced the real income of workers.

The Limitations of Perestroika

Gorbachev's Perestroika presented anew the hope for a democratic and humanistic socialism; it led to the thawing out of social issues which had been frozen in the history of the Soviet bloc; it revived the expression of political opinions and the formation of social movements aiming to deal with ecology, feminism, trade unions, and national or ethnic problems. Internationally, Gorbachev propounded a new world view based on 'universal human values', aiming at the end of the cold war through a series of negotiations with the USA for arms reductions. Although this policy was necessitated by the onerous burden of military expenditures in a deepening economic crisis, and it certainly obscured the socialist view of global class struggle, it also had a positive side in actually ending the tensions of the cold war, accepting self-determination for every nation, and attempting to restore friendly relations with China, 'the Eastern great socialist country'.

Despite all this, Perestroika failed to achieve its fundamental goal of reviving the Soviet economy. On the one hand, the actual process of Perestroika revealed how difficult it was, given its bureaucratic institutions and functioning, to re-activate the Soviet centrally planned economy, and to switch toward a more intensive and flexible type of accumulation. The restoration of workers' discipline and morale was itself hard to achieve under Soviet bureaucratic control which generated the feeling of alienation among people.

On the other hand, the process of Perestroika also showed that a market economy cannot materialise in a short period of time simply through political commands, or by legislation from above. The formation of a market economy has to be quite different from that of a centrally planned economy. Many social institutions at various levels, various specialised and trained persons, such as traders, managers, accountants, and lawyers, have to be in place for a market economy to function. Even the formation of non-State collective, co-operative, private, and joint-stock enterprises through the decomposition of State enterprises, was a very complicated and difficult project to realise under the existing bureaucratic system. Indeed, the full-scale transition to a market economy, proposed in the third step of Perestroika, would have been in substance identical to a transition to a capitalist market economy, if with some ameliorating welfare and macroeconomic policies. If Perestroika was in fact aimed at the transition to a capitalist market economy, it would indeed require comprehensive socioeconomic changes to be promoted by a strong political power, and lasting for a long period of time. These changes would, through social struggle, lead to the formation of new classes, in a process similar to that analysed by Marx in the theory of 'primitive accumulation' during the formation of the capitalist mode of production.

As far as the contents of the third step of economic reform is concerned, Gorbachev's Perestroika was not only too hasty, but also inconsistent with its initial goal of a better socialism. Perestroika became simultaneously fragile and unrealistic as Gorbachev's political leadership was shaken by a wave of nationalism and ethnic problems.

Nationalism and Ethnic Problems

The Soviet Union had always been a multi-ethnic country, and from the beginning it faced serious, but sometimes latent, national and ethnic problems. Prior to the Russian Revolution there were two strands of opinion among Marxists on how to deal with nationalist and ethnic problems. The first stood for the view that the socialist movement should treasure the variety of culture and the specificity of nations and peoples. In this view, only by mutually respecting diverse cultures, including different languages, could socialism bring about a humane world society. Thus, in the process of destroying the dominion of capital, the socialist movement should fully respect the basic self-determination of nations with a variety of cultures, and so create real socialist co-operation and solidarity among people of different nations and peoples. O. Bauer presented this view in *Die Nationalitätenfrage und die Sozialdemokratie* (1907).[2]

The second opinion argued, in opposition to the first, that workers have a more fundamental common problem namely, their social position as an oppressed class under capitalism. The central issue for socialists is the universal class struggle between workers and capitalists. The road to socialism through class struggle would make it more likely that workers would achieve their self-emancipation into universal human beings. Therefore, rivalries and differences among nations and peoples have to be resolved within the socialist liberation movement of the working class. R. Luxemburg, among others, stood for this view.[3] In this view, the differences among nations and peoples would be reduced and eventually disappear as socialism progressed.

Lenin was initially favourable to this latter view. He supported Stalin's *Marxism and the National Question* (1913)[4] which put across this line of argument, and appointed Stalin to the chair of the People's Committee for Racial Problems after the Revolution. However, Lenin also emphasised the importance of the right of nations to self-determination, and, particularly in the last two years of his life (1922–3), he became very concerned about maintaining the independence of the Soviet republics of Ukraine, Belorussia, Azerbaidjan, Georgia, and Armenia. He struggled seriously in his sickbed against Stalin's crude policy of absorbing these republics into the Russian Soviet Socialist Republic. Lenin's intention was to form a Soviet Union of European and Asian Republics by uniting these republics with the Russian Soviet Socialist Republic on an equal footing and with an equal right to sovereignty.[5] Thus, Lenin's final position was closer to the first strand, namely, that socialism should admit a variety of national and ethnic cultures aiming at international co-operation.

Lenin's struggle was not successful, and Stalin's policy of neglecting the autonomy of different nations and peoples, and giving priority to the construction of socialism in a single unified country, became dominant. As a result, the Russian culture, language, and political power dominated the whole Soviet Union. Under the Stalin regime, masses of Western Ukrainians, Lithuanians, Latvians, Estonians, among many others, were forced to move to Siberia and other areas in accordance with the needs of industrial development. The policy of Russification of other nations and peoples within the Soviet Union under the domination of Russian political and military power certainly created strong feelings of indignation and discontent among the nations and peoples of the republics.

A similar attitude was adopted toward the allied countries which established socialist or communist governments, as well as toward the communist or socialist movements in other countries. Under the pretext of communist internationalism, the Soviet Communist Party tended to give directions to and to control socialist countries and foreign communist movements, frequently serving its own narrow interests, and not sufficiently appreciating the historically specific circumstances of each country. This tendency was one of the origins of the Eastern European dissident movements, as well as of the Moscow–Beijing rift, and repeatedly caused turmoil and splits within the socialist or communist movements of various countries.

Indignation and discontent within the non-Russian republics and peoples of the Soviet Union, as well as in Eastern Europe, were kept latent as long as domestic and international co-operation for the construction of socialist societies seemed meaningful and, especially, delivered improvements in the economic conditions of life. This precondition for co-operation evaporated when economic stagnation deepened throughout the 1980s without any sign of recovery, despite the efforts of Perestroika. Gorbachev's approval of the right to self-determination of nations and peoples gave confidence to anti-establishment movements in Eastern Europe and in the non-Russian republics of the Soviet Union to demand independence and democratic self-determination without fear of military intervention.

The Dissolution of the Soviet Union

Thus, the national and ethnic question, latent for a long historical period, surfaced as the political expression of the deepening crisis of the Soviet economy. When the first oil shock hit the capitalist world, the political leaders of Eastern Europe believed, and officially stated, that their countries were definitely immune to this problem since they had access to cheap oil imports from the Soviet Union through the COMECON (Council for Mutual Economic Assistance) international co-operation system. The shock to Eastern Europeans was great, therefore, when the price of Russian oil was subsequently brought up to the international level. Although the increase in the oil price reflected the tendency to shortages of supply even within the Soviet economy, the shock exacerbated the economic difficulties of Eastern Europe and added to the indignation of the people toward the Soviet regime.

The rise of the Solidarity trade union democratisation movement in Poland in 1980–1 was put down by a military government under the threat of Soviet military intervention. However, as Perestroika proceeded, the movement revived together with similar workers' and citizens' movements in other Eastern European countries, and led to a series of Eastern European revolutions in 1989.

Following the Eastern European revolutions, democratisation and independence movements in Estonia, Latvia, and Lithuania (the three Baltic countries), and similar movements in the other republics of the Soviet Union, gained strength. Uneven economic conditions with differential access to Western markets intensified the desire for independence in the course of the deepening of the economic crisis in the Soviet Union. This came on top of the traditional latent discontent in non-Russian republics against Russification. Gorbachev tried to preserve the Soviet Union, but failed to stabilise the political crisis caused by the independence movements. B. Yeltsin was elected president of the Russian Republic and promoted radical reforms, including the secession of the republics from the Soviet Union. The failure of the 'conservative' coup d'état of August 1991 to defend the Soviet Union and Communist Party rule against the Yeltsin line of reforms led to the rapid disintegration of the Soviet Communist Party. The disintegration of the Soviet Union itself was also inevitable, as 11 countries out of the old Soviet constituent republics became independent and formed CIS (Commonwealth of Independent States) in December 1991.

The Deepening Russian Economic Crisis

After the secession of the Russian Federation from the Soviet Union, Yeltsin pressed on with radical economic reforms aiming at rapid and comprehensive marketisation. Yeltsin's economic reforms were clearly no longer aiming at reforming socialism: the aim of comprehensive marketisation was to transform the Russian economic order into a capitalist market economy. The radical neo-liberal strand of neo-classical economics was openly proclaimed to be the theory behind Yeltsin's reforms. This type of economics believes that a free market can bring about the most efficient and harmonious economy, and can automatically solve all economic problems. By applying this type of economics to the Russian economy, the radical economic reformers in Yeltsin's government, such as Y. Gaidar, asserted that the existence of fixed prices and the absence of a free market in the centrally planned economy had caused distortions, stagnation, and inefficiency. As a corollary, they strongly recommended liberalisation of trade in goods and services, and the freeing of prices as the way of restoring the vitality of the Russian economy. It was argued that this transition to the free market system should be done swiftly in order to reduce confusion and social pain.

Yeltsin adopted this 'shock therapy', freed prices and attempted to move to a full market economy from the beginning of 1992. The result was an evident failure. In the process of political upheaval, real national income in the Soviet Union had already declined by 5 percent in 1990 and 11 percent in 1991. After 1992 the decline accelerated in the Russian Republic and proceeded at the annual rate of 15–20 percent. Such a severe and continuous decline of productive activity is almost unprecedented historically, except for the comparable great economic crisis in the USA in the 1930s.

The liberalisation of prices did not promote increases in the supply of primary products and raw materials, and so caused vicious inflation starting with the means of production. The giant State enterprises tried not to reduce employment and production by obtaining raw materials as far as possible, despite the fall in sales and confusion in the distribution of their products. Given that the Russian State aimed at securing international aid and loans, and so strove to follow World Bank and IMF advice not to increase the budget deficit by advancing subsidies and loans to State enterprises, these enterprises maintained their level of operation by mutually extending inter-firm commercial credit. In the Soviet economy each firm used to specialise in large-scale production of a certain model of a single product, and so occupied a monopoly position within the bureaucratic managerial system. It is a new and difficult operation for these firms flexibly to alter and multiply their products according to changes in social needs, even if price movements have been liberalised. The existence of inflexible monopolistic firms is also reminiscent of the difficulties faced by capitalism in reviving after the Great Depression in the 1930s.

In the Soviet bloc the organic system of reproduction was constructed in a planned way among specialised firms located in various countries and republics. Therefore, the collapse of COMECON and of the Soviet Union inevitably disturbed and obstructed the distributional part of reproduction. For example, batteries produced in another republic became difficult to obtain by a tractor factory in the Russian Federation, impeding production activity in both the tractor and the battery factory. The peripheral smaller States of the CIS are inevitably suffering disproportionately because of the destruction of the organic reproduction system.

The shock therapy of freeing prices compounded by expanding inter-firm credit, an increasing supply of roubles, and declining production in turmoil, exacerbated inflation. Rapidly rising inflation in turn became a source of further disruption of production, and decline in the economic life of people. In the first six months of 1992 the prices of consumer goods and services rose by a factor of 10 compared to December 1991. Nominal wages also rose during the same period, but only by a factor of four. As a result, real wages fell rapidly to 40 percent of the December 1991 level. The exchange rate of the rouble which stood at 400 yen to the rouble fell to below 1 yen to the rouble. Russian average nominal wages in June 1992 were 4400 roubles a month, and became extremely low by international comparison. Inflation further continued and by the end of 1992 the price level was 23 times that of the previous year.

Rapid inflation allowed a small number of speculators to profit and made Russian economic life full of inequalities. On the whole, however, its destructive macroeconomic effect was obviously much greater than that of the vicious inflation experienced in the capitalist world during the period of the oil shocks.

Privatisation

The Gaidar neo-liberal reform programme initially contained a plan for the rapid and comprehensive privatisation of State enterprises. At the beginning of 1992, the Russian Federation had 21,945 State-owned industrial enterprises accounting for 96 percent of industrial production.

One of the major difficulties faced by the privatisation programme was the shortage of money owned by the people which would have allowed them to purchase the shares or stocks of privatised enterprises. Therefore, in October 1992 vouchers of 10,000 roubles per person were equitably distributed among the people in order to be used for the purchase of stocks or small shops. Simultaneously, the privatisation of 2000 State enterprises and 100,000 small shops was planned. By that time, however, the initial radical programme for privatisation was significantly softened since it had met with difficulties and objections. Apart from the shortage of money, managers and workers also wanted to secure their rights and positions in the existing enterprises. Local government, furthermore, demanded substantial rights to the enterprises in their areas. Thus, concessions were made, giving priority to managers and workers to purchase up to 45 percent of their enterprises, limiting purchases by vouchers to within 35 percent of the total payment, and allocating a considerable part of the net revenue from the sale of shares to local government. The Russian people profoundly distrust the strong controlling power of the bureaucrats in the State committee for privatisation because it provides ample opportunities for corruption.

The handling and the actual results of the privatisation programme turned out quite different from the neo-liberal ideal. The massive issue of negotiable vouchers, amounting to 1 1/2 trillion roubles, clearly accelerated inflation. Contrary to initial expectations, the sale of shares of enterprises did not significantly help in resolving the crisis of the State budget deficit. The actual speed of privatisation was much slower than was initially intended. Managers and workers can now expect to maintain, and even increase, their autonomous control over the enterprise by, to a certain degree, deciding when and how to privatise their enterprises. Thus, the process of privatisation became quite different from the initial neo-liberal idea of making privatisation a smooth, straight road to capitalism. It has turned out to be a complex social class struggle between the federal and local politicians and bureaucrats, the foreign and the emerging domestic bourgeoisie, the industrial managerial Nomenklatura, and the workers.[6]

The dynamics of this struggle are complicated because of co-operative alliances formed between the workers and the industrial managerial Nomenklatura aiming at opposing the neo-liberal radical reforms. These alliances are commonly called 'conservative' in the Western Press. We should note that the opportunity exists for workers to establish their own rights and to control the enterprises they work at, by forming social relations of production which are different not only from those in the old Soviet regime but also from capitalist ones.

In agriculture, which still employs 35 percent of the total working population, farmers in the 26,000 collective large farms voted in 1992 on the type of farm which they wanted to form. In about 16,000 farms, with approximately two thirds of the total farm land, farmers declared a preference for family ownership of farmland, and so wanted to run either small family farms, or collective farms based on family-owned farmland. In another 10,000 farms farmers opted for co-operative collective farms. In the remaining 2600 farms, they decided to maintain the existing form of collective farms.

It is remarkable that so many farmers, including many in the first category, did not choose straightforward private family management of farms, and wanted to hold on to some form of collective farming. To some extent this must be related to the difficulty of using the existing large-size agricultural machines, such as tractors, on a small private basis. However, it also signifies the survival of a certain element of the socialist tradition which can help to create a new social formation based on farmers' self-management. This is similar to the industrial workers' inclination to strengthen their control over the enterprises within new social relations.

The Failure of Neo-liberalism

Although it is still too early to predict the nature of the socioeconomic order which will emerge from the severe economic crisis in Russia, one thing at least seems clear. That is, the straight neo-liberal economic reforms of Gaidar aiming at creating a capitalist free market economy in a short period of time, and fully supported by Yeltsin, have failed to achieve economic stabilisation, much less the revival of the Russian economy. It can even be said that the reforms actually compounded the crisis. Neo-liberal economists do not fully explain why the application of their theories failed, and tend to argue that the trouble arose from insufficient marketisation.

It has to be said that, on the one hand, the existing social and historical conditions inimical to immediate privatisation and to the smooth functioning of a market economy will not be easily dissolved. As in the historical experience of the transition from feudalism to capitalism through primitive accumulation, the transformation leading to a market economy will take quite a long time. The process may involve political upheavals and require the midwife services of violence, it may entail the decomposition of old dominant interests, such as those of the the various levels of the Nomenklatura, may foster the emergence of new social classes as well as new types of skills and specialists, and it may even rely on great changes in the behavioural patterns of the people at large. The neo-classical theory of the market economy, relied upon by Gaidar and other neo-liberals, lacks the necessary theoretical framework to deal with such socio–historical conditions of economic life.

On the other hand, unlike the centrally planned economy, a market economy is impossible to construct from above by simply using State power. A market economy is not something mechanically designed, but, rather a set of spontaneous, organic, and fundamentally anarchical, socioeconomic relations. On top of the many social and institutional preconditions necessary to a market order, an individual person's willingness to participate in a market economy has to be developed, sometimes over generations, for the law of value to function smoothly. For a full-scale market economy of the capitalist type, a class of wage workers without property or social rights to the means of production has to be created. Without flexibility in hiring and firing workers, firms cannot adjust production according to the changes in market demand. Such conditions cannot prevail without severe struggle in the process of forming new social classes, and it is not yet clear that they are actually going to be established in Russia.

The failure of the neo-liberal reform programme has revealed afresh the fundamental nature and the necessary preconditions for a complete market economy. A transition from a centrally planned economy to a full-scale capitalist market economy involves a long and painful process of social transformation, and there is no guarantee that it will be successful. This type of transformation in an environment of deepening and severe economic crisis is full of tension and actual struggle regarding the determination of social rights and the position of workers. Although a revival of the old centrally planned economy is probably out of the question in Russia, the introduction of a market order and the process of privatisation may well be combined with several types of collectivist relations of production. The outcome can be different from a capitalist mode of production, and could eventually be re-directed to a new form of socialism. The content of the theoretical arguments of this book, opposing both neo-classicism and the Soviet type of Marxism, serves to suggest and to examine this perspective.

Yeltsin's political position has been shaken and much weakened, due mainly to the failure of his neo-liberal economic policies, and he seems to have lost all sense of direction of economic policy, as well as all control over the deepening Russian socioeconomic crisis. The critics of Yeltsin's government have gained in prestige and popularity. In order to break the 'conservatives', Yeltsin did not hesitate to bomb the Russian Supreme Council in October 1993. In a remarkable demonstration of double standards, the governments of the major capitalist countries, which had severely condemned the Chinese government over the Tienanmen incident of 1989, did not condemn this destruction of the Russian Parliament. In the following general election of December 1993, the party closest to Yeltsin, 'Russia's Choice', was rejected by the popular vote, obtaining only 14 percent of the parliamentary seats. Although the ultra-right Liberal Democratic Party led by V. Zhirinovsky gained considerably more seats than originally expected, the left Russian Agrarian Party and the Communist party of the Russian Federation also received considerable popular support, together securing almost 20 percent of the parliamentary seats, this despite their boycott campaign against voting for this election.

The signs of recovery for the left are still feeble, and left-wing parties are not yet clear either in their economic programmes or in their broader theoretical foundations. However, the election results seem to signal the end of Yeltsin's ability to govern easily, as well as the end of neo-liberal economic reforms of the shock therapy type. We will have to wait and see how new hope for the future of socialism can revive out of the historically long and painful struggle of socialists and workers in Russia and the CIS.

EASTERN EUROPEAN REVOLUTIONS AND SYSTEMIC CHANGE

In 1989 a series of stormy social revolutions occurred in Eastern Europe which shattered their Soviet-style centrally planned economies operating under one-party rule. There were three main causative factors which the revolutions shared; (1) stagnation and crisis in economic life, (2) demands for self-determination from the oppressive overlordship of the Soviet Union, (3) demands for liberalisation and democratisation of the Soviet-style oppressive social order within each country. The socioeconomic reforms which took place after the Eastern European revolutions had to tackle these issues.

The Role of Economic Difficulties

In May–June 1990 the author visited Warsaw, Berlin, Prague, and Budapest and in the course of several interviews with many economists became convinced that economic difficulties were not a primary direct cause of the 1989 revolutions. Claims for political and social freedom, for democracy and self-determination were more important as a direct motivation for people's movements.

The *per capita* GNP of these countries was lower than that of the advanced capitalist countries. However, even in Poland, with GNP *per capita* lower than in eastern Germany, Czechoslovakia and Hungary, and about the same as in the Soviet Union, the level was above one third of the OECD average. The standard of living of ordinary people was stable and far removed from the absolute poverty which often generates revolutionary movements in third world countries. Under the egalitarian socialist order, workers were immune from the threat of unemployment, and were supplied with relatively cheap basic means of consumption. Given a relatively equitable distribution of income, based on the payment of pensions after retirement, and free or cheap nurseries, schooling, transport, housing and medical services, the people's economic life was stable, if stagnant.

The level of economic life in the collective farms, unlike the Soviet Union and China, was generally rather higher than that of urban workers, especially in Czechoslovakia and Hungary. This was achieved, at least partly, through subsidising the prices of agricultural goods. Thus the Communist Party and its policies tended to be popular among the rural population.

Had Eastern European countries been perfectly isolated from the rest of the world, economic life would not have been, by itself, a serious source of complaint and social unrest. However, by geographical position and cultural tradition, these countries are close to Western European countries and it was impossible to black out information regarding Western consumption patterns. The demonstration effect of the gap between Eastern and Western consumer goods became greater and greater in the 1970s and 1980s. While the Soviet type of planned economy was stagnant with regard to the qualitative improvement of products, the Western capitalist countries raised the sophistication and multiplied the models of consumer durables, such as personal cars, audio equipment and so forth. This was done through the introduction of ME technologies under the pressure of competitive restructuring. Access to such Western consumer goods, including cosmetics, women's dresses and suchlike, was limited to the privileged politicians and bureaucrats. Under these circumstances, the privileges afforded by some social positions became significantly greater than before, and ordinary people began to feel even more strongly that the existing social order was unfair, restrictive, and intolerable.

The impact which Soviet economic problems were having on Eastern Europe was also important. A short while after the first oil shock the price of Soviet oil significantly increased and was brought to the level prevailing in the capitalist world. Although this rise in the price of oil was actually related to the relative shortage of supply of oil in the Soviet Union itself, as we have already argued, the shock was great and led to severe complaints about the international order within the Eastern bloc. Furthermore, it became difficult to export to the Soviet Union as the Soviet economy fell into stagnation and crisis.

As a result, the majority of the Eastern European countries in the 1970s considerably increased their financial debt to Western countries, partly in order to pay for the increased import costs of oil and means of production, and partly in order to finance the construction of modern factories to produce goods for export. The continuing economic depression in the West had led to a shortage of safe and profitable investment opportunities for greatly increased financial funds, and so the latter positively poured into Eastern Europe. Such international loans enabled Eastern European countries to maintain acceptable economic growth in the 1970s more successfully than the Soviet Union.

However, in the 1980s the economic depression of the capitalist world worsened, real rates of interest rose very high, the expectation of increased export to the Western world failed to materialise, and the cumulative debt of Eastern Europe turned into a heavy burden, in a manner similar to the international debt of many third world countries.[7] In order to pay the interest and principal due, Eastern European countries often had to reduce imports of raw materials and to alter the price system so as to restrict domestic consumption. This added to the tendency toward shortage phenomena, and exacerbated the dissatisfaction of the people with the existing Soviet type of government.

Revolutions for Democratic Socialism

Dissident reform movements in Eastern Europe countries have a long and tragic history. Such movements kept repeatedly appearing, and demanded a more democratic and humane socialism, the self-determination of people, fundamental human rights of freedom and democracy, the lessening of the domination by the Soviet Union and its bureaucratic top-down social order. The Hungarian upheaval of 1956, the Prague Spring of 1968, and the Polish Solidarity movement of 1980–1, represent the peak moments of such reform movements. Direct Soviet military intervention suppressed the first two, and the threat of intervention initiated the suppression of the third. However, it was evident that the participation of the masses in the reform movement increased from Hungary to Czechoslovakia to Poland. Probably as a result of this, the form of suppression became milder, and the number of lives lost in each case declined dramatically.

Market socialism theories of Eastern European origin, as we have seen in Chapter 4, were developed mostly in an effort to replace the 'orthodox' Soviet model of centrally planned economy. Market economies were not only supposed to be more efficient, but also more suitable for democratic socialism.

The Eastern European social movements of 1989 were the heirs to these historical experiences and theories, and generally aimed at realising democratic socialism through a combination of market and planning, although a naive pro-market climate against any form of socialism or state intervention also tended to acquire popularity. The sense of worsening economic impasse due to the policies of the existing socialist governments certainly facilitated the spread of dissident democratisation movements among workers and citizens, even if it was not the main direct cause for the uprisings. The direct cause was, rather, the people's aspirations to political democracy, freedom, self-determination, and fundamental human rights. Many people, however, also tended to assume that democratisation would also resolve the economic impasse through market socialism free from Soviet control.

Gorbachev's Perestroika, with its Glasnost, democratisation and tendency toward marketisation (itself much influenced by Eastern European ideas and theories of reform), served as an encouraging international background for Eastern European movements. The potential for change in the Soviet type of socialism had already been presented in the Soviet Union. Moreover, in June 1989 Gorbachev, in a joint statement with the West German Chancellor H. Kohl, openly declared that the Soviet Union would respect people's fundamental right to self-determination. This made the participants in Eastern European reform movements confident that Soviet intervention would no longer suppress their attempts at reform.

The 1989 Eastern European revolutions, however, were quite different from Perestroika in their form. Drawing on the long history of dissident democratisation movements, the revolutions took the form of mass grass-roots movements. Their propagation across the Eastern bloc certainly owed something to the influence of the modern mass media, particularly the impact of TV images. The bicentennial of the French Revolution in 1989 was also important in reminding people of their fundamental right, as well as their power, to stand up and revolutionise an unfair and oppressive socio–political order. At the same time, these revolutions demonstrated afresh that it is feasible, as Rosa Luxemburg had argued, to bring democratic change to the political system through the workers' mass movement, though the change they actually brought about was in a direction very different from that intended by Luxemburg.

The fact that large numbers of workers and citizens participated in the reform movement shattered the legitimacy of the existing one-party rule, and destroyed the confidence of leaders in the ruling Communist Party or similar parties with a different name. It was not rare even for highly placed leaders in the ruling parties to join the Solidarity movement in Poland, or the Citizens' Forum in Czechoslovakia and Hungary. At the final stage of the turmoil, the ruling communist parties could not offer any further resistance, and simply collapsed. The armed forces kept neutral and silent in 1989, reluctant to suppress the people's movements. As the transformation was achieved with little violence and blood, it was called a Velvet Revolution in Czechoslovakia. These features were more or less common to all the 1989 East European revolutions.

What made possible the velvet-like character of the revolutions was, above all, the popularity and support which the reform movements enjoyed among the mass of the people. Enthusiasm rose across the world as it became clear that people's own power had the potential to change history. It is worth stressing that in preparing for the 1989 revolutions, and in bringing the revolutions to fruition, the popular mass movements were spontaneously organised from below, aiming at the democratisation of socialism and not at its destruction. In this respect the goal of the revolutions seemed almost identical to that of Gorbachev's Perestroika. The popularity and the goals of the mass movements contributed to the erosion of the legitimacy of the communist party leaders, who were supposed to be in their positions in the name of a workers' State for socialism.

The Turn to Neo-liberalism

After the revolutions, however, and in the process of general elections with a multiplicity of political parties, the reform movement in the East European countries underwent a significant change. Most of the new governments which emerged from the general elections, often as coalitions among parties, adopted neo-liberal economic policies, and openly aimed at comprehensive marketisation in the direction of capitalism. The parties born out of the reform movement competed for popular support during the general elections, by intensifying the 'radical' reform current aiming at comprehensive marketisation away from socialism. A naive admiration for the free market gained popularity as the most consistent alternative for the discredited statism.

In retrospect, it is an amazing fact that the various theories of democratic market socialism, developed in Eastern Europe over many decades, and having served as a weapon against the Soviet type of centrally planned economic order during the growth of the reform movement, were neither adopted nor attempted to be put into practice after the 1989 revolutions.

Neo-liberalism, favouring privatisation, deregulation and a free market with less government intervention, happened to be the dominant economic current in the capitalist world in the 1980s, following the failure of Keynesianism. Economic advisers from the World Bank (IBRD), IMF and elsewhere in the Western world, strongly recommended such neo-liberal policies to the new governments in Eastern Europe. It was argued that such policies were the only appropriate path to restoring economic efficiency, and to securing access to Western aid and loans.

Since the Eastern European countries hoped considerably to increase their economic relations with the West through economic aid and loans, the dominant neo-liberalism in the West, expressed through the suggestions of the economic advisers, materially influenced (if they did not over-rule) the economic policies of the new governments.

Thus, within a short period of time the dominant political economy of Eastern Europe seemed to have undertaken a dramatic double jump from socialist central planning to democratic market socialism to neo-liberal capitalist marketisation. The newly adopted neo-liberalism was turned into a State ideology, required to be taught at the universities by almost the same bureaucratic system as under the old regime. Conscientious Marxist economists, who led and supported the democratisation movements, could not swim with the tide and, once again, found themselves in the position of dissidents under the new regimes.

Failures and the Signs of Revival of Socialism

Both the tempo and the consequences of liberalisation in the direction of a full market economy were complex and quite different for each Eastern European country. Systemic change freeing prices and foreign trade in order to create a market economy in these countries did not bring about the expected results in terms of economic efficiency and growth. Rather, change generally fuelled inflation, depressed industrial activity (partly due to increased imports), created mass unemployment, and made the economic life of the people full of inequalities. Differences in political and economic conditions among Eastern European countries were also considerably widened.

East Germany

Of all the countries of the Eastern bloc East Germany seemed to be in the most favourable situation since she was the most industrialised country in Eastern Europe, and was united to West Germany at an exchange rate of one to one with the Deutchemark as well as a guaranteed welfare safety net. However, the number of workers in employment in East Germany decreased rapidly from 9.2 million in September 1989 to 7.5 million in July 1991, raising the number of the unemployed to over 1 million (an unemployment rate of 13.5 percent), according to official data.[8] By 1992 the government of the united Germany had spent 180 billion Deutchemarks to support the area of old East Germany, creating a huge budget deficit, roughly 6 percent of GNP. Under this heavy burden, the German economy could no more serve as the powerful locomotive of the EU, and began to record negative growth rates from the beginning of 1993. Disillusionment with reunification spread and fed social unrest, including chauvinistic attacks on refugees and migrant workers from other Eastern European countries. The Social Democratic Party now has an opportunity to increase support for its policies of more socially controlled economic stability, and opposition to chauvinism and neo-liberalism.

Poland

Poland opted for the shock therapy type of radical market reform in October 1989, thus preceding Gaidar's Russian reform of 1992. Prices and trading in goods and services were widely freed, and private economic activities were broadly allowed, including foreign trade. However, the expectation that economic recovery would follow after a brief shock proved unfounded, and the Polish economy fell further into deep crisis. Inflation at an annual rate of 70 percent, induced wild speculation, confused productive activities, and much reduced real wages. Unemployment increased, industrial production fell, and GDP declined. The budget deficit and the foreign debt swelled, limiting the availability of aid and loans from the World Bank and the IMF.

Such disappointing economic confusion and crisis after shock therapy started to be called the Poland phenomenon, and already at the general election of 1991 started to give rise to political reactions of two kinds. First, the rate of abstention from voting was very high, reflecting people's disillusionment with reform. Abstention was even more remarkable since it followed hard on the heels of systemic change in the direction of democracy caused by a mass popular movement. Secondly, in the overwhelming majority of electoral areas, one or the other of the two parties born out of the process of renewal of the Polish United Workers' Party (PUWP, corresponding to the Communist Party in the Soviet Union), came first. Even if the support gained was usually little more than 10 percent, as there were dozens of competing small parties, the election result was a clear sign of revived and renewed socialism.

The coalition government, which did not yet include these two socialist parties, had to reconsider its shock therapy type of economic policies, and began to increase State control over the economy from the beginning of 1992. This policy change following the failure of the neo-liberal shock therapy allowed the Polish economy to stabilise after 1992, though still in severe depression.

In 1993, Polish GDP grew by 4 percent, but the rate of inflation still stood at 35 percent depressing real wages. The rate of unemployment remained very high at about 15 percent, and the disparities in the economic condition among people and geographical areas obviously increased. In the general election of October 1993, the two socialist parties together won an absolute majority in the House of Representatives, and formed a Left Alliance government. The new government intended to form 'a socialist market economy' through more moderate reform policies coupled with welfare and employment policies. Thus, the signs of revival of socialism based on a socialist market economy became clearer, expressed through the people's democratic choice.

Yugoslavia

Yugoslavia was another Eastern European country which adopted shock therapy after its systemic change. As in Poland, the economy was severely shaken and rapidly deteriorated. Economic crisis fuelled religious and ethnic conflicts, which had already considerably worsened under the decentralised economic order with workers' self-management, particularly after the death of former President Tito (1892–1980).

Of the six Republics of Yugoslavia, the relatively rich Slovenia and Croatia declared independence in June 1991, and had received international recognition by the spring of 1992. In Croatia, however, a civil war with the country's Serbs continues, and a third of the country is subject to the protection of a Peace Keeping Operation by the United Nations. Macedonia declared independence in September 1991, but it has not yet been internationally recognised. Bosnia–Herzegovina declared independence in March 1992, after which a civil war between Serbs, Muslims and Croats broke out. To complete the dissolution of Yugoslavia, Serbia and Montenegro united and formed New Yugoslavia. The EU and the USA have not recognised New Yugoslavia, and have imposed sanctions on it because Serbia has intervened in the Bosnian civil war. An Albanian independence movement and other ethnic conflicts are also present within New Yugoslavia.

These ethnic conflicts and civil wars certainly added to the confusion in economic life. What is clear is that neo-liberal shock therapy was neither successful nor appropriate for Yugoslavia, but, rather, induced the tragic politico–military turbulence and was unable to resolve the country's resultant socioeconomic crisis. It is arguable that military intervention by the United Nations will exacerbate military tension and violence in this area; some form of inter-regional co-operation must be recreated, transcending the anarchical market and hopefully in the traditional spirit of humanistic socialism. However, it has to be said that the omens are not yet auspicious.

Czechoslovakia

In Czechoslovakia, neo-liberal economic policies were introduced in a milder and more practical way compared to radical shock therapy. As a result, the country's economic crisis was milder. Still, real economic growth was negative in 1990, falling to -15.9 percent in 1991, and − 7 percent in 1992. Given these economic difficulties, the national differences between Czech and Slovaks began to increase.

The Czech Republic is more industrialised, tends to attract the bulk of investment from Western countries, and is consequently more receptive to neo-liberal marketisation policies. Slovakia is traditionally more agricultural, and has had closer economic relations with the Soviet Union through military production. Systemic change worked unfavourably for Slovakia, the economic situation rapidly worsening and the rate of unemployment rising. Neo-liberal policies of comprehensive marketisation seemed unsuitable to Slovakia.

As a result of these differences Slovakia plumped for independence after the Czechoslovak general election of June 1992, and the Czechs agreed. In January 1993, the Federation was dissolved by a 'velvet divorce' (after the Velvet Revolution). Whereas in the Czech Republic neo-liberal economic reforms have been pushed forward by prime minister Klaus, in Slovakia political powers in favour of democratic socialism, or social democracy, have played an important role. Two different lines of economic reform in Eastern Europe were thus followed by the Czech Republic and Slovakia, corresponding to their characteristic economic conditions.

As part of the neo-liberal marketisation policies in Czechoslovakia, a large-scale privatisation of State enterprises started in 1992 through the equitable distribution of privatisation vouchers to the tune of 1000 points per person. The vouchers can only be used to purchase shares of the State enterprises which will be turned into joint-stock companies. It was expected that this device would help people's capitalism materialise, with the largest proportion of share holders in the world. Within a short period of time, however, as many as 437 investment trusts emerged and collected two thirds of the vouchers. They were helped by utterly speculative promises of the type 'let us increase the value of your voucher by ten times in a year'. It is possible that such speculative operations could eventually cause disillusionment with reform, induce bankruptcies, and add to the instability of an already fragile and depressed economy. The pace of privatisation of State enterprises has also been much delayed. Thus, even in the Czech Republic, the success of the drive toward capitalist marketisation, whether in the form of people's capitalism or not, is neither certain nor predictable.

Hungary

Hungary could have been one of the least damaged economies after the Eastern European systemic change. Already before the change the country had the highest degree of privatisation among Eastern European countries, comparable only to that of Poland. Hungary did not adopt shock therapy policies, but took more measured steps toward transformation, although still under the influence of neo-liberalism. The country was also fortunate in avoiding open national and ethnic conflicts.

Nevertheless, as the neo-liberal marketisation policies were implemented, enterprises were forced to 'rationalise', and were either privatised or given more managerial autonomy. Imports were extensively liberalised, and prices were freed. As a result, the Hungarian economy received a serious shock. Industrial activity declined because of competition with cheaper imported commodities and disturbingly rapid inflation. Unemployment rose from 80,000 at the beginning of 1991 to 660,000 (12 percent) in 1992. As farmland was privatised, agricultural production, which had been relatively successful under collective farming during the previous 30 years, fell precipitously in 1992–3. In the three years to 1993, Hungarian national product dropped by 19 percent, and industrial production fell by 36 percent. Thus, the Hungarian economy also found itself in a serious crisis.

With regard to the privatisation programme, the initial issue was whether State firms should be returned to the original owners. After a long debate it was decided that State property should not returned, with the exception of limited property in land. The government then constructed a neo-liberal programme aiming at the privatisation of 2200 State firms possessing 30–35 percent of the total State assets within three years. By April 1993, only 760 companies, or one third of the number planned, had been sold to private individuals. The majority of buyers were foreigners, and the total revenue from the sale was between one third and one fourth of the acknowledged book value.[9] Given the depressed economic conditions, it was not easy to sell State firms, especially to Hungarian people. Thus the privatisation programme failed to achieve its initial goal, and turned out to be unrealistic even in Hungary.

After three years of neo-liberal marketisation and privatisation policies, the depressed economy and mass unemployment led to the disillusionment of the Hungarian people. The rate of inflation in 1993 still stood at about 20 percent, and the rate of unemployment stood at 12 percent. The second general election following systemic change took place in May 1994, and it clearly was a confidence vote on neo-liberal economic policies. The result was a collapse of the former coalition government parties and a resurgence of the Hungarian Socialist Party. The latter is the successor to the Communist Party and had campaigned for democratic socialism with welfare and employment policies. From being the fourth party in terms of electoral support prior to the election, it now stands as the most popular party in Hungary, with the absolute majority of seats in the parliament. After Poland, here is also a clear sign of the revival of contemporary socialism. People rejected the neo-liberal radical reforms aiming at rapid and full marketisation, and opted for milder and more egalitarian democratic socialist reforms.

The Failure of Neo-liberalism and the Turn to New Socialism

It is clear by now that neo-liberal economic policies, whether of the shock therapy type or not, have failed to solve the economic difficulties of Eastern European countries, and actually exacerbated the economic crisis by adding new features, such as vicious inflation, mass unemployment, and trade and budget deficits. The introduction of a market economy turned out to necessitate many preconditions which would take a long time to develop, such as changes in social institutions, property rights, and the education and training of professionals. The transition from a centrally planned economy to a capitalist market economy is almost comparable to the transition from feudalism to capitalism, completed in England through the process of primitive accumulation lasting more than three centuries. Although a late-comer to capitalism, such as Japan, could considerably reduce its length, the transition still involved tremendous social change, lasting some generations and had to be ruthlessly promoted by a strong centralised political power.

The application of abstract neo-liberal economic theories to Eastern European ignored the difficulties in creating the social preconditions for a full market economy. As a result, neo-liberal policies proved inappropriate to the existing socioeconomic conditions in these countries. In a typical pattern, free foreign trade tended to depress industrial activities, and a free market in currency led to falling exchange rates against Western currencies, leading to higher import prices and accelerating inflation. The elastic expansion of currency and credit in order to meet the transactions needs of the free market also promoted inflation, and so reduced real wages.

Even in Poland and Hungary, where privatisation had been most advanced, at the time systemic change took place the proportion of private enterprises in total GDP was only about 15 percent. The overwhelming presence of State enterprises was hard to change, and quite obstructive to the workings of a competitive market economy. State enterprises were truly monopolistic in their fields of activity, and could employ a pricing policy of mark-up over rising costs, thus spreading inflation and maladjustment throughout the economy. Neo-liberal economic policies were not match for these conditions.

The governments elected in most Eastern European countries after the 1989 revolutions were relatively weak, as they were often based on coalitions of relatively small parties. Since they arose out of popular democratic movements in opposition to strong Communist governments, they were apt to dislike heavy-handed political behaviour. Neo-liberalism suited them, as it promised to deal with economic problems through the workings of the free market and away from politics. However, forming the preconditions of a fully competitive capitalist market economy actually requires the presence of a strong and stable political power, as seen during the process of primitive accumulation. For instance, in order to transform State enterprises into private companies, opposition by State bureaucrats with vested interests, and by the people incensed due to the uneven redistribution of State assets, has to be dealt with by a strong political leadership. Absence of such a strong political leadership is one of the fundamental problems in the actual process of marketisation in Eastern Europe.

Therefore, it is not surprising to witness widespread disillusionment with neo-liberalism in Eastern Europe, as well as some clear signs of recovery of democratic socialism. Indeed, the Polish and Hungarian people's preference for reformed socialist parties advocating a socialist market economy with welfare and employment policies suits the needs of economic reform given the actual conditions of these societies. This turn of events can be expected to influence other Eastern European countries facing similar conditions. The most important question now is whether the turn to a new type of socialism, distinct from the old Soviet type, can be viable and successful. It is a fascinating question whether Marxist thought and theories can be employed afresh in this new situation, and whether effective international co-operation can be rebuilt among the reviving socialist powers of Eastern Europe, CIS and China, all similarly aiming towards a socialist market economy.

ECONOMIC REFORMS IN CHINA

Successful Reforms with High Economic Growth

In comparison with the economic reforms in the Soviet Union and Eastern Europe, reforms in China have been quite successful in terms of economic growth. In 1978 the Chinese Communist Party decided to deal with the economic turmoil of the Cultural Revolution and to modernise the Chinese economy. Thus, economic reforms in China began seven years earlier than Perestroika. The reforms were initiated from above, as for Perestroika, and unlike the changes wrought by the Eastern European reform movements. Furthermore, while Perestroika and the Eastern European revolutions stressed the democratisation of the political system, Chinese systemic change from the very beginning strongly emphasised economic reforms. The task of democratisation of the political and social system has been postponed, and strong leadership by the Chinese Communist Party has been maintained.

The Chinese systemic change pioneered the road to privatisation and marketisation away from the centrally planned economy, but its steps were gradual, accompanied by considerable State control as, for instance, on foreign trade and foreign exchange. Change in China was far from the shock therapy type of radical and hasty marketisation. At the start of the reforms it was planned to double the Chinese real national income in each of the two decades to the end of the century (the double doubling programme). This was to be achieved through the four modernisations: agriculture, industry, defence, science and technology. A double doubling of real national income requires real annual economic growth of the order of 7.2 percent and this was generally seen as too ambitious at the time. However, during the first decade the Chinese economy actually grew at an average annual rate of 9.9 percent. After two years of confusion in 1989–90, marked by a rate of growth of 4 percent level, the Chinese economy returned to an even higher growth pattern of more than 10 percent annual growth.

The fact that the huge Chinese economy with more than 1 billion people, could grow so rapidly and for so long, in a way reminiscent of the Japanese historic High Growth Period of 1951–1973, is worthy of close attention. Below we will consider the main features of the Chinese economic reforms which made possible such remarkable growth in the midst of a world-wide depression.

Reforms in Agriculture

Chinese economic reforms began with systemic change in agriculture. People's communes, a mode of farming more thoroughly collective in production and consumption than even the Soviet collective farms, started to be dissolved after 1979. Instead, peasant family production was generally introduced through entrusting the management of a portion of farmland to a family for a term of 15 years. Each family could then decide what crops to plant and what kind of livestock to raise. State ownership of land has remained, and each family's farm land is supposed to be returned to the State at the end of the term, but it is generally expected that the plot would be rented out again to the same family as long as it had been well cultivated.

Accompanying this transformation was a careful revision of the relative prices of agricultural products in terms favourable to the peasants. The motivation and the incentive to improve agricultural production were, as a result, restored and strengthened. Chinese agricultural production, which had been so depressed during the Cultural Revolution as to necessitate the import of foodstuffs, recovered some vitality, and actually grew at the annual rate of 8.1 percent during the 1980s.

Since about 800 million Chinese people (out of a total of a little over 1 billion at the beginning of the 1980s) still live in agricultural villages, this revival and strong growth of agricultural production were very significant for the economic growth of the whole of China. An increased agricultural surplus under a contract production system facilitated the expansion of the market economy, both within the rural areas and between rural agricultural and urban industrial areas. This development is reminiscent of Adam Smith's formulation regarding the natural course of progress for opulence. According to Smith,

> As subsistence is, in the nature of things, prior to convenience and luxury, so the industry which produces the former, must necessarily be prior to that which ministers to the latter. The cultivation and improvement of the country, therefore, which affords subsistence,

must, necessarily, be prior to the increase of town, which furnishes only the means of conveniences and luxury. It is the surplus produce of the country only, or what is over and above the maintenance of the cultivators, that constitutes the subsistence of town, which can therefore increase, only with the increase of this surplus produce.[10]

Thus, Smith assumed that the growth of rural agricultural production would enable the expansion of urban industrial production, and the growth of the market economy, on the grounds of this major social division of labour.

Small Enterprises in Villages

In addition to reforms in agriculture, the Chinese government promoted the creation of small private, or collective, enterprises in manufacturing, trade, transport, and other industries in rural villages. It is estimated that more than 18 million of such rural enterprises had been created by the end of the 1980s. More than 95 million jobs were generated absorbing the surplus labour-force in peasant families.

While increased agricultural income facilitated the creation of small enterprises in the rural areas, working in those enterprises added to the pecuniary income of peasant families. An important source of high economic growth in China has obviously been the vitality of small enterprises in the rural villages. By gaining an income from both agriculture and working in the non-agricultural small enterprises, a great many peasant families became able to purchase such consumer durables as refrigerators, washing machines, and colour TVs. At the same time, rural enterprises often produce parts of these consumer durables, or offer repair services. It is thus evident that the activation of a Chinese market economy has taken place from below in the rural villages, as well as in the trading between villages and cities.

The Chinese government has campaigned to promote small enterprises in rural areas with such slogans as 'leaving from agriculture, but not from villages' and 'entering into factories, but not into cities'. Thus the government intends to attract manufacturing into the rural villages. This intention arose, on the one hand, from the fear of a likely huge internal migration of the surplus rural working population if manufacturing continued to develop only in the cities. On the other hand, the policy has an affinity with the traditional socialist ideal of unifying agriculture and manufacturing after their unfortunate separation in the process of capitalist development. The formation of so many small enterprises in villages realises this ideal in a practical way.

Management by Contract

The system of management by contract spread from the farming areas to State enterprises in the cities. In the 1980s, managerial authority and responsibility in the State enterprises were shifted into the hands of factory managers through a system of contracts. A factory manager is allowed to renew employment contracts with workers every two years, and can dismiss idle workers according to his or her judgement.

During a visit to China by the author in 1986, it transpired that the standard way of dividing the surplus gained by such contract management of a factory was: 55 percent of the total was paid to the State, and of the remaining 45 percent, 40 percent was used to expand production, 20 percent paid bonuses on top of normal wages, 20 percent aimed at workers' welfare, and 20 percent was directed to research and development. Chinese State enterprises offer cheap accommodation to workers and pay pensions to retired workers as a part of their welfare expenditure.

As more and more prices were freed and trade in goods and services was liberalised, the system of management by contract became attractive to both managers and workers, and strengthened their motivation to work. By the beginning of 1993, the proportion of manufactured products still subject to planned prices fell to about 15 percent of the total.

However, in some key industries producing energy and construction materials, such as coal, oil, steel, and cement, norms must still be fulfilled at officially fixed (relatively low) prices. As a result, the large State enterprises in these industries are often making deficits, and so they are criticised as inefficient. Their deficits are subsidised by the State through soft budget constraints in the manner we have already discussed for enterprises in a centrally planned economy. Such deficits are frequently due to the low fixed prices, and so the State rather than the enterprise is really responsible for the existence of a deficit. At the same time the low and fixed prices of energy and construction materials facilitate both the setting up of small enterprises in rural villages, and the activities of contract management in various urban industries. In the case of contemporary China these prices thus work as a supporting foundation for the growth of a market economy.

Rivalry Among Local Economies

As well as gradually expanding the role of autonomous management by contract, raising the weight of the market economy, systemic change in China has also brought about a considerable decentralisation of the political and economic order.[11] A large part of decision-making, particularly on economic matters, such as the licensing of business, has been transferred from the central government to local governments in the prefectures or provinces. The State budget as a proportion of Gross National Income correspondingly fell from 31.9 percent in 1979 to 19 percent in 1988.

As a result, local governments have began to rival each other and have striven to increase the prosperity of their own particular administrative areas. Work on infrastructure and investment in new factories, are planned and undertaken in competition with each other, often outside the control of the centre, or of a unified plan. Colour TV assembly plants, for example, have proliferated as a result of rivalry among local administrative areas, and now more than 50 brands exist. Many Chinese economists think of this as an inefficient outcome, and the decentralised local economies are often compared to the old semi-independent feudal economic areas of China.

However, in the contemporary Chinese economy, administrative rivalry among local governments serves as to promote, rather than obstruct, growth and vitality. Such rivalry generates an additional motive to compete which is outside the economic order of the market, though it also serves to activate the market economy.

Turmoil and the Tienanmen Incident

After a decade of high economic growth, the Chinese economy became overheated and economic turmoil emerged. As a result of the competitive expansion of investment by local administrative areas and enterprises, the supply of construction and raw materials became relatively scarce. Prices of such goods began to rise rapidly in 1988. Excessive investment plans also induced the emergence of a budget deficit, and growth in the volume of currency. These conditions worked together to generate rapid inflation. Speculative trading and stockpiling spread as prices rose, and, in turn, exacerbated the relative shortage of goods in the market. Not a few bureaucrats took advantage of their official position illegally to profit by channelling raw material trade into unofficial routes.

Thus, in 1988–9 the Chinese economy was faced with inflation of more than 10 percent annually, and at the same time the whole economy went into turmoil. Many observers tended to think at that time that the Chinese economy was facing deadlock and crisis in the manner of the Soviet and the Eastern European economies.

The Tienanmen incident of June 1989 strengthened this impression. The student movement for democratisation opposed the corruption of Communist Party cadres and bureaucrats, particularly activities such as illegal trade in goods for private benefit, or placing one's own children in high positions of State. Indeed, this movement seemed similar to Perestroika and the Eastern European democratisation movement in its demand for political democratisation. When Gorbachev visited Beijing in May 1989 he was very popular among students. The Chinese Communist Party leaders regarded the movement as a threat to the leadership of their party. The continuing mass meeting and demonstrations at Beijing's Tienanmen square became the focal point of protest. After repeated but fruitless orders to disperse, the Chinese government violently suppressed the protest by mobilising the People's Liberation Army to shoot at the students. There is no doubt that a milder and more democratic way of resolving the problem should have been found; the violent and bloody suppression of the moment was condemned across the world. At the same time, however, there is room to suspect that the student movement's demands for democratisation similar to Perestroika and to the Eastern European reform movements did not really have broad social foundations in China, and it could have possibly lead to a catastrophe similar to that which followed Perestroika.

It has to be noted that the Chinese Communist government could still retain the support of the People's Liberation Army. This means that the government could rely on the support of large numbers of the working people in the rural and urban areas, among whose families the soldiers are recruited. In point of fact, the majority of working people remained rather passive and calm during the Tienanmen incident. Unlike the Eastern European democratisation movements, the student movement in China could not involve the mass of workers and peasants in the drive for democratisation. In my view this was mainly because strong economic growth gave to the broad masses of the Chinese people an optimistic perspective for the future, as well as maintaining the credibility of the existing government. Besides, the proportion of the university students and intelligentsia who support the democratisation movement is still relatively small in China. The basic difference between the Soviet/Eastern European and the Chinese systemic change can be seen in precisely these points.

Most advanced capitalist countries protested and imposed economic sanctions on the Chinese government after the Tienanmen incident. As a result, economic aid, loans, and investment from the advanced capitalist countries were discontinued. This compounded the difficulties which the overheating and turmoil had created for the Chinese economy, and brought the open-door economic policy to a standstill for a period.

Readjustment and Return to the Double Doubling Plan

The strong political authority and leadership of the Chinese Communist government permitted the suppression of the student movement, and promoted the cooling down of the overheated economy. Speculative trading for private profit, especially illegal trading in goods by bureaucrats, was severely condemned and punished. Economic discipline at various levels was tightened and restored. These readjustment policies were effective in reducing inflation and in restoring order to prices once again.

The slowdown of growth because of economic overheating also contributed to dampening excessive aggregate demand and inflation. In this regard, the readjustment of the Chinese economy in this period contained a somewhat similar dialectical logic to the restoration of economic order through a crisis in the normal course of the capitalist business cycle. Ironically, the cessation of investment, aid and loans from abroad after the Tien An Men Incident also helped to dampen and readjust the Chinese economy. The readjustment process was remarkably successful. Rapid inflation was overcome within two years, the annual rate falling to below 3 percent in 1990. It is even more remarkable that the Chinese economy maintained a real annual growth rate above 4 percent even in 1989–90, i.e. the very years of turmoil and readjustment.

Given the successful readjustment, the National Council of People's Commissioners declared in March 1991 that China would return to the double doubling plan, and so achieve a real GNP four times as high as that of the late 1970s by the end of this century. In order to achieve this, the Chinese economy needs to grow in real terms at about 6 percent annually throughout the 1990s, since the annual growth rate in the 1980s had greatly exceeded the planned rate of 7.2 percent. The new plan seems quite feasible in view of the growth rate actually observed even during 1988–90.

The plan also looks feasible given the present conditions favourable to economic growth in China. These include the large size of the latent surplus population in agriculture which can be mobilised for urban and rural industrialisation. Furthermore, China still has a flexible supply of natural resources such as coal, iron ore, and petroleum. For instance, although the Da Quin oil field is nearly peaking out, the recently discovered large-scale oil field in the Shinkian Uighur area will probably mitigate the energy constraint on the growing Chinese economy for a considerable period of time. Compared to the labour and natural resource supply problems of the Soviet economy in its last phase of stagnation, the Chinese economy continues to enjoy much more favourable conditions for industrialisation.

Availability of industrial technologies and a latent demand for consumer durables, which are being imported from the developed countries, is also immense. This is reminiscent of the Japanese economy during the High Growth Period in the 1950s and 1960s. The open-door modernisation policies have created fresh incentives to use new technologies and new models of consumer goods. The general attempt to raise the level of education further enables the Chinese people to use such new technologies, and to enjoy consumer goods from abroad. The incentive to work for a better life may indeed be one of the strongest factors explaining Chinese economic vitality. Attracted by the expanding Chinese market and the potential for exports, foreign investment from advanced capitalist countries has been resumed and is now increasing, thus tending to facilitate Chinese economic growth.

The Socialist Market Economy

Once the turmoil was overcome the Chinese economy again began to grow faster than the rates targeted in the double doubling plan. In 1992–3 the economy grew at an annual rate above 10 percent in real terms. The market economy continues to thrive, especially in South China and the coastal cities. Spurred on by the revitalisation of economic activity, the National Council of People's Commissioners decided in March 1993 to revise the Constitutional Law, and expressly stipulated that China is constructing a socialist market economy. At the same time, the planned target growth rate was raised from 6 percent to 8–9 percent in order to complete the double doubling plan sooner, i.e. within the next five years.

In the course of economic reforms after 1978 the Chinese government had avoided defining the country's economic transformation as the creation of a market economy since the latter was regarded as capitalistic. Indeed, Chinese systemic change was supposed to be based on four basic principles; (1) the road to socialism, (2) the people's democratic dictatorship, (3) the leadership of the Communist Party, and (4) Marxism–Leninism and the thought of Mao. It used to be argued that the commodity economy would be a bird kept within the cage of these four principles. The official definition of China's economic order was the stage of the socialist commodity economy. However, since marketisation proceeded successfully and had reduced the proportion of manufactured goods with planned prices to only 15 percent by 1993, the Chinese government proposed to take a step forward and move to a socialist market economy.

What this implies is that, on the one hand, the entire system of a market economy and not only partial commodity exchanges, should be more widely and openly turned into the driving force of Chinese economic growth. On the other hand, however, and unlike the unlimited conception of marketisation to be found in the Eastern European and Russian neo-liberal radical economic reforms, marketisation should not proceed to fully developed capitalism. The road to socialism should be firmly adhered to. Thus, the concept of a socialist market economy was newly put forward. The socialist content of this conception is provided by (1) the public ownership of land and the major means of production, such as those employed by State and other public enterprises, (2) the egalitarian distribution of income to maintain an egalitarian economic life as far as possible, and (3) the leadership of the Communist Party.

Although the leadership of the Communist Party has played a valuable role, there remains the problem of whether the Chinese Communist Party (CCP) can continue to monopolise political power, given the growth of a more and more powerful private sector. It is still hard to offer a definite answer to this question. If it is impossible to do so, the CCP may relinquish power voluntarily, form a coalition government, or be overthrown. Further, the CCP may leave office only to return to it with popular support after free elections, as we have seen in Poland and Hungary.

Market Economy and Socialism

The forms of market economy originate in the economic relations between societies, and are, therefore, theoretically independent of the specific social relations of production. Throughout this volume, this fundamental recognition, deriving from Marx, has been applied to the issues of socialism. The point of this was to demonstrate the feasibility of different models of socialist economic order, not confined to a fully planned economy, but comprising models employing the forms of a market economy in a different way. Although the concept of a socialist market economy seems to contradict classical Marxist theory, in which socialism was identified with a fully planned economy excluding the market, as in the Soviet Union, the basic argument of this volume demonstrated its theoretical feasibility. However, as we have also argued, unlike a pure capitalist market economy or a fully planned socialist economy, there cannot be a theoretical best solution regarding how to combine socialist planning with a market economy. Political and practical policy judgements regarding this combination, arrived at in the light of the historical and social conditions of each country, must necessarily play a fundamental role. Systemic change away from the centrally planned economy has demonstrated the importance of such political discretion in order to introduce a market economy.

In contrast to the tragic failure of abstract neo-classical theories of rapid marketisation in Eastern Europe and the Soviet Union, the Chinese economic reforms, more gradual, practical and based on the actually existing socio–political conditions, were much more successful. Western public opinion tends simply to condemn the lack of democracy in China, as shown by the violence of the Tien An Men incident. Here is, without a doubt, an important problem that has to be solved in the future. We should not forget, however, that strong leadership by the Communist Party has been one of the key factors behind the high economic growth of the period of marketisation in China. Management by contract both in agriculture and in public enterprises has increased inequality among peasant families, enterprises and regional areas, and would have caused much discontent and social unrest if it were not for the presence of strong political leadership. Strong government was also instrumental in dealing with turmoil, overheating of the market economy, and bureaucratic corruption in 1989–90.

Thus, ironically the transition to a market economy has been performed rather successfully under the strong authority of the Communist Party in China, whereas it failed and destroyed economic activity under the neo-liberal governments of Eastern Europe and Russia. A similarly successful transition seems to be underway in Vietnam in the 1990s. The strength of Communist Party leadership may be sustained by popular support so long as economic growth is maintained.

These developments suggest that systemic change in the direction of a market economy has a complex character. The process of marketisation requires various social and institutional changes to be brought about by a strong non-market political authority. Economic inequality which inevitably arises as a result of marketisation can precipitate severe social conflicts and the struggle for the formation of different classes, as in capitalism's primitive accumulation phase. This can be socially accepted as a condition of successful change only under a stable political order. The political and social order for a successful transformation can be socialist or communist since the market can be, both theoretically and practically, articulated with very different social relations of production, including socialist collective ownership of the means of production, public enterprises, private or capitalist enterprises, or a mixture of these.

There is, certainly, a danger that the socialist foundations under the Communist government would be eroded through the very process of successful economic growth with increasing marketisation. For instance, the proportion of State enterprises in the total output of manufacturing in China fell from 78 percent in 1978 to 55 percent in 1993. Many of these State enterprises are running deficits. Increased economic inequality is inconsistent with socialist egalitarian principles, and so it could feed popular discontent with the government. Economic growth tends to be unstable and to result recurrently in overheating and rapid inflation through the increased influence of the market economy. With a liberalised market economy and an open-door policy, international cultural and political pressure against the socialist political and social order can possibly rise. Such pressure could also be intensified, directly or indirectly, by the influence of advanced capitalist countries.

There is no simple solution to the problem of a stable and consistent balance between promoting the growth of the market economy and achieving socialism. The balance must be empirically found by the Chinese leaders and people as they experiment with the socialist market economy. Since we live in a completely marketised capitalist economy, and have experienced and understood its fundamental contradictions, instability, and oppression of working people, we cannot but be interested in how the principles of socialism, rather than capitalism, are carried through in Chinese society. In this regard, the Chinese experiment of the socialist market economy is worth careful observation, freed from prejudiced one-sided condemnations of its socialist aspects, particularly in view of the failure of shock therapy in Eastern Europe and CIS, including the Russian Federation.

China as a socialist power, with her successful gradual economic reforms, has definitely increased its importance for the smaller socialist countries, as well as for liberation movements across the world. Its official shift toward the socialist market economy preceded, and probably contributed to, the recovery of democratic socialist parties with similar policies in Poland and Hungary. Although the Chinese economic reforms need still to be studied and theorised much more thoroughly, even from the point of view of Marxism, their actual success in economic growth already presents impressive historical lessons. These lessons have to be learnt in order to stabilise the economic crisis, and to bring about effective economic reforms in the Eastern European and CIS economies in a more gradual and socialist way, with a democratic constitution.

Concluding Remarks

What does political economy for socialism mean for those of us who live in capitalist countries? During the cold war era, socialism used to signify not only the political movement and the set of ideas which envisaged a new social order belonging to working people, but also a concrete model of the planned economy to be found in the actually existing socialist countries. It was generally believed that the Soviet socio-economic order represented an advanced model of scientific socialism, or Marxism in practice, as its leaders asserted. Scientific socialism was believed to be a workers' state without social oppression and discrimination of working people, and immune from the economic crises and stagnations which ravage economic life in capitalism.

Disillusionment was immense when the social problems and the economic impasse of actually existing socialism became increasingly revealed in the 1970s and 1980s. The East European revolutions and the dissolution of the Soviet Union increased this disillusionment and sense of shock among people. The subsequent systemic change in the direction of neo-liberal marketisation, and the Chinese reforms in the direction of a market economy, were also seen by many as definitive evidence of the end of socialism and the victory of the capitalist market economy.

The failure of the centrally planned economies generally discredited socialist ideas and movements in the capitalist countries. Since much of the socialist tradition in the capitalist countries was already very critical of the Soviet type of society, and independent of Soviet and Chinese Marxism, this development was partly unjustified and unexpected. However, the general feeling of disillusionment with socialism among people actually added extra pressure on militant socialists in workers' and citizens' movements, on top of that generated by capitalist restructuring and neo-liberal privatisation policies in the course of the economic depression which started in 1973.

The change toward a market economy in Eastern Europe, the Soviet Union and China inevitably led to a serious crisis of Marxism, as the latter lost its actually existing model of an alternative social order. Marxism thus became less attractive to the mass of workers and citizens of the capitalist counties, at least for the time being. As a result, political parties which have traditionally represented trade unions and workers movements, such as the British Labour Party and the Japanese

Socialist Party, have shed some of their left-wing credentials and moved toward the centre accepting the confines of the existing social order. Nonetheless, this shift has failed to increase the popularity of these parties, indeed often reducing it further since their identity became not to be easily distinguished from that of other liberal parties.

However, the apparent victory of neo-liberalism and the capitalist market economy over socialism did not last for long. After a short period of euphoria, marked by the swelling of economic bubbles in the West and the failure of the Soviet type of socialism in the East, the severe recession after 1991 has once again struck the basic keynote of depression in the capitalist world after 1973. It was once again shown that, the free market is far from a natural and harmonious economic order, but fundamentally unstable and crisis-ridden. According to the official statistics of the OECD there are now more than 35 million unemployed people in the advanced capitalist countries. According to a report by ILO in 1994, the global number of unemployed or underemployed people unable to sustain the minimum standard of living reached 820 million, which is 30 percent of the total working population, the worst outcome since the Great Depression of the 1930s. This is indeed some achievement by the victorious capitalist market economy.

Even workers fortunate enough to have jobs are generally far from enjoying a democratic order at the workplace, since democracy stops at the factory gate today as much as in Marx's time. The majority of workers have no guarantee of stable economic life and live under the incessant threat of unemployment, illness, the loss or reduction of income after retirement, and the burden of debt to buy a car and a small flat for their family. The capitalist market economy has no answer for these unstable and poor economic conditions of life for the majority of workers, while at the same time creating a very uneven distribution of income and wealth. This is true even of the most advanced capitalist countries, including Japan.

Moreover, the capitalist market economy cannot even try to tackle systematically the destruction of the ecological conditions of life. The deleterious effects of the gradual accumulation of carbon dioxide in the atmosphere, acid rain, the depopulation of rural areas as well as the overcrowding of the urban areas, and decreasing mineral resources such as oil, are clearly impossible for capitalism to deal with, motivated as it is by private profit.

Thus, in our *fin de siècle* age of the presumed victory of capitalism over socialism, capitalism has also revealed its fundamental limitations and weaknesses as a socio-economic order. Our age does indeed seem an age of chaos. Are we to resign ourselves to cynical and nihilistic disillusionment with both socialism and capitalism? Should we abstain from trying to strive for a better world with more democracy and sustainable economic growth?

Modern socialism, as we have seen, was borne and developed out of the critique of the existing capitalist social order. Socialism, as the priciple of hope for a better world, will not die away as long as the capitalist market economy continues to maltreat working people and nature. Social movements such as trade unions, consumer and worker co-operatives, citizens' associations and groups dealing with social and political issues, all attempt to resist the deleterious effects of capitalism, contain the potential for a more systematic critique of capitalism, and carry the promise of socialism. Therefore, for socialist political economy to be useful to such social movements, it should continuously endeavour to improve the scientific understanding of the workings and the limitations of the capitalist economy, starting from the very basic level of theory and leading to the concrete level of empirical research of contemporary reality.

At the same time, political economy for socialism in our age should strive to reconsider and condense the entire stream of ideas, theories, and historical reality of socialism, in order to restore the fundamental vitality of socialism for the new century. This volume is devoted to this task and has attempted to show that socialism is a viable idea for the future once it has been freed from the old Soviet interpretation. Marx's theories of political economy are useful not only as basic principles for understanding capitalism, but also as basic theories for understanding socialism in a much more flexible way than used to be the case. Various models of socialism, combining plan and market, or with a variety of property rights in the means of production, as well as organisational forms of enterprises, are theoretically feasible. This has been the mainstay of our interpretation of Marx's theories, at least as far as the medium term of historically different societies is concerned. Although Marx's own image of communism was of an associational society without a market and treating social labour time in a simple and transparent way, his basic theories of the forms of the market economy and capitalism can be more flexibly employed to deliver various models of socialism. In this regard, the Chinese experiment of the socialist market economy, as well as the policy re-orientation of Poland and Hungary in the same direction, does not necessarily contradict Marx's theories.

From this view of Marxist political economy for socialism, the conditions of growth as well as the failure of the Soviet type of socialism can be more properly understood in all their significance and limitations. The unfortunate splits within the socialist movement in many capitalist countries often originated in their different positions with respect to the Soviet Union and China. Given the deep crisis of socialism, this type of division as well as the nihilistic neglect of the ideas and theories of socialism, must be overcome by a proper and scientific reconsideration of the Soviet type of centrally planned economy. Our interpretation of political economy for socialism would enable the flexible co-operation of socialists in the capitalist countries, despite differences as regards the best economic order for the long future, since it offers a broad rage of democratic choices for people in the medium term. Unlike Soviet 'orthodoxy', we need not any more define an exclusive 'correct' model, nor a single road to socialism for the foreseeable future.

With flexible theoretical models of a socialist economic order, Marxists would also be able more easily to co-operate, not only among themselves, but also with social democrats, radical democrats, or left-wing Keynesians on certain political and economic issues. Disagreements regarding the best social order for the future would become less obstructive as far as co-operation on very contemporary urgent issues is concerned. However, a theoretical difference would remain between social democrats, who limit their demands mainly to redistributive taxation, and socialists, who hope for a radical change of property rights in the means of production. Thus, political economy for socialism must restrengthen the socialist arguments in a broad sense. If the current confused yearnings for a better world are not to be taken advantage of by reactionary and conservative political trends, and so should not fail to break out of the capitalist social order, political economy for socialism must provide a workable frame of reference for understanding the past and the future of socialism, as well as of capitalism.

This volume intended to contribute to the work of revitalising the political economy for socialism, hoping that it can, even a little, indicate a brighter and more hopeful perspective for social life in the midst of our chaotic *fin de siècle*. How far this intention has been realised must now be left to the readers' assessment. The author looks forward to the readers' co-operative response for the future.

Notes

Throughout this volume, for books and papers published in Japanese, and some other languages, but not in English, I have translated the titles.

Introduction: Socialism at Stake

1. More concretely and in detail, see M. Itoh, *The World Economic Crisis and Japanese Capitalism* (London: Macmillan, 1990).
2. See K. Uno, *Principles of Political Economy*, trans T. Sekine (Brighton: Harvester Press, Atlantic Highlands: Humanities Press, 1980), and R. Albritton, *A Japanese Reconstruction of Marxist Theory* (London: Macmillan, 1986).
3. See Itoh, (1990), Chs 8, 9, 10.

1 Origins of Socialism

1. M. Beer, *History of British Socialism* (1940; Nottingham: Russel Press, 1984).
2. K. Marx and F. Engels, *The Manifesto of the Communist Party* (1848, *Marx–Engels Collected Works*, 6; Moscow: Progress Publishers, 1976. Hereafter, reference to the *Collected Works* will be given in the form *MECW*).
3. K. Marx, *Capital*, vol. I, II, III (1867, 1885, 1894, trans B. Fowkes and D. Fernbach) (Harmondsworth: Penguin, 1976, 1978, 1981. Hereafter, references to *Capital* will include, volume and page of this Penguin edition).
4. F. Engels, *Socialism: Utopian and Scientific* (1892; *MECW*, 24).
5. E. Bernstein, *Die Voraussetzungen des Sozialismus und die Aufgaben der Sozialdemocratie* (Stuttgart: Dietz, 1899).
6. K. Kautsky, *Bernstein und das Sozialdemokratische Programm* (Stuttgart: Dietz, 1899).
7. For detail, see H. Bix, *Peasant Protest in Japan 1590–1884* (New Haven: Yale University Press, 1986).
8. S. Ando, *Complete Works of Shoeki Ando* vol. 1–21 plus 1, ed. the Association for Studying Shoeki Ando (Tokyo: Nousan-gyoson Bunka Kyokai, 1983–7, in Japanese).
9. T. More, *Utopia* (1516); Japanese version trans M. Hirai (Tokyo: Iwanami-shoten, 1957).
10. J. Locke, *Two Treatises on Civil Government* (1690; Cambridge: Cambridge University Press, 1967).
11. C.-H. de R. Saint-Simon, *Catéchisme Politique des Industriels* (1823–4); *Nouveau Christianisme* (1825), both in *Oeuvre de Saint-Simon et d'Enfantin* (Paris: Dentu, 1865–76).
12. F.M.C. Fourier, *Le Nouveau Monde Industriel et Sociétaire ou Invention*

du Procédé d'Industrie Attrayante et Naturelle Distribuée en Serie Passionées (1822), in Oeuvre Complètes de Ch. Fourier (Paris: La Librairie Sociétaire, 1845, t.6).
13. J.C.L. Simonde de Sismondi, *Nouveaux Principes d'Economie Politique* (Paris: Delaunay, 1819).

2 Modern Socialism

1. R. Owen, *A New View of Society* (1813–14), in *The Life of Robert Owen Written by Himself*, vol. I (New York: A.M. Kelly, 1976).
2. Marx criticised 'the shallow utopianism of the idea of "labour-money" in a society founded on the production of commodities', as labour cannot be directly social labour in such a society. Nevertheless, it is noteworthy that Marx distinguished between Owen's experiment with labour-money and the utopian idea of labour-money. He offered the following favourable comment on the former:

   > Owen's 'labour-money' . . . is no more money than a theatre ticket is. Owen presupposes directly socialised labour, a form of production diametrically opposed to the production of commodities. The certificate of labour is merely evidence of the part taken by the individual in the common labour, and his claim to a certain portion of the common product which has been set aside for consumption. But Owen never made the mistake of presupposing the production of commodities, while, at the same time, by juggling with money, trying to circumvent the necessary conditions of that form of production (*Capital*, I, pp. 188–9).

   Marx's assessment of Owen's view here is more relevant to Owen's experiments with labour-money in New Harmony than to the National Equitable Labour Exchange.
3. J.S. Mill, *Principles of Political Economy* (1848), ed. W.J. Ashley (London: Longmans, Green, 1921, pp. 199–200).
4. B. Shaw (ed), *Fabian Essays in Socialism* (London: Fabian Society and Allen, 1889).
5. A famous and brief summary of historical materialism is given in the Preface of K. Marx, *A Contribution to the Critique of Political Economy* (1859), trans S.W. Ryazanskaya (Moscow: Progress Publishers, 1970).
6. E. Bernstein, *Die Voraussetzungen des Sozialismus und die Aufgaben der Sozialdemocratie* (Stuttgart: Dietz, 1899).
7. For more in detail on K. Uno's methodology, see M. Itoh, *Value and Crisis* (London: Pluto Press, New York: Monthly Review Press, 1980, Ch. 1); *The Basic Theory of Capitalism* (London: Macmillan, Totowa, N.J.: Barnes & Noble, 1988, Ch. 3); R. Albritton, *A Japanese Reconstruction of Marxist Theory* (London: Macmillan, 1986); and T. Sekine, 'Uno-Riron: A Japanese Contribution to Marian Political Economy', *Journal of Economic Literature*, 13 (3) (September 1975).
8. K. Kautsky, *Bernstein und das Sozialdemokratische Programm* (Stuttgart: Dietz, 1899a).

9. K. Kautsky, *The Agrarian Question* (1899b), vol. 1–2, trans P. Burgess (London and Winchester, Mass.: Zwan Publications, 1988).
10. R. Luxemburg, *Sozialreform oder Revolution?* (1899) (Leipzig: Vulkan-Verlag, 1919).
11. E.g. in K. Kautsky, 'Der Imperialismus', *Neue Zeit*, 32 (2) (1914); 'Zwei Schriften zum Umlernen', *Neue Zeit*, 33 (2) (1915); 'Der Imperialistische Krieg', *Neue Zeit*, 35 (1) (1917).
12. V.I. Lenin, *Imperialism; the Highest Stage of Capitalism* (1917) (Peking: Foreign languages Press, 1965).
13. R. Luxemburg, *Die Russische Revolution* (1918) (Berlin: Gesellschaft und Erziehung, 1922).
14. A. Gramsci, *Selections from the Prison Notebooks of Antonio Gramsci*, ed. and trans Q. Hoare and G.N. Smith (London: Lawrence & Wishart, 1971).

3 Marx's Socialism

1. To emphasise the importance of the dialectic, Engels stated that

   the metaphysical mode of thought, justifiable and even necessary as it is in a number of domains whose extent varies according to the nature of the particular object of investigation, sooner or later reaches a limit, beyond which it becomes one-sided, restricted, abstract, lost in insoluble contradictions. In the contemplation of individual things, it forgets the connection between them; in the contemplation of their existence, it forgets the beginning and end of that existence; of their repose, it forgets their motion. It cannot see the wood for trees (Anti-Dühring, in *MECW*, 25, pp. 22–3).

   Citing these passages, P. Sweezy commented that 'I am distressed by the extent to which the metaphysical mode of thought, the nature and limitations of which Engels so clearly exposes, has invaded present-day Marxism' (*Four Lectures on Marxism*, New York: Monthly Review Press, 1981, p. 19). Indeed, metaphysical interpretations of Marx's thought and theories have caused various distortions and confusions in the arguments for and against Marxism. A secure way out of these problems can be found in the scientific study of the political economy of capitalism as well as of socialism.
2. This point was emphasised by K. Uno in his *Methodology of Political Economy* (Tokyo: The University of Tokyo Press, 1962, Part III, in Japanese).
3. K. Marx, *A Contribution to the Critique of Political Economy* (1859), trans. S.W. Ryazanskaya (Moscow: Progress Publishers, 1970, pp. 20–2).
4. K. Marx and F. Engels *The Manifesto of the Communist Party* (1848) (*MECW*, 6, 1976, p. 482). In the English edition of 1888 Engels noted 'That is, all written history. In 1847, the pre-history of society, the social organisation existing previous to recorded history, was all but unknown'.
5. There are two other attempts to apply the formula of historical materialism in order to show the inevitability of the end of capitalism. One of

them is based on Marx's law of the tendency of the rate of profit to fall (TRPF) due to the rising organic composition of capital. H. Grossmann, *Das Akkumulations- und Zusammenbruchsgezetz des Kapitalistischen Systems* (Leipzig: Hirschfeld, 1929) is a typical example of this line of argument. However, Marx's law of TRPF, unlike Ricardo's TRPF, can well contain a continuous increase in the absolute amount of surplus-value and of capital, even if at a reduced pace, and therefore it cannot by itself show the inevitability of a dead end for capitalist accumulation. Grossmann was mistaken in this. Another attempt can be found in the argument that the productive forces of our age are already out of the control of private capitalist firms. Thus, they threaten the continuing existence of human society because of the progressive destruction of the ecological environment and of human health. This argument is exemplified by the work of N. Okishio on this point, (N. Okishio and M. Itoh, *Economic Theories and Contemporary Capitalism*, Tokyo: Iwanami-shoten, 1987, Ch. IX, in Japanese), which also seriously examines the reasons for ending capitalism and transforming it into socialism. This, however, is not identical with the logical inevitability of the collapse of capitalism, nor with the transition to socialism. Using some forms of state policy, capitalism may continue to function by attempting to limit the dangers to human existence. Alternatively, it may fail to do this and finally destroy humanity. Anyway, in my view the point is that the subjective social factor, the growth of the power of working people to organise, is indispensable for the transformation of capitalism into socialism. This moment is not directly guaranteed within the realm of basic economic theories.
6. K. Marx, *Critique of the Gotha Programme* (written in 1875, *MECW*, 24, p. 95).
7. The first act by virtue of which the state really constitutes itself the representative of the whole of society – taking possession of the means of production in the name of society – that is, at the same time, its last independent act as a state. State interference in social relations becomes, in one domain after another, superfluous, and then dies out of itself; the government of persons is replaced by the administration of things, and by the conduct of the process of production. The state is not 'abolished'. It dies out (F. Engels, *Anti-Dühring*, 1878, in *MECW*, 25, p. 268).
8. A. Smith, *An Inquiry into the Nature and Causes of the Wealth of Nations*, vol. I. (1776), ed. E. Cannan (London; Methuen, 1922, p. 15).
9. The amount of labour embodied in the total joint product can be theoretically determined if the products are treated as a combined product. The ratio alloting the labour-substance in joint products can be treated as determined by the relative prices of these products in a market economy. In the case of a socialist economy without market pricing, these ratios can be determined so as to reduce the volume of unused products and to reduce the social demand for products in relative shortage. See more in detail M. Itoh, *The Basic Theory of Capitalism* (London: Macmillan, 1988, pp. 175–8).
10. As for the relation between the law of value and prices of production, see Itoh, (1988, Ch. 7, section 1).

11. Smith, (1776, vol. II, p. 267).
12. K. Marx and F. Engels, *The German Ideology* (written in 1845–6, in *MECW*, 5, p. 47).
13. For instance Lenin says that

    The whole society will have become a sigle office and a single factory, with equality of labour and pay. But this 'factory' discipline, which the proletariat will extend to the whole society, is by no means our ideal, or our ultimate goal (V.I. Lenin, *The State and Revolution*, 1918, in *Lenin Collected Works*, 25, Moscow: Progress Publishers, 1964, p. 474).

14. M. Hironishi raised this problem in his book *Mistranslation of 'Capital'* (Tokyo: Seiyu-sha, 1966, pp. 65–73, in Japanese).
15. K. Marx, *The Poverty of Philosophy* (1846–7, in *MECW* 6, p. 184).
16. See more in detail Itoh (1988, pp. 144–5).
17. See also Itoh (1988, pp. 240–3).
18. Marx assumed that the labour values of the products of land are higher than their prices of production as the organic composition of capital in agriculture is generally lower than the social average. He defined a theoretical limit to absolute rent for those products within the range of 'the excess value over and above the price of production' (III, p. 898). However, I do not see any strong reason why the composition of capital in agriculture is always lower (or why the turnover of capital there is more rapid) than the social average, or why the range of absolute rent should remain within the labour-substance embodied in the land concerned. The limit of absolute rent must be given by the possible increase in the supply of products of the land by additional investment in the existing leaseholds.
19. In the first four chapters (Chs 21–24) of Part V of Volume III of *Capital*, Marx examines the theoretical relation between profit and interest, starting with the assumption of a money capitalist who does not function as industrial or commercial capitalist, and a functioning capitalist who does not own any capital. Interest paid out of the profit earned by a functioning capitalist provides the economic foundation for the moneyed capitalist class within the traditional view of the classical school. By contrast, Marx's theory of the credit system after Chapter 25 in Part V, explains interest as a part of surplus-value redistributed among real capitals through the mechanism of the mutual utilisation of idle capital. In its substantial functions this aspect of Marx's theory of interest is clearly more applicable to a socialist economy, where moneyed capitalists must be absent.
20. Engels, *Anti-Dühring* (in *MECW*, 25, p. 263).
21. V.I. Lenin, *A Characterisation of Economic Romanticism* (1897), in *Lenin Collected Works*, 2 (Moscow: Progress Publishers, 1963, p. 87).
22. The tendency to general shortage in a centrally planned economy is analysed in J. Kornai, *The Socialist System* (Princeton: Princeton University Press, 1992).
23. Already in *The Manifesto of the Communist Party* Marx and Engels referred

to the 'Establishment of a industrial armies, especially for agriculture' (*MECW*, 6, p. 505) as one of the tasks to be achieved by the proletariat at the very beginning of the construction of communism. The necessity of having a socialist form of the industrial reserve army for a flexible allocation of labour should be recognised more broadly, and it should not be limited to seasonal labour for agriculture.

4 Market Economy and Socialism

1. D. Lavoie, *Rivalry and Central Planning: The Socialist Calculation Debate Reconsidered* (Cambridge: Cambridge University Press, 1985) presents a good survey of the debates which we shall consider in the following two sections (pp. 83–105). Lavoie's position, stressing the importance of the Austrian theoretical tradition in underlining the role of rivalry in the market economy, is ineteresting but different from mine.
2. N.G. Pierson, 'The Problem of Value in the Socialist Society' (1902), in F.A. Hayek (ed.), *Collectivist Economic Planning* (London: Routledge & Kegan Paul, 1935, p. 27). Hereafter quotes from this book shall be given in the form *H* and page.
3. For instance A. Emmanuel, *Unequal Exchange*, trans by B. Pearce (New York and London: Monthly Review Press, 1972) theoretically stressed that such an exploitative international relation is inevitable due to two forms of the law of unequal exchange. The first form relates to Marx's theory of prices of production where a part of surplus labour must be transferred from the industries with lower composition of capital (labour intensive industries) to industries with higher composition of capital so as to equalise the rates of profit. Generally the industries in the third world countries tend to have a lower composition of capital, and so send some surplus labour abroad even in transactions based on equalised competitive conditions. The second form of unequal exchange comes from much lower wages with higher rates of surplus value in the third world countries compared to the advanced countries. Under these conditions, exchange by prices of production (cost prices plus average profit) would certainly result in exploitative and unequal international exchange of labour. The factors which enforce exploitative international trade, however, cannot be limited to such a basic rationale. Among such factors, the gap in the level of education of the people and the clientelist nature of the state must be also important reasons for underdevelopment in many countries. We have to note at the same time that not a few third world countries, such as those in Asia, have increased their GDPs quite fast especially in the past two decades.
4. In P. Sweezy (ed.), *Karl Marx and the Close of His System by E. von Böhm-Bawerk and Böhm-Bawerk's Criticism of Karl Marx by R. Hilferding* (New York: M. Kelly, 1966).
5. M. Weber, *Economy and Society* (1921), ed. G. Roth and C. Wittich (New York: Bedminster Press, 1968, p. 108).
6. Weber (1968, p. 110).
7. H.D. Dickinson, 'Price Formation in a Socialist Community', *Economic Journal* (December, 1933).

8. For example, F.A. Hayek, *Individualism and Economic Order* (London: Routledge & Kegan Paul, 1949).
9. H.D. Dickinson (1933, p. 240).
10. Dickinson (1933, p. 241).
11. Dickinson (1933, p. 242).
12. Dickinson (1933, p. 247).
13. Dickinson (1933, p. 243).
14. F.M. Taylor, 'The Guidance of Production in a Socialist State', *American Economic Journal* (March 1929) and in B.E. Lippincott (ed.), *On the Economic Theory of Socialism* (Minnesota: The University of Minnesota Press, 1938, p. 45).
15. O. Lange, 'On the Economic Theory of Socialism', *Review of Economic Studies* (October 1936, February 1937) and in B.E. Lippincott (ed.) (1938, p. 73).
16. Lange (1938, p. 88).
17. Lange (1938, p. 91).
18. F.A. Hayek, *The Road to Serfdom* (1944; Chicago: University of Chicago Press, 1972).
19. M. Dobb, 'Economic Theory and the Problems of a Socialist Economy', *Economic Journal* (December 1933).
20. M. Dobb, *Political Economy and Capitalism* (London: Routledge & Kegan Paul, 1937, p. 272).
21. Dobb (1937, pp. 295–7).
22. Dobb (1937, p. 299).
23. Dobb (1937, p. 303).
24. Dobb (1937, p. 314).
25. Dobb (1937, p. 319).
26. Dobb (1937, p. 325).
27. P. Sweezy, *Socialism* (New York: McGraw-Hill, 1949, p. 232).
28. Sweezy (1949, p. 233).
29. Sweezy (1949, p. 238).
30. Sweezy (1949, p. 239).
31. O. Lange, 'The Computer and the Market', in C. Feinstein (ed.), *Capitalism, Socialism, and Economic Growth* (Cambridge: Cambridge University Press, 1967, p. 158).
32. Lange (1967, p. 161).
33. E.G. Liberman, 'Plan, Profit, and Bonus' (1962b), in K. Nonomura, N. Miyanabe and H. Shimizu (eds and trans), The Soviet Economy and Profit (Tokyo: Nihonhyoron-sha, 1966, in Japanese).
34. W. Brus *Ogolne problemy funkcjowowania gospodarski socijalistycznej* (Warszawa PWN, 1961), trans S. Tsuruoka, The Functional Model of Socialism (Tokyo: Godo-shuppan-sha, 1971, in Japanese).
35. W. Brus, *The Economics and Politics of Socialism* (London and Boston: Routledge & Kegan Paul, 1973) presents this political implication more clearly.
36. J. Kornai, *Economics of 'Shortage'* (Collection of papers 1980–3), ed. and trans T. Morita (Tokyo: Iwanami-shoten, 1984, in Japanese); *Economics of Shortage* (Amsterdam: North-Holland, 1980); *The Political Economy of Communism* (Princeton: Princeton University Press, 1992).

37. Kornai (1992, p. 291).
38. Particularly in J. Kornai, *The Road to a Free Economy – Shifting from a Socialist System* (New York: W.W. Norton, 1990).
39. R. Selucky, *Marxism, Socialism, Freedom* (London: Macmillan, 1979, p. xi).
40. K. Marx and F. Engels, *The German Ideology* (1845–6) (in *MECW* 5, p. 47).
41. Selucky (1979, p. 30).
42. Selucky (1979, p. 179).
43. A. Nove, *The Economics of Feasible Socialism* (London: Macmillan, 1983, p. 14).
44. Nove (1983, p. 21).
45. Nove (1983, p. 33–4).
46. Nove (1983, p. 41).
47. Nove (1983, p. 52).
48. Nove (1983, p. 59).
49. Nove (1983, p. 204).
50. Nove (1983, p. 206).
51. Nove (1983, p. 208).
52. Nove (1983, p. 208).
53. Nove (1983, p. 213).
54. Nove (1983, p. 228).
55. E. Mandel, 'In Defence of Socialist Planning', *New Left Review*, 159 (September/October 1986, p. 11).
56. Mandel (1986, p. 25).
57. A. Nove, 'Markets and Socialism', *New Left Review* 161 (January/February 1987).
58. E. Mandel, 'The Myth of Market Socialism', *New Left Review*, 169 (May/June 1988).
59. C. Harman, 'The Myth of Market Socialism', *International Socialism* (Spring 1989).
60. P. Auerbach, M. Desai and A. Shamsavari, 'The Transition from Actually Existing Capitalism', *New Left Review*, 170 (July/August 1988, p. 72).
61. Auerbach *et al.* (1988, p. 76).
62. Auerbach *et al.* (1988, p. 78).
63. D. Elson, 'Market Socialism or Socialisation of the Market?', *New Left Review*, 172 (November/December 1988, p. 17).
64. Elson (1988, p. 10).
65. A. Okun, *Prices and Quantities*, (Oxford: Basil Blackwell, 1981, p. 89).
66. J. Robinson, 'Consumer's Sovereignty in a Planned Economy' (1964), in A. Nove and M. Nuti (eds), *Socialist Economics* (Harmondsworth: Penguin, 1972. p. 274).
67. R. Blackburn, 'Fin de Siecle: Socialism after the Crash', in R. Blackburn (ed.), *After the Fall* (London: Verso, 1991, p. 66).
68. P.K. Bardhan and J.E. Roemer (eds), *Market Socialism: The Current Debate* (New York and Oxford: Oxford University Press, 1993, Introduction, p. 7).
69. J.E. Roemer, 'Can There be Socialism after Socialism?' in Bardhan and Roemer (eds) (1993, p. 90).

70. Bardhan and Roemer (1993, Introduction, p. 11).
71. Roemer (1993, p. 90).
72. D. Elson, 'The Value Theory of Labour', in D. Elson (ed.), *Value* (London: CSE Books, 1979).
73. M. Itoh, *The World Economic Crisis and Japanese Capitalism* (London: Macmillan, 1990, Ch. 8 in particular).
74. For instance in the ten years since 1975 (1975 = 100), the index of productivity of Japanese manufacturing rose to 217 (while that of West Germany rose to 135), but the index of real wages remained stagnant at 105.9 (while that of West Germany rose to 131.7). It must be noted, however, that the index of 'product wages' in Japanese manufacturing, to be calculated by dividing nominal wages by the manufacturing GDP deflator, instead of by the consumer price index, rose to 211 in the same period, pararell to the index of productivity (see Table 8.1 in Itoh, 1990, p. 182). As a result, the profit share of the Japanese manufacturing sector did not recover. This means that the costs of consumer goods and services, including retail distribution costs, have been constantly rising relative to that of manufacturing goods, and also that the prices of manufactured goods have been reduced continuously so as to intensify international competitive power in the face of the appreciating yen.

5 The Nature of the Soviet Type of Society

1. Nomenklatura, or nomenclature, originally meant a system of names. In the Soviet Union it signified specifically a list of candidates for the various positions in the Communist Party and administrative offices. It was further used as an apellation for privileged persons whose names could enter this special list.
2. I. Fujita, *The Theory of Socialist Societies* (Tokyo: The University of Tokyo Press, 1980, in Japanese).
3. R. Medvedev, *Let History Judge: The Origins and Consequences of Stalinism*, 2 vols, ed. and trans G. Shriver (Oxford: Oxford University Press, 1989).
4. J. Elleinstein, *The Stalin Phenomenon*, trans P. Lantham (London: R & Lawrence & Wishart, 1976).
5. L. Trotsky, *The Revolution Betrayed*, trans M. Eastman (London: Faber & Faber, 1937).
6. E. Mandel, 'On the Nature of the Soviet State', *New Left Review*, 108 (March–April 1978).
7. P. Sweezy, *Post-Revolutionary Society* (New York and London: Monthly Review Press, 1980, Ch. 8).
8. A. Hegedüs, *Socialism and the Bureaucratic System*, Japanese version trans K. Hiraizumi (Tokyo: Otsuki-shoten, 1980).
9. C. Bettelheim, *Les Luttes de classes en USSR*, 4 vols (Paris: Seuil et Maspero, 1974, 1977, 1982, 1983).
10. P. Sweezy (1980).
11. R. Bahro, *Die Alternative* (Köln: Bund Verlag, 1977), trans D. Fernbach, *The Alternative in Eastern Europe* (London: NLB, 1978).
12. S. Amin, 'Crisis, Nationalism, and Socialism', in S. Amin *et al.*, *Dynamics*

of Global Crisis (London and Basingstoke: Macmillan, 1982, pp. 205–6); 'The Prospects for Socialism', in M. Nicolic (ed.), *Socialism on the Threshold of the Twenty-first Century* (London: Verso, 1985, p. 23). At the same time, Amin also characterises the nature of Soviet type of societies as 'the statist mode of production' in his works.

13. M.S. Voslensky, *Nomenklatura – Die herrschende Klasse der Sowjetunion* (Vienna-Munich-Zurich and Innsbruck: Verlag Fritz Molden, 1980).
14. D. Singer, *The Road to Gdansk: Poland and the U.S.S.R.* (New York and London: Monthly Review Press, 1981).
15. O. Sik, *Argumente für den Dritten Weg* (Hamburg: Hoffman und Campe, 1973).
16. J. Kosta, *Sozialistische Planwirtschaft: Theorie und Praxis* (Westdeutscher Verlag, 1974).
17. W. Brus, *The Economics and Politics of Socialism* (London and Boston: Routledge & Kegan Paul, 1973).
18. F. Fejto, *Histoire de Démocraties Populaires après Staline* (1972), Japanese version trans R. Kumada, (Tokyo: Iwanami-shoten, 1978).
19. M. Bleaney, *Do Socialist Economies Work?* (Oxford: Basil Blackwell, 1988, p. 138).
20. E. Kardelj, *Pravci razvoja politickog sistema samoupravljanija* (Beograd: Izdavacki Centar Komunist, 1977, 1978) Trans H. Yamazaki, *Self-Management and Democracy*, (Tokyo: Otsuki-shoten,1981).
21. T. Ouchi, *A Study of a New Vision of Socialism* (Tokyo: The Research Center for Labour and Social Problems, 1979 in Japanese).

6 Achievements and Crisis

1. M. Bleaney, *Do Socialist Economies Work?* (Oxford: Basil Blackwell, 1988, p. 15).
2. B. Selunin and G. Hanin, 'Cunning Number', *Novye Mir* (February 1987, in Russian).
3. S. Miyazaki, S. Okumura and K. Morita (eds), *An Outline of Modern International Economy* (Tokyo: The University of Tokyo Press, 1981, p. 238, in Japanese).
4. M. Gorbachev, *Perestroika* (New York, Cambridge and others: Harper & Row, 1987, pp. 18–19).
5. See in more detail in M. Itoh, *The World Economic Crisis and Japanese Capitalism* (London: Macmillan, New York: St Martin's, 1990, Chs 2 and 3).
6. P. Sweezy and H. Magdoff, 'Perestroika and the Future of Socialism II', *Monthly Review* (April 1990, p. 4).
7. Sweezy and Magdoff (1990, p. 5).
8. J. Kornai, *Economics of Shortage* (Amsterdam: North-Holland, 1980); *The Political Economy of Communism* (Princeton: Princeton University Press, 1992). As I have explained in Chapter 4 (p. 110), Kornai did not examine the problem of how the Soviet economy could maintain relatively high economic growth before it fell into stagnation which aggravated the economy of shortage after the late 1970s.
9. B. Chavance, *Le Système Economique Soviétique* (Paris: Edition Nathan,

1990), Japanese version trans H. Saito (Tokyo: Omura-shoten, 1992, p. 16).
10. Chavance (1992, Japanese version, p. 193).
11. S. Kojima and M. Maruyama, *Modern and Contemporary History of China* (Tokyo: Iwanami-shoten, 1986, p. 228, in Japanese).

7 The Reforms and Systemic Change

1. M. Gorbachev, *Perestroika* (New York, Cambridge and others: Harper & Row, 1987, p. 37).
2. O. Bauer, 'Die Nationalitätenfrage und die Sozialdemokratie', *Marx-Studien*, Bd.2 (1907).
3. R. Luxemburg, *Die Industrielle Entwicklung Polens* (Leipzig: Duncker und Humboldt, 1898). H.B. Davis (ed.), *The National Question – Selected Writings by R. Luxemburg* (New York. Monthly Review Press, 1976).
4. J.V. Stalin, *Marxism and the National Question* (1913), in *Stalin Works*, vol. 2, Japanese version, trans the Association for Stalin Works Publication (Tokyo: Otuki-shoten, 1952, vol. 2).
5. M. Lewin, *Le Dernier Combat de Lenin* (1967), Japanese version trans H. Kawai (Tokyo: Iwanami-shoten, 1969).
6. S. Clarke, 'Privatization and the Development of Capitalism in Russia', *New Left Review*, 196 (1992).
7. G. Frank, in his *Reflections on the World Economic Crisis* (New York and London: Monthly Review Press, 1981a) and *Crisis in the World Economy* (London: Heinemann, 1981b), formulated the conception of a single and unified global cisis originating in the main advanced capitalist countries by emphasising this common difficulties for both third world countries and actually existing socialist countries. Although interesting, this conception is too simplistic and unduly neglects the internal logic of the Soviet economic crisis, as well as its impact on Eastern European countries. Nevertheless, it is important to understand, although beyond the scope of this volume, how the crisis and the turmoil of economic reforms in the former Soviet bloc relate to the economic difficulties of the advanced capitalist countries and many non-Asian third world countries. In this respect the crisis of the old socialist countries forms an integral part of the global crisis of our age.
8. W. Glatzer und H. Herbert (eds), *Lebensverhältnisse in Deutchland* (Frankfurt am Main: Campus Verlag, 1992), Japanese version trans S. Nagasaka and S. Omiya (Tokyo: Keiso-shobo, 1994, pp. 12–15).
9. G. Bakos, 'Hungarian Transition after 3 Years' (paper for Inaugural Symposium, Centre of European Studies, Nanzan University, December 1993).
10. A. Smith, *An Inquiry into the Nature and Causes of the Wealth of Nations* (1776) ed. E. Cannan (London: Methuen, 1922, vol. I, Book III, Chapter 1, p. 356).
11. This aspect is made concretely clear in E.F. Vogel, *One Step Ahead in China* (Cambridge, Mass.: Harvard University Press, 1989).

Bibliography

ALBRITTON, R., *A Japanese Reconstruction of Marxist Theory* (London: Macmillan, 1986).
AMIN, S., 'Crisis, Nationalism, and Socialism', in S. Amin *et al.*, *Dynamics of Global Crisis* (London and Basingstoke: Macmillan, 1982).
────── 'The Prospects for Socialism', in M. Nicolic (ed.), *Socialism on the Threshold of the Twenty-first Century* (London: Verso, 1985).
ANDO, S., *Complete Works of Shoeki Ando* vol. 1–21 plus 1, ed. the Association for Studying Shoeki Ando (Tokyo: Nousan-gyoson Bunka Kyokai, 1983–7 in Japanese).
AUERBACH, P., DESAI, M. and SHAMSAVARI, A., 'The Transition from Actually Existing Capitalism', *New Left Review*, 170 (July/August 1988).
BAKOS, G., 'Hungarian Transition after 3 Years' (paper for Inaugural Symposium, Centre of European Studies, Nanzan University, December 1993).
BAHRO, R., *The Alternative in Eastern Europe*, trans D. Fernbach (London: NLB, 1978).
BARDHAN, P.K. and ROEMER, J.E. (eds), *Market Socialism: The Current Debate* (New York and Oxford: Oxford University Press, 1993).
BARONE, E., 'The Ministry of Production in the Collectivist State', (1908), in Hayek (ed.), *Collectivist Economic Planning*.
BAUER, O., 'Die Nationalitätenfrage und die Sozialdemokratie', *Marx-Studien*, Bd. 2 (1907).
BEER, M., *History of British Socialism* (1940; Nottingham: Russel Press 1984).
BERNSTEIN, E., *Die Voraussetzungen des Sozialismus und die Aufgaben der Sozialdemokratie* (Stuttgart: Dietz, 1899).
BETTELHEIM, C., *Les Luttes de Classes en USSR*, 4 vols (Paris: Maspero Seuil, 1974).
BIX, H., *Peasant Protest in Japan 1590–1884* (New Haven: Yale University Press, 1986).
BLACKBURN, R., 'Fin de Siecle: Socialism after the Crash', in R. Blackburn (ed.), *After the Fall* (London: Verso, 1991).
BLEANEY, M., *Do Socialist Economies Work?* (Oxford: Basil Blackwell,1988).
BRUCAN, S., *World Socialism at the Crossroads* (New York: Praeger, 1987).
BRUS, W., *Ogolne problemy funkcjonowania gospodarski socjalistycznej* (Warszawa PWN, 1961), trans S. Tsuruoka, *The Functional Model of Socialism* (Tokyo: Godo-shuppan-sha, 1971 in Japanese).
────── *The Economics and Politics of Socialism* (London and Boston: Routledge & Kegan Paul, 1973).
BRUS, W. AND LASKI, K., *From Marx to Market* (Oxford: Clarendon Press,1988).
CHAVANCE, B., *Le Système Economique Soviétique* (Paris: Edition Nathan, 1990), Japanese version trans H. Saito (Tokyo: Omura-shoten, 1992).
CLARKE, S., 'Privatization and the Development of Capitalism in Russia', *New Left Review*, 196 (1992).

DAVIS, H.B. (ed.), *The National Question – Selected Writings by R. Luxemburg* (New York: Monthly Review Press, 1976).
DICKINSON, H.D. 'Price Formation in a Socialist Community', *Economic Journal* (December 1933).
DOBB, M., 'Economic Theory and the Problems of a Socialist Economy', *Economic Journal* (December 1933).
────── *Political Economy and Capitalism* (London: Routledge & Kegan Paul, 1937).
ELLEINSTEIN, J., *The Stalin Phenomenon*, trans P. Lantham (London: Lawrence & Wishart, 1976).
ELLMAN, M., *Socialist Planning* (Cambridge: Cambridge University Press,1979).
ELSON D., 'The Value Theory of Labour', in D. Elson (ed.), *Value* (London: CSE Books, 1979).
────── 'Market Socialism or Socialisation of the Market?', *New Left Review*, 172 (November/December 1988).
EMMANUEL, E., *Unequal Exchange*, trans B. Pearce (New York and London: Monthly Review Press, 1972).
ENGELS, F., *Herrn Eugen Dühring's Revolution in Science (Anti-Dühring)* (1878) (*MECW*, 25).
────── *Socialism: Utopian and Scientific* (1882) (*MECW*, 24).
FEJTO, F., *Historie des Démocraties Populaires après Stalin* (1972), Japanese version trans R. Kumada (Tokyo: Iwanami-shoten, 1978).
FRANK, G., *Reflections on the World Economic Crisis* (New York and London: Monthly Review Press, 1981a).
────── *Crisis in the World Economy* (London: Heinemann, 1981b).
FOURIER, F.M.C., *Le Nouveau Monde Industriel et Sociétaire ou Invention du Procédé d'Industrie Attrayante et Naturelle Distribuée en Series Passionnées* (1822), in *Oeuvre Complètes de Ch. Fourier* (Paris: La Librairie Sociétaire, 1845, t.6).
FUJITA, I, *The Theory of Socialist Societies* (Tokyo: The University of Tokyo Press, 1980, in Japanese).
GLATZER, W. and HERBERT, H. (eds), *Lebensverhältnisse in Deutchland* (Frankfurt am Main: Campus Verlag, 1992), Japanese version trans S. Nagasaka and S. Omiya (Tokyo: Keiso-shobo, 1994)
GORBACHEV, M., *Perestroika* (New York, Cambridge and others: Harper & Row, 1987).
GRAMSCI, A., *Selections from the Prison Notebooks of Antonio Gramsci*, ed. and trans Q. Hoare and G.N. Smith (London: Lawrence & Wishart, 1971).
GROSSMANN, H., *Das Akkumulations- und Zusammenbruchsgezetz des Kapitalistischen Systems* (Leipzig: Hirschfeld, 1929).
HALM, G., 'Further Considerations on the Possibility of Adequate Calculation in a Socialist Community' (1935), in Hayek (ed.), *Collectivist Economic Planning*.
HARMAN, C., 'The Myth of Market Socialism', *International Socialism* (Spring 1989).
HAYEK, F.A. (ed.), *Collectivist Economic Planning* (London: Routledge & Kegan Paul, 1935).

―――― *The Road to Serfdom* (1944; Chicago: University of Chicago Press, 1972).
―――― *Individualism and Economic Order* (London: Routledge & Kegan Paul, 1949).
HEGEDÜS, A., *Socialism and the Bureaucratic System*, Japanese version trans K. Hiraizumi (Tokyo: Otsuki-shoten, 1980).
HIRONISHI, M., *Mistranslation of 'Capital'* (Tokyo: Seiyu-sha, 1966, in Japanese).
HU, CHIAO-MU, 'Observe Economic Laws, Speed up the Four Modernizations', *Peking Review*, 45–47 (10–24 November 1978).
ITOH, M., *Value and Crisis* (London: Pluto Press, New York: Monthly Review Press, 1980).
―――― *The Basic Theory of Capitalism* (London: Macmillan, Totowa, N.J.: Barnes & Noble, 1988).
―――― *The World Economic Crisis and Japanese Capitalism* (London: Macmillan, New York: St Martin's, 1990).
―――― *Contemporary Socialism* (Tokyo: Kodansha, 1992, in Japanese).
KARDELJ, E., *Pravci razvoja politickog sistema samoupravljanija* (Beograd: Izdavacki Centar Komunist, 1977, 1978) trans H. Yamazaki, *Self-Management and Democracy*, (Tokyo: Otsuki-shoten, 1981).
KAUTSKY, K., *Bernstein und das Sozialdemokratische Programm* (Stuttgart: Dietz, 1899a).
―――― *The Agrarian Question* (1899b), vol. 1–2, trans P. Burgess (London and Winchester, Mass.: Zwan Publications, 1988).
―――― 'Der Imperialismus', *Neue Zeit*, 32(2) (1914).
―――― 'Zwei Schriften zum Umlernen', *Neue Zeit*, 33(2) (1915).
―――― 'Der Imperialistische Krieg', *Neue Zeit*, 35(1), (1917).
KOJIMA, S. and MARUYAMA, M., *Modern and Contemporary History of China* (Tokyo: Iwanami-shoten, 1986).
KORNAI, J., *Economics of Shortage* (Amsterdam: North-Holland, 1980).
―――― *Economics of 'Shortage'* (Collection of Papers 1980–3), ed. and trans T. Morita (Tokyo: Iwanami-shoten, 1984, in Japanese).
―――― *The Road to a Free Economy – Shifting from a Socialist System: The Case of Hungary* (New York: W.W. Norton, 1990).
―――― *The Political Economy of Communism* (Princeton: Princeton University Press, 1992).
KOSTA, J., *Sozialistische Planwirtschaft: Theorie und Praxis* (Westdeutscher Verlag, 1974).
LANGE, O., 'On the Economic Theory of Socialism', *Review of Economic Studies* (October 1936, February 1937) and in B.E. Lippincott (ed.), *On the Economic Theory of Socialism* (Minnesota: The University of Minnesota Press, 1938).
―――― 'The Computer and the Market', in C. Feinstein (ed.), *Capitalism, Socialism and Economic Growth* (Cambridge: Cambridge University Press, 1967).
LAVOIE D., *Rivalry and Central Planning: The Socialist Calculation Debate Reconsidered* (Cambridge: Cambridge University Press, 1985).
LENIN, V.I., *Imperialism: The Highest Stage of Capitalism* (1917) (Peking: Foreign Languages Press, 1965).

―――― *The State and Revolution* (1918) (*Levin Collected Works*, 25, Moscow: Progress Publishers, 1964).
―――― *A Characterisation of Economic Romanticism* (1897) (*Lenin Collected Works*, 2, Moscow: Progress Publishers, 1963).
LEWIN, M., *Le Dernier Combat de Lenin* (1967), Japanese version trans H. Kawai (Tokyo: Iwanami-shoten, 1969).
LIBERMAN, E.G., 'Plan, Profit and Bonus' (1962b), in K. Nonomura, N. Miyanabe and H. Shimizu eds and trans, *The Soviet Economy and Profit* (Tokyo: Nihonhyoron-sha, 1966, in Japanese).
LIPPINCOTT, B.E. (ed.), *On the Economic Theory of Socialism* (Minnesota: The University of Minnesota Press,1938).
LOCKE, J., *Two Treatises of Civil Government* (1690) (Cambridge: Cambridge University Press, 1967).
LUXEMBURG, R., *Die Industrielle Entwicklung Polens* (Leipzig: Duncker und Humboldt, 1898).
―――― *Sozialreform oder Revolution?* (1899) (Leipzig: Vulkan-Verlag, 1919).
―――― *Die Russische Revolution* (1918) (Berlin: Gesellschaft und Erziehung, 1922).
MANDEL, E., 'On the Nature of the Soviet State', *New Left Review*, 108 (March/April 1978).
―――― 'In Defence of Socialist Planning', *New Left Review*, 159 (September/October 1986).
―――― 'The Myth of Market Socialism', *New Left Review*, 169 (May/June 1988).
MARSHALL, A., *Principles of Economics* (London: Macmillan, 1890).
MARX, K., *A Contribution to the Critique of Political Economy* (1859), trans S.W. Ryazanskaya, (Moscow: Progress Publishers, 1970).
MARX, K., 'The Poverty of Philosophy', (1846–47) (*MECW*, 6).
―――― *Capital*, vol. I, II, III (1867, 1885, 1894), trans B. Fowkes and D. Fernbach, (Harmondsworth: Penguin, 1976, 1978, 1981).
――――, 'Critique of the Gotha Programme', (1875) (*MECW*, 24).
MARX, K. and ENGELS, F., *The German Ideology*, (1845–6) (*MECW*, 5).
―――― *The Manifesto of the Communist Party* (1848), (*MECW*, 6).
MEDVEDEV, R.A., *Let History Judge: The Origins and Consequences of Stalinism*, 2 vols, ed. and trans G. Shriver (Oxford:Oxford University Press, 1989).
MILL, J.S., *Principles of Political Economy* (1848), ed. W.J. Ashley (London: Longmans, Green, 1921).
MISES, L. VON., 'Economic Calculation in the Socialist Commonwealth', (1920), in Hayek (ed.), *Collectivist Economic Planning*.
MIYAZAKI, S., OKUMURA, S. and MORITA, K., (eds), *An Outline of Modern International Economy* (Tokyo: The University of Tokyo Press, 1981, in Japanese).
MLYNAR, Z., *Nachtfrost–Erfahrungen auf dem Weg vom Realen zum Menschlichen Sozialismus* (Köln and Frankfurt am Main: Europäische Verlag, 1978).
MORE, T., *Utopia* (1516), Japanese version trans by M. Hirai (Tokyo: Iwanami-shoten, 1957).
NOVE, A., *The Economics of Feasible Socialism* (London: Macmillan, 1983).

———— 'Markets and Socialism', *New Left Review*, 161 (January/February 1987).
NOVE, A. AND NUTI, D.M. (eds), *Socialist Economics* (Harmondsworth: Penguin, 1972).
OWEN, R., *A New View of Society* (1813–14), in *The Life of Robert Owen Written by Himself*, vol. I (New York: A.M. Kelly, 1976).
OKISHIO, N. and ITOH, M., *Economic Theories and Contemporary Capitalism* (Tokyo: Iwanami-shoten, 1987, in Japanese).
OKUN, A., *Price and Quantities* (Oxford: Basil Blackwell, 1981).
OUCHI, T., *A Study of a New Image of Socialism* (Tokyo: The Research Center for Labour and Social Problems, 1979, in Japanese).
PIERSON, N.G., 'The Problem of Value in the Socialist Society, (1902), in Hayek (ed.), *Collectivist Economic Planning*.
POLANYI, K., 'Sozialistische Rechnungslegung', *Archiv für Sozialwissenschaft und Sozialpolitik*, 49 (1922).
———— 'Die Funktionelle Theorie der Gesellschaft und das Problem der Sozialistischen Rechnungslegung', *Archiv für Sozialwissenschaft und Sozialpolitik*, 52 (1924).
ROBINSON, J., 'Consumer's Sovereignty in a Planned Economy' (1964), in A. Nove and M. Nuti (eds), *Socialist Economics*.
ROEMER, J.E., 'Can There be Socialism after Socialism?', in P.K. Bardhan and J.E. Roemer (eds), *Market Socialism: The Current Debate* (New York and Oxford: Oxford University Press, 1993).
SAINT-SIMON, C.-H. de R., *Catéchisme Politique des Industriels* (1823–4), in *Oeuvre de Saint-Simon et d'Enfantin* (Paris: Dentu, 1865–76).
———— *Nouveau Christianisme* (1825), in *Oeuvre de Saint-Simon et d'Enfantin* (Paris: Dentu, 1865–76).
SCHUMPETER, J.A., *Capitalism, Socialism and Democracy* (New York: Harper, 1942).
SEKINE, T., 'Uno-Riron: A Japanese Contribution to Marxian Political Economy', *Journal of Economic Literature*, 13(3) (September 1975).
SELUCKY, R., *Marxism, Socialism, Freedom* (London: Macmillan, 1979).
SELUNIN, B. and HANIN, G., 'Cunning Number', *Novye Mir* (February 1987 in Russian).
SHAW, G.B. (ed.), *Fabian Essays in Socialism* (London: Fabian Society and Allen, 1889).
SIK, O., *Argumente für den Dritten Weg* (Hamburg: Hoffman und Campe, 1973).
SIMONDE de SISMONDI, J.C.L., *Nouveaux Principes d'Economie Politique* (Paris: Delaunay, 1819).
SINGER, D., *The Road to Gdansk: Poland and the U.S.S.R.* (New York and London: Monthly Review Press, 1981).
SMITH, A., *An Inquiry into the Nature and Causes of the Wealth of Nations*, vol. I, II (1776), ed. E. Cannan, (London: Methuen, 1922).
STALIN, J.V., *Marxism and the National Question* (1913), in *Stalin Works*, vol. 2, Japanese version, trans the Association for Stalin Works Publication (Tokyo: Otuki-shoten, 1952).
———— *Economic Problems of Socialism in the U.S.S.R.* (1952, Peking: Foreign Languages Press, 1972).
SWEEZY, P.M., *Socialism* (New York: McGraw-Hill, 1949).

——— (ed.), *Karl Marx and the Close of his System by E. von Böhm-Bawerk and Böhm-Bawerk's Criticism of Karl Marx by R. Hilferding* (New York: M. Kelly, 1966).
——— *Post-Revolutionary Society* (New York and London: Monthly Review Press, 1980).
——— *Four Lectures on Marxism* (New York: Monthly Review Press, 1981).
SWEEZY, P.M. and MAGDOFF, H., 'Perestroika and the Future of Socialism I, II', *Monthly Review* (March–April 1990).
TAYLOR, F.M., 'The Guidance of Production in a Socialist State', *American Economic Journal* (March 1929) and in B.E. Lippincott (ed.), *On the Economic Theory of Socialism* (Minnesota: The University of Minnesota Press, 1938).
TROTSKY, L., *The Revolution Betrayed*, trans M. Eastman (London: Faber & Faber, 1937).
UNO, K., *Methodology of Political Economy* (Tokyo: The University of Tokyo Press, 1962, in Japanese).
——— *Principles of Political Economy*, trans T. Sekine (Brighton: Harvester Press, Atlantic Highlands: Humanities Press, 1980).
VOGEL, E.F., *One Step Ahead in China* (Cambridge, Mass: Harvard University Press, 1989).
VOSLENSKY, M.S., *Nomenklatura – Die Herrschende Klasse der Sowjetunion* (Vienna, Munich, Zurich and Innsbruck: Fritz Molden, 1980).
WEBB, SIDNEY and BEATRICE, *Industrial Democracy* (1897) (London, New York and Bombay: Longmans, Green, 1920).
WEBER, M., *Economy and Society* (1921), ed. G. Roth and C. Wittich (New York: Bedminster Press, 1968).

Index

Absolute s-rent 74
Adjustment policies 173
Agency problems 127
Albritton, R. 217, 218
Alexander of Hales 8
Alternative technologies 158
Amin, S. 150
Anarchism 3
Ando, S. 8
Anti-Dühring 44
Asiatic mode of production 150, 151
Association of free men 133
Auerbach, P. 120
Automobile society 158

Bahro, R. 150
Bakos, G. 227
Bakunin, M.A. 3
Ball, J. 8
Bank credit 75
Bardhan, P.K. 126
Barone, E. 90
Bauer, O. 180
Beer, M. 3
Bernstein, E. 6, 25
Bettelheim, C. 149
Bix, H. 217
Blackburn, R. 125
Bleaney, M. 226
Bolsheviks 27
Bourgeois revolution 12
Brezhnev, L.I. 146, 148
Brus, W. 106, 136, 154, 156
Business cycles 78

Capital 41
Capitalist law of population 78
Centrally planned economies 160
Chartism 19, 20
Chavance, B. 227
China 50, 201

Chinese Communist Party 209
Chinese Cultural Revolution 144, 149, 173
CIS (Commonwealth of Independent States) 183
Citizens' Forum 192
Clarke, S. 227
Class struggle 41
  history of 38
Classic socialism 109
Contradictions of capitalism 77
Co-operation of workers 165
Co-operative movement 138
Cold war 166
  end of 179
COMECON 182
Comintern 6
Commercial credit 75
Communism 4
  higher phase of 57
  lower phase of 56
Communist Manifesto 38
Complex labour 53, 54, 131, 132
Comte, A. 14
Conservative coup d'état 183
Consumer sovereignty 125
Consumer Union 124
Contract production system 202
Contracted managers 134
Contradictions of capitalism 77
Costs of education 56, 171
Crisis 77, 80, 207
  excess capital theories of 77
  excess commodities theories of 77
  of Marxism 213
Critique of Christianity 33
Critique of the Gotha Programme 43, 54
Czechoslovakia 197

De-Stalinisation 144, 148

234

Decentralisation 153, 154
Democracy 111
Democratic socialism 111, 125, 191, 199
Democratisation 153, 206
Democratisation movements 191, 192, 194, 206
Deng Xiaoping 175
Desai, M. 120
Detailed knowledge 92
Dickinson, H.D. 83, 93, 126
Dictatorship of the proletariat 43
Different types of prices 84
Differential groundrent 21
Differential s-rent 74, 131
Disfigured socialism 151
Dispersed knowledge 137
Disproportionality 78
Division of labour 57
  evils of 58
Dobb, M. 83, 99
Dynamic flexibility 81

East Germany 194
Eastern European revolutions 145, 192
Ecological
  conditions of life 214
  crises 38
Economism 41
Education system 150
Egalitarian principle 132
Egalitarianism 9
Electronic computers 104
Electronic information systems 69
Elleinstein, J. 147
Elson, D. 122, 134
Emmanuel, A. 222
Enfantin, B.P. 14
Engels, F. 4, 22, 78, 143
Enlightenment 9
Epoch of social revolution 34
Erfurt Programme 25
Ethnic problems 180
Euro-communism 154
Euro-socialism 154
Extra s-profit 71, 98, 131
Extra surplus value 69
Extra-economic factors 87

Fabianism 6, 20, 21
False social value 73
Feasible models of socialism 135
Fejto, F. 154
Feminism 21
Feuerbach, L.A. 33
Flexible adjustment 82
Forms of property ownership 81, 134
Forms of value 45, 129
Four basic principles 209
Four modernisation policies 175
Fourier, F.M.C. 3, 14, 15, 16
Frank, G. 227
Free association 111
French Revolution 13, 192
Friedman, M. 135
Fujita, I. 147
Full s-wage model 52, 67, 101
Fundamental human rights 12

Gaidar, Y. 183, 187
German Social Democratic
  Party 6, 25
Glasnost 176, 177
Glorious Revolution 12
Glyn, A. vii
Godwin, W. 3
Gorbachev, M. 144, 167, 176, 192, 206
Gosplan 160
Gossnab 160
Gramsci, A. 28
Gray, J. 19
Great Leap Forward 173
Grossmann, H. 220

Halm, G. 90
Harman, C. 224
Harnin, G. 162, 163
Hayek, F.A. xvii, 83, 91, 98, 125, 126, 135, 137
Hegedüs, A. 148, 155
Hegel, G.W.F. 33
Hironishi, M. 221
Historical materialism 4, 5, 23, 34, 146, 150
Horizontal shortage 107
Humanistic socialism 179

Hungarian upheaval 191
Hungary 198
Hus, J. 8

Idle funds 75
Ikko Ikki 8
Imperialism 27
Incentive 127, 131
Information networks 124
Information technologies 130
Inter-firm shortage 108
Interest 77
  role of 95
International trade 85
Invisible handshake 123
Isidor, H. 8
Itoh, M. 218, 220, 221, 226

Jacobins 13
Japanese
  economic system 137
  economy xviii, 139
  labour management 55
  type of management 127

Kalecki, M. 124
Kanban system 121
Kardelj, E. 154
Karoshi xv, 16, 139
Kautsky, K. 6, 26
Keiretsu 127
Khrushchev, N.S. 146
Kojima, S. 227
Kolkhozes 164
Kornai, J. 107, 126, 169
Kosta, J. 154

Labour certificate 75, 84
Labour Party 21
Labour process 45
Labour-money 19
Labour-time embodied 47
Lagour theory of value 129, 132
Lange, O. xviii, 83, 96, 103, 126
Lapavitsas, C. xi
Laski, K. 136
Lavoie, D. viii
Law of impoverishment 25, 26
Lenin, V.I. 6, 27, 78, 181

Lewin, M. 227
Liberation theology 8
Liberman, E. 105
Lippincott, B.E. 223
Locke, J. 12,
Luther, M. 8
Luxemburg, R. 6, 26, 28, 192

Malthus, T.R. 17
Management by contract 204
Mandel, E. 117, 148
Manpower planning 122
Manufacture 58, 59
Mao Zedong 144, 173
Market socialism 72, 105, 112, 114, 126, 130, 156, 192
Maruyama, M. 227
Marx, K. 4, 22, 31, 143, 215
Marxism 6, 22, 31, 213
Medvedev, R.A. 147
ME (micro-electronic) information technologies xv, 60
Military expenditure 162
Military industry 169
Mill, J.S. 20, 21
Mises, L. von xvii, 83, 86, 161
Mlynar, Z. 145
Money capitalist 221
Moneyed capitalist class 75
Moonlighting 170
More, T. 10
Motivation 131
Motive for innovation 98
Multiple models of socialism 133
Müntzer, T. 8

Narodniks 17
Nationalisation 79
Natural human right 9
Natural law 9
Necessary labour 65
Neo-liberal policies xiv
Neo-liberalism 92, 193, 200
Neo-Marxism 154
Neo-Stalinism 148
New class society 152
New Harmony 19
Nomenklatura 144, 150, 170, 186, 187

Index

Norms 160, 165, 171
Nove, A. 112
Nuti, D.M. 224

Officially fixed prices 48, 49, 161
Okishio, N. viii, 220
Okun, A. 123
One nation, one factory 61, 62, 221
Orthodox Marxism 133
Ouchi, T. 154
Overproduction 17
Owen, R. 3, 18

Paris Commune 43
Partial information 92
Pattern of consumption 159
Perestroika 144, 167, 176
Pierson, N.G. 83, 84
Plekhanov, G.V. 26
Poland 195
Poland phenomenon 195
Polish Solidarity movement 144, 191
Politics of use-values 122, 159
POS (point of sales) information system 138
Post-Revolutionary Society 150
Prague Spring 145, 154, 191
Prehistory of human society 35, 36
Price form 45
Primitive accumulation 180, 187, 200
Primitive communist societies 9
Privatisation 185, 197, 199
Productive forces 34
Promotion mechanism 150
Property right 12
   by labour 12
   variety of 215
Proudhon, P.J. 3
Public banks 76
Public debt 76
Puritan Revolution 12

Quasi-money 48
Quasi-prices 48

Rate of interest 76

Reagan, D. 169
Real consumers' sovereignty 68, 125
Realm of necessity 66
Relations of production 34
Religious fetishism 33
Renaissance of Marxism 28
Research and development (R & D) 70, 204
Revisionism 6, 25
Ricardo, D. 4
Robespierre, M.F. de 13
Robinson, J. 124
Roemer, J.E. 126
Role of education 110
Romantic socialism 3, 17
Rowthorn, B. viii
Russian Social Democratic Party 6

s-capital 68, 105
s-interest 105
s-money 50, 75
s-prices 49, 51, 68, 126, 132, 156
s-profit 67, 68, 105
s-profit rate 68
s-rent 74, 131
s-taxes 156
s-wages 51, 52, 67, 101, 130
Sachs, J. 179
Safety net 134
Saint-Simon, C.-H. de R. 3, 13
Scientific socialism 4, 5, 22, 31, 213
Second International 6, 27
Sekine, T. 218
Selucky, R. 111
Selunin, B. 162, 163
Semi-monetised economy 109
Shamsavari, A. 120
Shaw, G.B. 21
Shock therapy 184, 195, 196, 199
Shortage economy 107, 169
Shortage syndrome 109
Sik, O. 154
Simonde de Sismondi, J.C.L. 3, 16
Singer, D. 150
Skilled labour 53, 54, 131, 132
Smith, A. 4, 46, 57, 58, 150, 202

Social democracy x, 5, 6, 126, 163, 216
Social freedom 112
Socialisation of the market 122, 124, 134
Socialism 1, 3, 21, 22, 213, 216
Socialist credit mechanism 75
Socialist economic calculation debate viii, 83
Socialist ethic 65
Socialist form of the industrial reserve army 80, 131
Socialist market economy 196, 201, 208
Socialist wages 67
Soft budget constraint 108, 161
Solidarity movement 192
Soviet 6, 143
Soviet type of socialism 128
Soviet–Chinese split 144
Soviet-type Marxism 42, 146
Sovkhozes 164
Spontaneous market 137
Stalin's Constitutional Law 146
Stalin, J.V. 6, 147, 181
Stalinism 148
Star Wars 169
State capitalism 149
State class 150
Statism 44, 158
Substance of value 45
Superstructure 34, 35
Surplus labour 63
Sweezy, P.M. vii, 83, 102, 148, 150
Systemic change 210, 213

Taylor system 60
Taylor, F.M. xviii, 21, 83, 96
Third alternative way 119
Third International 6
Thompson, W. 19
Three levels of research xvii

Tienanmen incident 205–7
Transition to a market economy 178
Transitional economies 118
Trial and error procedure 96, 97
Trotsky, L. 148

Under-consumption theory 17
Underground economy 171
Unequal exchange 222
Unit of economic accounting 47, 49
Universal human values 179
Uno, K. xvii, 26
Utopian socialism 3, 10, 16

Value of skilled labour-power 55
Value theory 117, 128
Value theory of labour 129
Vanguard party 27
Velvet divorce 197
Velvet Revolution 192
Vertical shortage 108
Victory of capitalism xv, xviii, 214
Vogel, E.F. 227
Voslensky, M.S. 143, 150

Webb, Sidney and Beatrice 21
Weber, M. 83, 89
Weisskopf, T.E. 126
Welfare state 163
Wicliff, J. 8
William of Wykeham 8
Workers' loyalty 137
Workers' self-management 106, 125, 153

Yeltsin, B. 183, 187, 188
Yugoslavia 50, 105, 154, 196

Zhirinovsky, V. 188

LEWIS AND CLARK COLLEGE LIBRARY
PORTLAND, OREGON 97219